T0065657

CLIMB YOUR OWN LADDER

101 HOME BUSINESSES
THAT CAN
MAKE YOU WEALTHY

BY

Allen Lieberoff

A FIRESIDE BOOK
Published by Simon and Schuster
New York

To good friends.
Without them, you have nothing.

Also by Allen Lieberoff

Good Jobs:
High Paying Opportunities
Working for Yourself or for Others

Copyright © 1982 by Allen Lieberoff
All rights reserved
including the right of reproduction
in whole or in part in any form
A Fireside Book
Published by Simon & Schuster, Inc.
Simon & Schuster Building
Rockefeller Center
1230 Avenue of the Americas
New York, New York 10020
FIRESIDE and colophon are registered trademarks of Simon & Schuster, Inc.
Designed by Elaine Golt Gongora
Manufactured in the United States of America
Printed and bound by Fairfield Graphics
10 9 8 7 6 5 4 3
Library of Congress Cataloging in Publication Data
Lieberoff, Allen J.
   Climb your own ladder.

   "A fireside book."
   1. Home-based businesses.   2. Part-time employment.   I. Title.
HD2341.L49   1982   658'.041   82-10655
ISBN 0-671-45477-3

CONTENTS

INTRODUCTION   vii

*A FEW IMPORTANT
NOTES*   ix

1

WRITING OPPORTUNITIES   1

Advertising Copywriting   1
Fund-Raising Writing   4
Writing Articles for
    Magazines   6
Speech Writing for Politicians
    and Business People   8
Writing Greeting Card
    Verse   10
Comedy Writing   11
Resumé Writing   13
Manuscript Typing   18
Letter-Writing Businesses   20
    Business Correspondence
        (Secretarial Service) 20
    Sales Letter Writing   23
    Complaint Letter
        Writing   24
Prize Contests   29
Publishing   30

2

SERVICES REQUIRING SPECIAL VEHICLES   32

Local Moving—Light   32
Local Moving—Heavy   33

Door-to-Door Advertising
    Distribution Service   35
Dry Cleaning Service Route   37

3

AUTOMOTIVE SERVICES   40

Mobile Car Waxing Service   40
Mobile Car Washing Service   42
Mobile Lube and
    Oil-Changing Service   46
Theft-Proofing Cars   48

4

MANUAL AND MECHANICAL SERVICES   52

Painting and Paperhanging   52
Custom Picture Framing   55
Key Duplicating Service   57
Rubber Stamp
    Manufacturing   59
Stenciling House Numbers
    on Curbs   61
Antique Restoration and
    Furniture Refinishing   62

5

CLEANING SERVICES   65

General Janitorial Work   65
Rug Cleaning   67

CONTENTS

Upholstery Cleaning 69
Stain Removal Service 70
Window Washing 70
Industrial Cleaning 72

6

CREATIVE AND ARTISTIC ENDEAVORS 75

Personal Catering 75
Sandwich and Salad
  Business 77
Calligraphy 81
Sign Making 83
Jewelry Manufacturing 85
Makeup/Eyelash/Nail Artist 86
Child Photography 89
Selling and Maintaining
  Indoor Plants 90
Mural Painting 92
Mosaic Mural Making 94
Typesetting 96
Screen Printing 100
Direct Advertising
  Production 106
Fashion Design and
  Manufacturing 108

7

CLERICAL SERVICES 116

Tax Preparation Service 116
Bookkeeping Service 119
Collating and Binding
  Service 120
Mailing Service 122
Word Processing 126
Inventory Service 129
Insurance Inventorying 133

8

FIELD WORK 135

Process Serving 135
Market Research
  Interviewing 137

9

SELLING 141

Agenting 141
Direct Selling 144
Outside Car Salesperson 149
"Swap Meets" or
  "Flea Markets" 152
Gift Service 155
Mail Order Business 158
Advertising Representative
  for Newspapers and
  Magazines 162
Telephone Sales 165
Industry Recruiting 168

10

VENTURES THAT REQUIRE ADMINISTRATIVE SKILL 172

Retail Art Show 172
Consignment Shop 174
Special Purchase Broker 176
Apartment House Manager 179

11

PROMOTIONAL SERVICES 182

Product Demonstration and
  Modeling 182

CONTENTS

Product Demonstration and
   Modeling Agency   184

12

THE
ENTERTAINMENT
FIELD   188

Personal Manager   188
Artist's Manager or
   Booking Agent   190
Concert Promoter   193
Theatrical Producer   196
Television Record
   Packaging   198
Film Showing Business   202

13

INSTRUCTIONAL
SERVICES   206

Photography   208
Advertising Copywriting   208
Arts and Crafts   208
Fashion Design   208
Assertiveness Training   209
Gourmet Cooking   209
Tennis   209

Self-Defense   209
Exercise Classes   210
Tutoring High School
   Students   210

14

TRAVEL SERVICES   213

Camper and Recreational
   Vehicle Guide   213
Touring Service   216
Travel Agent   219

15

UNIQUE AND
INTERESTING
SERVICES   226

Astrology Reading   226
Handwriting Analysis
   (Graphology)   228
Singles Dances   230
Party Entertainment
   Service   234
Child Attending for
   Shoppers   237
Sex Surrogate   239

INTRODUCTION

The corporate ladder is not the only way to the top. You can build and climb your own personal ladder in the attainment of your goals. Any venture can be exciting and lucrative—it all depends upon how it is approached. Everyone has at least one unique talent which, when realized and properly nurtured, can be both emotionally and financially rewarding.

Climb Your Own Ladder will show you how to put imagination and creativity into a wide variety of service businesses. These ventures can be started inexpensively in or from your home. They can be continued on a part-time basis as a source of additional income for further investment in real estate, securities, commodities, fine art, and other growth opportunities. Or, later, the simplest venture can be expanded into a large and sophisticated full-time enterprise.

Many people are successful because they think and plan in concepts. Each activity they engage in leads to, supports, and enhances a succeeding endeavor of greater magnitude. This is the process by which small business operations grow into gigantic enterprises. In this book you will be shown how one endeavor can lead to larger opportunities in the same field. When a number of services in a field are integrated and provided as a full-service "package," the potential for success becomes immense. We live in a constantly changing environment providing opportunities that previously did not exist.

A freelance copywriter can eventually develop his or her own advertising agency. A freelance business or political speechwriter can find him or herself in the upper rungs of the business and political world. The operator of a dry cleaning service route can develop a large chain of dry cleaning stores serving both individual consumers and large commercial establishments. The operator of a mobile lubricating and oil service for automobiles can become the owner of a chain of "lube and oil" concessions in self-service gasoline stations. A sex surrogate can advance to becoming a professionally licensed sex therapist. Security is an important concern in any organization, and a handwriting analyst (graphologist) can help a client corporation screen all levels of job applicants as to their personality, honesty, and other characteristics important to the operation of a well-organized company. A rug cleaning business can be started by one person with little capital and grow into a million dollar enterprise by securing assignments in the corporate world. These are but a few of the numerous opportunities discussed in this book. The possibilities are almost limitless.

As inflation increases, so let your income increase. The *junior or middle management executive* can put his or her expertise into the marketing and growth of many of the ventures that will be discussed. A *housewife* can learn a new skill or adapt a former skill or hobby into an exciting business venture.

A *college student* can work his or her way through school via independent ventures that are compatible with and enhance the college program being undertaken. Many of the business and marketing courses taken in school can assist the success of an independent business. And in turn, self-employment in college allows you to fully appreciate the academic program you are undergoing. Many of today's corporate heads expanded a college venture into a successful enterprise following graduation.

The *male head of household* can supplement the family income during his spare time. In fact, there are many instances where a man has successfully left his full-time job to pursue a more lucrative career developed from his part-time venture.

Working people who seldom enjoy the tax benefits of the wealthy can create their own tax write-offs by deducting apartment, automobile, telephone, and entertainment expenses required to develop their part-time or full-time businesses.

There are many opportunities in which the *entire family* can participate, with each member contributing his or her special talents in the promotion and success of the business. This type of cooperative venture can add a new dimension to the family structure.

Despite the increasingly competitive business world with all its sophisticated computers, success still lies with the talents, creativity, and determination of the individual. Showing you how you can best use your talents to win success is the purpose of this book.

—*Allen Lieberoff*

A FEW
IMPORTANT NOTES

All the businesses discussed in this book are relatively simple to operate. Nevertheless, all business endeavors require a certain amount of paperwork and record keeping. The following are a few important points to consider when starting your business venture:

Almost all communities require a *business license* for the operation of an independent venture. Contact your city hall to obtain such a license.

The usual fee for a business license is $65 per year. If your business involves the selling of a product or products for which there is a *state sales tax* charge, it will be your responsibility to collect this tax from your customers, keep accurate records of these transactions, and periodically turn these tax revenues over to the state. All this is accomplished through the local office of your state's Board of Equalization. If your state charges a sales tax for the residents of that state, contact the local office of your State Board of Equalization. They will arrange for the convenient payment of all state sales taxes due them.

To keep track of your profits, and as a basis for paying income taxes, *accurate business records* should be kept, and it is advisable that you enlist the services of an accountant, a bookkeeping service, or both to assist you in this. The fees you will pay them will be well worth it. The services these professionals can render will allow you more free time for the running of your business and the creation of more profits. To make it easy to work with a good accountant or bookkeeping service, establish a *commercial checking account* under your business name. All incoming business revenues should be recorded and deposited in this checking account. Likewise, all business expenditures should be itemized and paid out of this checking account. In this manner, your accountant can use your itemized check stubs as a guide to preparing important financial statements and tax records. Accumulated profits can always be deposited in bank accounts or money funds providing greater interest.

As your business enterprise expands, you may want to hire additional people to assist you in the attainment of your goals. Obviously, there is always the possibility of one of your employees getting ill on the job. To protect your employees financially (medical bills, time lost from work, compensation for continued suffering), and to protect yourself from devastating lawsuits, all states require that employers carry *liability insurance* on their employees. Many private insurance companies offer liability insurance policies covering various occupational hazards. However, not all companies will insure for every occupational risk. In this case, all states have a Worker's Compensation Fund to provide insurance coverage that cannot be obtained in the private sector. Whether you insure privately or with your state, premiums are determined by the accident statistics on the particular type of work. For example, the premium for clerical workers (a relatively safe occupation) is approximately 35¢ per $100 paid them. Painters and wallpaperers require a premium of about $7.50 per $100 paid them. Movers of house furnishings and heavy equipment, because they can more readily injure themselves lifting heavy objects, require a premium of $15 per $100 paid them. These fees should be considered when determining your overhead and charges for your goods or services. It is possible to make arrangements with your State Worker's Compensation Department or private carrier to make your payments in a manner that will always allow you to hire extra individuals spontaneously and have them covered automatically.

The expenses incurred in setting up and operating a business can usually be deducted from your income tax. In addition, if you operate your business from your home or apartment, or use your automobile or telephone in conducting your business, part of these expenses can be included in these tax-deductable expenses. Contact your accountant or local Internal Revenue office for exact rules and details for each year.

All the opportunities discussed in this book were researched in 1981 and 1982. These opportunities will continue to exist in the years to follow as they cater to the daily needs of consumers and industry. Because of inflation, however, projected expenses and profits will most likely increase. To calculate future expenses and profits for each opportunity, multiply the quoted figures by the inflation rate.

REFERENCE BOOKS

In many of the endeavors discussed in this book, I direct you to various reference books to assist you in getting started or acquiring clients. These books can be found in most community and college libraries in your area. If your library does not have one of the reference books cited, ask the librarian to call around to find a branch that does carry it.

Ulrich's International Periodicals Directory—This reference lists magazines and newspapers according to subject matter. It will direct you to publications that contain general information about many industries, trades, and professions and the names of some of the individuals who work in them (your potential clients).

Standard Rate and Data—This reference lists all magazines according to industry, trade, or profession, giving the circulation and subject matter. It is especially helpful if you're looking for likely publications in which to advertise.

Note: If you have difficulty in locating a particular magazine listed in one of the above reference books, write to the publisher informing him that you are considering subscribing to or advertising in his journal, and to please send you some sample copies for review. They will usually send you a couple of copies, and these can help you decide if subscribing to that publication will be profitable to you.

The Thomas Register—This series of books lists almost every manufacturer in the country, classifying them by product. It is an extremely useful aid when selecting equipment for your business or items you may want to purchase or sell.

Encyclopedia of Associations—This large book lists according to function every association or organization in the country, giving the address of the headquarters of each. Listings include trade groups, professional associations, athletic groups, philanthropic organizations, and medical associations, to name just a few. This encyclopedia is an invaluable aid in targeting specific interest groups who may want to buy your product or service.

By the way, your local librarian might be the most important resource you have for your business. Librarians are highly trained professionals who make it their business to keep abreast of every source book available that can give people important information in conducting their business or profession. If there is something you need to know, ask your librarian. He or she will know how to help you.

ON BECOMING BONDED

In many of the endeavors discussed in this book, you will have to convince your potential clients of your honesty and reliability. One of the best ways to do so is through a bond. A bond is an assurance against theft, granted by an insurance company. It protects a client against any possible theft that could be committed by the person he or she is doing business with (in this case you). It is up to you to obtain the bond. Before granting you a bond, the insurance (bonding) company interviews previous employers and investigates police files to assure themselves that you have no record of theft. If your record is clean you are usually eligible for bonding. The fee for bonding is approximately $35 per year for $1,000 worth of protection for your client's valuables. Thus, your client knows that if you steal something, they will receive up to $1,000 in compensation from your bonding company. You can obtain $10,000 worth of protection for your clients for approximately $145 a year. Nevertheless, you know you are not going to steal. You just want to give your client assurance that you have no criminal record and that you are trustworthy. Thus, if you just take out $1,000 worth of insurance for the $35, you will be allowed to put the words "Bonded by (the name of your bonding company)" on your business card. To find bonding companies, just look in the Yellow Pages under "Bonding Companies" or "Business Service Bonds."

BUSINESS CARDS

Another tool to project an image of professionalism and credibility is a business card. The information given on the card can be quite simple: the name of your business, its function, any slogans that you might have, your own name, title, address and telephone number. If you are bonded, include that information. Business cards serve to remind potential clients of your service and to help them locate you. Any printing shop can make them up for you.

A FEW TIPS ON SALESMANSHIP

Every chapter in this book includes a discussion of the many ways you can build up a large clientele for the business being discussed. Nevertheless, when approaching potential clients, you still must sell yourself. Obviously, you can read books and attend seminars on "salesmanship." However, I would like to give you the basic rudiments for impressing and selling your client: Show an enthusiasm for your product or service and a sincere concern for the needs of your customer.

Everyone can be a tremendous salesperson when representing something he or she truly believes in. Unfortunately, it is not always easy to get a job representing a top-notch product or service. That is the beauty of this book. It allows you to create and develop your own service business—one you can be proud to represent.

If you want to do advertising copywriting for a company or agency, communicate your belief in that person's product. When soliciting customers for a mobile automobile lubricating and oil or waxing service, show that you are truly interested in extending the longevity of your customers' cars. A personal caterer should show clients that he or she would like to cater a dinner party that will impress that person's associates and enhance his or her image. As a part-time or full-time travel agent, take an interest in your client's vacation or business trip as if it were your own. Even if things are a little rough in the beginning, if you exhibit a belief in yourself and an interest in other people, everything will eventually fall into place.

1
WRITING OPPORTUNITIES

ADVERTISING COPYWRITING

WHY

Everything is sold through advertising. Copywriters create the headlines, slogans, and text that attract buyers to a product. Pick up any newspaper or magazine and look at the ads or listen to radio or television commercials. Every time someone tries to induce the public to purchase a product or utilize a service, whatever is said about that product is known as "copy" and is written by copywriters. Advertising agencies, large and small, will have some permanent copywriters on their staff. However, in order to cut down on business overhead, many copywriting assignments are contracted out to freelance copywriters. If you have a good command of the English language, possess a fairly decent literary style, and have a feel for what people will respond to, there is no reason you can't take advantage of these opportunities.

GETTING STARTED

People who have had a variety of jobs and experiences and are creative make excellent candidates for the advertising profession. Previous jobs, no matter what they were, make you more aware of the nature of people. After all, knowing how people react to certain stimuli is really what advertising is all about. The ad is the original stimulus. When people react positively to this stimulus (go out and purchase the product), the ad is successful.

To write an effective ad, learn as much about the product as possible. This can be accomplished easily by reading all of the client's literature on the product, followed up if necessary by personal interviews with the client. After you become familiar with the product, ask yourself how you can describe the benefits and advantages of the product. Make the text informative, but also as concise and brief as possible. Don't repeat any sentences or thoughts. Think up a headline or slogan that will catch the reader's attention and induce him or her to read further. If you're writing about a new kind of onion slicer, the caption might read: "AT LAST! NO MORE TEARS SLICING ONIONS." The ensuing copy should describe the benefits of using the product.

Taking a creative writing class in a college or high school adult education program can help to develop and supplement your own natural talents.

FINANCIAL REWARDS

The average fee scale for a freelance copywriter is anywhere from $25 to $100 an hour. Sometimes a package price is agreed upon for one individual assignment. The price might be $200 for an assignment no matter how slowly or quickly it is completed. As your reputation for fine work develops, you will be able to charge larger fees.

ACQUIRING CLIENTS

Your two sources of customers are advertising agencies needing copywriting services to serve their clients properly, and the manufacturers of goods who handle their own advertising needs (these are listed by product in *The Thomas Register*). Advertising agencies will be listed in the yellow pages of the phone book.

When going after your first assignment, naturally you will not have a portfolio of previous assignments to show prospective clients. This can be circumvented in two ways: first, pick out any product known to everyone. Make up your own creative "sample ad" to show your prospective client what you can do. Secondly, if an agency is deliberating on whether or not to give you a particular assignment, offer to write it with the option that if they are not pleased with your best effort, they won't have to pay you. Once you develop a reputation for creating good copy, however, you can command guaranteed payment.

One way to attract the attention of the manufacturers of goods and services is to look through newspapers and magazines, observing ads that are particularly impressive. Call or write the president of a company whose ad is well-done and compliment his or her agency. Discuss in your letter or conversation the possibility of handling some of the company's other needs. If you see an ad you think is not effective enough and you have some constructive criticism, call and suggest how the ad can can be improved. This will involve you in conversation that can result in an assignment. Also, call on product managers (the company operator will give you names) to find out what their needs are and offer them ideas for developing successful ads.

Do not be afraid to approach large companies. Most major industrial organizations who produce a variety of products usually decentralize their operations. Each major product line is under the supervision of a product manager. This individual has the responsibility of marketing the product and is usually given a free hand in determining what advertising sources to use.

Another means of soliciting clients is to attend conventions held by a particular industry. You can go from one exhibit booth to another to speak with the marketing people. Quite often it is possible to solicit the business of several noncompeting companies. You may want to serve several varied industries; or you may find it more convenient to specialize in one particular industry. For example, you may have had experience working with medical equipment. This knowledge would help you in communicating with manufacturers of medical equipment to solicit their business.

Publications read by almost everyone in the advertising profession are *Adweek* magazine and *Advertising Age* magazine, both found in most main libraries. Place an ad in these journals to make advertising agencies and manufacturing companies aware of your services.

FUTURE GAINS

After you become proficient in this area of the profession, you might want to start your own advertising agency. In this capacity, you would not only produce advertising copy, but would also be responsible for providing the artwork for the ad and arranging for it's production. Just as other ad agencies utilized your services to provide the copy, you can subcontract the artistic and production requirements for the ad to specialists in that field. Eventually, if desired, you yourself can become proficient in these areas or hire skilled personnel to work for you.

Operating a well-run agency can be very lucrative. In general, you take your copywriting, artistic, and production costs and double them to arrive at a professional fee for your clients. In addition, you receive an extra 15 percent "agency discount" from the publications in which you place your clients' ads. If an ad costs you $1000 to produce, your fee to the client would be $2000. If you place a one-page ad in four magazines who charge $3000 per page, this amounts to $12,000 in advertising fees. Your agency discount of 15 percent amounts to $1800 for a total gross profit of $2800. As your accounts grow in size and number, these professional fees can escalate considerably.

FUND-RAISING WRITING

WHY

There are numerous nonprofit organizations—charities, hospitals, medical research groups, churches, colleges and community causes—constantly trying to raise money for their worthwhile endeavors. Most people don't part with their money easily. That is why these groups will pay substantial amounts of money to people who can write bulletins and brochures to induce people to give money willingly to their causes. Writing for fund-raising projects and organizations utilizes the same principles as advertising copywriting, but in this case it is for a "good cause" instead of a product.

GETTING STARTED

There are books available that offer excellent instructions and guidelines for preparing an effective fund-raising campaign or writing brochures. One such book is *The Art of Fund Raising*, by Irving R. Warner, published by Harper & Row.

Most of the executives engaged in a fund-raising campaign are involved in the administrative end of the project. They don't have the time (or often the talent) to write the campaign literature. To do this effectively, you will have to research your work by reading literature on the problem the money is being raised for, talking to people directly or indirectly involved with the problem, and getting involved emotionally in the eventual solution of the problem.

To get the hang of campaign writing, study fund-raising literature already in existence. These brochures and slogans can provide excellent examples of approach, tone, and style.

When writing your copy, draw the reader right into the heart of the problem. For instance, if money is being raised to find a cure for and help the people already suffering from a disease, write a brief description of what the afflicted person has to go through and contend with during a typical day. Naturally, you don't want your text to be a tearjerker. Nevertheless, design your writing style to make the reader sit up and recognize the plight of others.

This can induce the most resistant person to reach into his or her pocket and give.

To improve your natural abilities in this kind of writing, it would be a good idea to attend some classes in psychology, art, science, and finance.

FINANCIAL REWARDS

There are two ways in which you may be paid for your services: by the hour or in one lump sum. Whichever method is used, the efforts for a good job should pay you from $25 to $100 an hour, or a total of $300 to $500 for a letter and $1000 to $2000 for a brochure.

ACQUIRING CLIENTS

When soliciting clients, don't call ahead for an appointment. Dress neatly and present yourself, boldly but politely, to the director's office. Most likely, the person in charge will see you. After all, you are there to show him or her how you can bring in more money than they already have. Who doesn't want to hear about this? Most important, though, have a sample outline of the steps you plan to take to increase their revenues.

Call on the heads of every religious group in your community. All churches and synagogues are constantly trying to raise funds to finance a multitude of meritorious projects, and most churches are small enough to be approached easily.

In most communities, all charitable groups seeking funds from the public are required to register their organization with the city to be screened for establishing their credibility. Contact your city hall to obtain a list of worthwhile charity groups for eventual contact.

FUTURE GAINS

Because so many functions depend on financial contributions, fund raising is "big business." Eventually you can extend your participation from writing copy to directing an entire campaign. In this capacity, you would originate and coordinate all the activities that go into a financially successful project. This would include writing brochures, distributing literature, and arranging fund-raising dinners, entertainment events, and the sale of special products—the proceeds of which are contributed to the campaign. The financial arrangements between you and your client can be flexible. An ideal situation is to receive $100 to $200 per hour plus a percentage of the revenues.

For more information on making fund raising a career, write:

American Association of
Fund Raising Council
25 W. 43rd St.
New York, N.Y. 10036

National Society of Fund
Raising Executives
1511 K St. N.W.
Washington, D.C. 20006

Fund Raising Management
Magazine

and

Direct Mail Marketing
Magazine
224 7th St.
Garden City, N.Y. 11530

These organizations and publications can give you current information on fund raising techniques, different methods of billing clients, and methods of distributing fund raising literature.

WRITING ARTICLES FOR MAGAZINES

WHY

Most magazines cannot afford to employ full-time reporting staffs to research and write all the articles they publish. If they did, they would go broke just from their high payroll. So most magazines and even many newspapers use the services of freelance reporters who investigate and write about topics of interest.

GETTING STARTED

A good source for guidance and information concerning article writing is the magazine *Writer's Digest,* published by Writer's Digest, 9933 Alliance Road, Cincinnati, Ohio 45242. A good book on the subject, *A Complete Guide to Marketing Magazine Articles,* by Duane Newcomb, is available from the same publisher.

In general, it is easier to sell nonfiction material than fiction. The mere mention of properly selected nonfiction topics elicits attention. There is a wide range of areas to draw upon as sources for good nonfiction.

Magazines and other periodicals want to capture the reader's attention. Always keep this question in mind: "Will the article sell magazines?" Personal interviews of prominent people always make interesting reading and are constantly in demand. The interview does not always have to be in-depth. Sometimes, just asking the person his feelings on one particular subject is sufficient. The *Guinness Book of World Records* is crammed with unusual people and feats. If any of the record holders live in your vicinity, they may be able to provide you with interesting infor-

6

mation about themselves, such as how they developed the skill that broke the record, or whether they plan to attempt to break their own record. Professors on a college campus who are experts in one particular field can provide an in-depth look at the latest trends, theories, or discoveries. For example, a psychology professor might discuss how to interpret dreams. Whenever a rock concert comes to your area, go backstage and try to get a quick interview with the stars; they have often been known to grant them. After all, they can always use more publicity to promote their records. The police station makes an excellent source for writing about unusual crimes. If a celebrity grew up in your area, go through old yearbooks in the library of the high school from which he or she graduated. Contact classmates who still live in the same town and ask them for "human interest" information about that celebrity. These people may even have some old pictures of the celebrity which many tabloids would pay a small fortune to print.

Go through magazines looking for small articles on interesting subjects which you could research further and expand upon for use by other magazines. Industries might be able to provide you with the latest news on new technological breakthroughs. Every industrial association is listed in the *Encyclopedia of Associations*, available in your library. You may find it very profitable to contact the officials of these organizations for information on new achievements.

Medical schools and college life-sciences research laboratories may be making interesting medical breakthroughs in areas such as genetics. Professional think-tanks are another source of new ideas and concepts that might be of value in the future. You can locate these places by consulting the *Research Centers Directory* or *Research and Development Directory* in your library. For help in becoming a better interviewer, consult *The Craft of Interviewing*, by John Brady, available from *Writer's Digest*.

FINANCIAL REWARDS

A good article will usually bring in anywhere from $100 to $1000 depending on the circulation and policies of the publication and the significance of the article. The average payment for an article is between $200 and $400.

ACQUIRING CLIENTS

Each year, *Writer's Digest* publishes a book entitled *Writer's Market*, which lists hundreds of magazine publishers, the type of articles they are looking for, and what they will pay for each article.

If you've already written an article, call up a likely magazine to find out the name of the editor who handles that subject. Contact that person, describe your article, and ask if he or she would like you to send it in. If it's at all appropriate, the editor will probably be willing to take a look. If not, he or she may refer you to either another editor at the magazine or another more appropriate publication.

One of the biggest users of freelance material is the *National Enquirer* newspaper, found on most newsstands and supermarket checkout counters. It has been reported that in 1976 they paid out more than $3,692,800 for freelance articles. They can provide you with some excellent information as to what a tabloid such as theirs is looking for. Write them for a copy of "Free-lancing for the *National Enquirer*" and their "Scale of Payment" Sheet. Their address is:

Director of Communication
National Enquirer
Lantana, Florida 33464.

Also, buy a couple of issues of the paper to familiarize yourself with their format.

FUTURE GAINS

Freelance magazine writing can be turned into a well-paying professional career. It has been reported that many freelance journalists make over $40,000 annually. You could eventually join the permanent staff of a newspaper or magazine and from there work your way up to executive editorial positions.

SPEECH WRITING FOR POLITICIANS AND BUSINESS PEOPLE

WHY

Business people and politicians often persuade others to accept their points of view through speeches. Quite often, however, they find it difficult to assemble and articulate their thoughts properly. This is your opportunity to help them do so.

GETTING STARTED

There are many ways for you to become informed about a particular subject for which you get an assignment. When writing business speeches, interview the client-speechmaker to find out the message he or she wants to get across to the audience. Read industry brochures and newsletters concerning the subject. Your local library can help you with this. A good encyclopedia can serve as an excellent source for preliminary information and background on the subject. Other people in the field can also provide you with information. Free-lancing as a political speech-writer is a bit more difficult, since most politicians rely on their staffers for their speeches. It is, however, possible. A background in newspaper work is valuable in getting you started. And, of course, you need to be informed about current events and your client's feelings and positions both on major national issues and those that specifically affect his or her constituency.

Valuable tools are your library's *Guide to Periodical Literature* and *Newspaper Index*, which can provide you with instant information on what your client's opponents are saying. This alone can give you valuable material for preparing interesting and effective speeches.

FINANCIAL REWARDS

A well-written business speech can bring anywhere from $200 to $2500 in fees. A political speech writer with good credentials can receive from $1,000 to $5,000 for a twenty minute speech.

ACQUIRING CLIENTS

The best place to attract the interest of business clients is to advertise in business and industry trade journals. A list of these publications can be found in *Ulrich's International Periodicals Directory.*

When soliciting political clients, contact the local Democratic or Republican parties' headquarters and inform them you would like to be of service to their candidates. Call on every officeholder in your community: councilmen, the mayor, state senators and assemblymen, the governor, federal congressmen and senators. They all have aspirations and need all the help they can get. Since you are a beginner, it might be advisable to prepare a sample speech to illustrate your knowledge and creativity.

When landing an assignment, you should not only ask the candidate what he or she wants to get across to the public, but also offer suggestions as to items you think are important and should not be overlooked.

FUTURE GAINS

Business-speech writers frequently obtain positions in the upper echelons of the business world themselves. Many people who have been speech writers for beginning politicians have ended up being their top advisors, confidants, and righthand people when they reached the top. Typical examples are Jody Powell and Hamilton Jordan, who started out with former President Carter when he was a gubernatorial candidate, and then followed him to the White House. Although President Carter is no longer in office, his important aides still command respect in society and are sought after to fill important roles.

WRITING
GREETING CARD VERSE

WHY

Greeting card manufacturers require a never-ending flow of prose, verse, ideas, and concepts for their creations. No longer do people buy greeting cards just for a person's birthday or a particular holiday. People are now buying greeting cards to relate thoughts to other people, whether they be serious, romantic, or humorous. Quite often, a person who is not planning to send a card will do so on impulse upon coming across a card that relates to a particular friend or acquaintance. The greeting card business is now a million-dollar-a-year industry. As in so many other businesses, much of the work is contracted out to freelance creators.

GETTING STARTED

If you are an aspiring poet, why not turn your talents toward the ever-growing greeting card world? Almost any thought you have can be directed to a particular market. There are numerous ways of expressing every type of human feeling and thought. To supplement your natural talent and interest in this field, it might be a good idea to purchase *The Greeting Card Writer's Handbook*, by H. Joseph Chadwick, published by *Writer's Digest* (see page 7 for address).

FINANCIAL REWARDS

A card company will customarily pay $1.50 to $3.00 per line of verse for everyday greeting cards, and from $15 to $75 for studio card ideas.

ACQUIRING CLIENTS

Almost every greeting card manufacturer in the country is a potential client. Even those who have their own full-time staffs can always be induced to utilize a new idea from an outsider who can give them an edge over the competition. The *Thomas Register of American Manufacturers*, located in your library, should contain a list of all the major greeting card manufacturers in this country.

FUTURE GAINS

As you become adept in this art, you can even start your own card company. At first you can distribute locally with just one card style or several different styles. Your line might consist just of humorous cards: You could come up with an idea for a cute cartoon-type animal with different messages for each occasion. Or if romance is your main interest, a series of romantic messages may serve to establish your identity. The possibilities are almost endless.

If you are artistic as well as poetic, you can design your own cards. If not, this task can always be contracted out to freelance artists. The actual manufacturing and printing of the cards can be subcontracted to a good printing company. If you do a good volume of business, a card that would wholesale for 50¢ and retail for $1.00 could end up costing you only 10¢ to print.

In the beginning, you can contact potential clients such as drugstores, department stores, supermarkets, liquor stores, stationery shops and boutiques by yourself. As business grows, you can hire freelance salespeople to represent you on a commission basis.

No matter what the state of the economy, greeting cards will always be used to convey messages and feelings.

COMEDY WRITING

WHY

Comedy occupies a large portion of the entertainment spectrum. Humor is often the foundation for night club acts, stage events, plays, movies, and television shows. Although delivered in a free-flowing manner, humor cannot always be spontaneous. In most cases, it takes the work of skilled comedy writers to create entertaining formats.

GETTING STARTED

How many times has someone told you to stop joking around? How often does a funny thought go through your mind, which you dismiss? Don't laugh—or better yet, do laugh! This is the essence of humor. There is no definite format for laughter. Everything has its humorous side. That's why there is such a wide variety of comedians and always room for more good ones. Comedians who come up with their own routines in the beginning of their careers, quite often utilize the services of good comedy writers as their careers begin to blossom and more performances and routines are required. It has been said that a good comedian or comedy writer is one who has a third eye or sixth sense in seeing the humor in almost any situation.

When thinking up jokes and routines, don't be afraid to write down even the most far-out thoughts that might pass through your mind. Chances are they are also going through the minds of many other people. And if you can construct a routine that can act as a mirror to other people's funny sides, you just might have a success on your hands.

Almost anything that happens in life is a source of humor. Read the newspapers. Many top comedy writers illustrate the humorous side of politics and world events. The ironic and controversial things that public officials do and say have been used by many comedians to break audiences into laughter. Does something in everyday life annoy you? Most likely it annoys everyone else, too, but no one says anything about it. Some examples are poor service in restaurants, airports, and department stores, or an obnoxious commercial on television. The problems of inflation, as frustrating as they may be, provide numerous opportunities for humor. For example, "Prices are so high, I saw a sign in the meat department of a supermarket saying: 'Financing available.'"

Just let your thoughts run free; write them down and see what results. The rewards can be most gratifying.

FINANCIAL REWARDS

Night club circuit entertainers will usually pay $10 to $20 for a joke, and for good routines $200 to $400 for one-minute monologues. Top comics will often pay $1500 and more a five-minute routine.

ACQUIRING CLIENTS

Whereas big-time comedians might be hard to approach in the

beginning, there are many comedians performing locally that might very well accept your talents. Watch their acts and talk to them backstage after they have finished. Show them some samples of your work. After you build up even a small reputation as a comedy writer, it will be possible to approach the bigger stars either personally or through their agents or managers. Also, as the younger comics you write for move up in the entertainment world, so will your reputation and fees.

To attract some of the bigger stars, advertise your services in the professional entertainment magazines such as *Variety* and *Hollywood Reporter.*

Lately, many products are being advertised in a humorous vein on radio and television. If you can think of a humorous approach to the marketing of any of today's consumer products, contact the advertising agencies representing those manufacturers. Writing humorous commercials can pay extremely well, especially if they are presented on a national scale.

FUTURE GAINS

There are tremendous amounts of money to be made writing for television situation comedies, known in the industry as sitcoms. You might create your own original sitcom, get hired as a staff writer for an established sitcom, or work freelance contributing individual episodes for the established comedies. Writers for situation comedies can earn anywhere from $1000 to $10,000 a show.

RESUMÉ WRITING

WHY

Each year, millions of people aspire to new jobs. It is difficult for employers to interview each applicant personally. Quite often they depend on reviewing resumés to decide who is qualified for a personal interview. A resumé is defined as a summary of a person's occupational and educational background. When properly written, it becomes a fantastic marketing tool in obtaining a desired position. In essence, a good resumé is a sales brochure with the job applicant as the product being sold.

If you can learn to write these personal "sales brochures," there is an excellent chance of developing a successful business in doing so. Some job applicants write their own resumés. But just like doing one's own income tax, it can become a perplexing and frustrating task. Just as it often takes a tax specialist to properly state a person's financial situation, it often requires a skilled communications expert to assess an individual's job qualifications and to then convey them on paper.

GETTING STARTED

Rather than teach you how to write resumés, we will discuss the essence of a good resumé and how to market your skills to the public. At the end of this section, we will list several books that do an excellent job of teaching resumé writing. Each book teaches a variety of styles. You might want to use one particular style most comfortable to you, a variety of styles appropriately selected for the needs of each individual applicant, or your own personal style developed as a composite of the styles you will read about. Whatever method you develop, there are several important rules in resumé writing: A good resumé is concise, to the point, and no more than two pages long. Anyone can write endlessly; it takes an expert to summarize. The resumé should cover your client's background, goals, job history, educational and military history, and some accomplishments and awards.

A good resumé requires a personal interview lasting from one hour to an hour and a half to give you an in-depth feeling for the talents of the client and how to communicate them on paper. The actual writing will require another hour to an hour and a half. Once you develop an expertise in this field, the interview and subsequent writing should not take more than one hour each.

CONDUCTING THE INTERVIEW

Believe it or not, most people, no matter how intelligent they may be, do not know how to express and communicate their true talents. This gives you an opportunity to stand out among any competitors. A good resumé interviewer should be somewhat of a job psychologist. You must know how to delve into a client's occupational background and draw out the accomplishments that will most impress an employer. Don't worry; if you truly like people and are interested in their success, this skill will develop quickly. In fact, it can become a lot of fun. Furthermore, a client receiving this attention will often inform his or her friends of your expertise.

WRITING TO SELL YOUR CLIENT

Some clients will have an impressive career background. These assignments will merely require a good writing style on your part. However, what about the individual whose accomplishments do not appear very impressive on the surface? Well, here again is an opportunity for you to establish your credentials in this field. No one is average or plain. As your ad or business card might say, everyone possesses something special about themselves and you bring it out. The supposedly average secretary might have been instrumental in untangling various administrative problems for his or her company. A purchasing agent might have been innovative in procuring some hard-to-find materials necessary in a company's manufacturing process. A plant manager might have developed a new manufacturing protocol that reduced a firm's expenses. Or maybe an advertising executive developed an ad campaign that dramatically increased a company's sales. When accomplishments such as these are elicited from a client and properly written down, they contribute an important dimension to the resumé.

Upon completing the resumé, if your client is not able to meet you to check and proofread it, call him or her on the phone for a verbal reading. It should not take you more than fifteen minutes to do so. After the client approves your work, it should be typed by a professional manuscript typist or at an independent secretarial service (endeavors also discussed in this book) on an IBM Selectric typewriter or similar machine to give it a professional look. To impress your clients with the completeness of your service, 100 copies of their resumé for eventual submission to potential employers should be printed on an offset printing press. Many instant print shops offer this accommodation. A secretarial service will charge approximately $10 for the typing. The offset printing will cost approximately another $10.

THE COVER LETTER

While it is quite permissible for a job applicant to send a commercially printed resumé to prospective employers, each resumé should be accompanied by a cover letter personally typed by the applicant. To embellish your services and professional reputation, offer to write a sample cover letter for your client. He or she can then use this as a guide each time a resumé is mailed out. A cover letter should be a brief introduction to the applicant, his or her aspirations, and the contributions he or she can make to the employer's organization.

BOOKS TO HELP YOU WRITE GOOD RESUMÉS

Resumés That Get Jobs
by Jean Reed
published by Arco
Publishing Co.
Resumés for Job Hunters
by Maury Shykind
published by Arco

Resumés for Hard Times
by Bob Weinstein
published by Fireside
Books,
Simon and Schuster

FINANCIAL REWARDS

Resumé fees range anywhere from $25 to $200. It has been my observation that resumés costing only $25 are nothing more than drab compilations of an individual's past experiences with a list of superlatives such as "greatest," "terrific," and "fantastic" added on. These resumés are unimpressive, suggest a shallowness on the part of the sender, and usually get thrown into the receiver's waste basket. A resumé that sends a subtle message to the reader is the one that usually gets results. For this type of creation, you are quite in line to charge at least $150 for your services. And by informing your client of what you want to accomplish for him or her, you should not meet any resistance in obtaining your fee.

One half of your fee should be collected after the interview. The other half should be collected when the finished copies are picked up. If you charge $150, after deducting the $10 for the professional typist and $10 for the offset printing, you are left with a profit of $130 for two to three hours of work.

ACQUIRING CLIENTS

DIRECT ADVERTISING

In developing a clientele, direct your efforts to the people most likely to be looking for jobs. Executives from all levels of the professional and commercial world are constantly seeking new career heights through upward job changes. Advertise your services in the local business and executive magazines circulated in the community. Your librarian can direct you to the best publications. People looking for new jobs constantly scan the "help wanted" and "executive career" sections in newspapers. Place announcements of your services there.

OUTPLACEMENT DEPARTMENTS

Because of the constantly changing needs of many corporations, it is often necessary to release an individual whose talents no longer fit the requirements of the company. At one time, it was quite common to abruptly fire such an employee. This policy is changing now, for several reasons. First of all, it is morally improper and hurts the morale of remaining employees. When people know their company cares about them, even in times of dismissal, it creates a feeling of camaraderie resulting in greater productivity. In addition, an employee who has to leave a company could quite possibly obtain an important position with a firm with whom his present employer would eventually like to do business. It therefore makes good business sense to leave departing employees with good feelings.

To assist employees who have to be dismissed, many firms have developed "outplacement departments" to help them prepare for and find new positions. Part of the process involves helping them write new resumés. If you can provide a resumé service for these outplacement departments, it can relieve them from this time-consuming responsibility and result in a substantial contribution to your own business.

Every company in your area is fair game for your services—banks, insurance companies, advertising agencies, retail store chains, television and radio stations, newspaper and magazine publishers, distributing and manufacturing companies, to name just a few. When approaching a commercial organization with an outplacement department, inform their personnel department that you can save them a lot of time and money by fulfilling their entire resumé requirements yourself. You can travel to the company to administer to their departing employees or the employees can be directed to your home or wherever else you might practice. In many cases, the company you work with might even pay your entire fee or part of it.

EMPLOYMENT AGENCIES

Many people use employment agencies to help them find jobs. Some agencies prefer their clients to provide them with a resumé which in turn can be forwarded to prospective client employers. Personally contact the managers of all executive employment agencies informing them of the services you can provide to their clients. Be sure to leave them several of your business cards for future referrals.

SELLING YOURSELF TO POTENTIAL CLIENTS

The best way to secure clients is to take a sincere interest in them. When they first call, ask what they do, what their goals are, what they've accomplished. Get excited about their aspirations. However, do not exaggerate your services. In fact, inform them that a good resumé does not get them a job; it just gets them an invitation for an interview with the proper people. This statement alone is a subtle sales talk on your part. It prevents them from expecting too much from you, but at the same time establishes the potential results of your skills. After they express a desire to see you, mention your fee and set up an appointment.

SUGGESTED COPY FOR AN AD OR BUSINESS CARD

RESUMÉS

Professional resumés for career advancement
Everyone possesses something special.
We work together to bring it out.

(Your name)
(phone number)

FUTURE GAINS

Doing from one to two resumés a day could result in an annual salary of from $30,000 to $60,000 a year. In addition, you will become familiar with numerous career fields, the financial rewards, the people looking for positions, and the employers looking for productive employees. This puts you in an advantageous position to eventually start your own executive placement agency. Fees charged in this type of business generally range from 20 to 30 percent of a placement's first year's salary (paid by the employer). It is not uncommon for the operator of a good placement agency to earn over $100,000 a year.

MANUSCRIPT TYPING

WHY

This country is filled with thousands upon thousands of authors—not just those attempting to write the "great novel," but college professors, teachers, scientists, businesspeople, and other types of educators involved in textbook writing. In addition, there are authorities in numerous fields who write "how to" and other informative books relating to their area of expertise.

Getting a book published is a very competitive undertaking.

The writer must have everything going for him or her. Not only must the material be informative and well written, but also expertly and neatly typed. While many writers are capable of turning out good copy, and most can even type, it is preferable that they let an expert typist type out the final draft for consideration by the publishing houses.

GETTING STARTED

If you can type at least 60 words per minute and are adept in English composition and proper punctuation, you are in an ideal position to set up your own manuscript typing business. To do this type of work, it is best to have a self-correcting IBM Selectric typewriter or similar instrument that can turn out professional looking copy. The average cost of such a writing machine is approximately $1000. Nevertheless, there are many typewriter stores that will rent them for as little as $50 a month. When your assignments develop into a full-time business, you can then purchase your own unit.

FINANCIAL REWARDS

The standard rate for manuscript typing is approximately $2.50 per double-spaced page. If you are reasonably fast and accurate, a page will take you approximately 10 to 15 minutes to complete. This allows you to work at the rate of $10 to $15 per hour.

ACQUIRING CLIENTS

Every writer in the United States is a potential client of yours. They can mail their manuscripts to you from their home locations for eventual typing and mail-back by you. Of course a few phone calls will be required to coordinate everything properly. These phone calls are usually charged to the client.

One way to announce your service to a large number of writers is to advertise in one of the world's leading magazines for writers, *Writer's Digest*, published in Cincinnati, Ohio. For approximately $40 you can place a six-line ad that will spread the word of your services to writers all over the country.

To reach the educational community, place small ads in the many educational magazines. The names and addresses of such publications can be obtained from your local library.

FUTURE GAINS

If you decide to develop your business into a full-time venture, you can hire freelance or even full-time secretaries to work under you.

As the work comes in, you can personally go through each manuscript to make any necessary corrections in punctuation and then have one of your employee secretaries type the final draft. You can pay your secretaries at the rate of $2.00 per page while charging your client $2.50 per page, thus pocketing a gross profit of 50¢ per page. A 500-page manuscript allows you a profit of $250. As your reputation and business increases, your profits can multiply.

You can also incorporate a manuscript typing business as part of a full-time secretarial service (discussed later in this book). Or, if you possess literary skills, there are opportunities in book editing. Many writers are good at assembling important information but are not very organized or creative about putting it down on paper. If you can rewrite a manuscript to make it more interesting and comprehensible, you can command fees of $1000 and more per book. This is in addition to the regular typing fee of $2.50 per page.

LETTER-WRITING BUSINESSES

There are three general areas of correspondence you can practice:

1. Business correspondence (secretarial service)
2. Sales letters
3. Complaint letters for consumers

Each one will be discussed separately in its entirety. As desired, each one can then be practiced as an individual specialty or as part of a full-service secretarial business.

Business Correspondence (Secretarial Service)

WHY

Almost every type of business transaction is accompanied by some form of written communication. This communication might be in the form of a request for business, the structuring of a business deal, a confirmation of business, amendments to a business agreement, correcting problems in a business relationship, or a host of other communiqués that facilitate achievements in the commercial world.

Every business organization is judged on the image it projects. Well-worded letters, expertly typed on professional looking business stationery, help to inspire the recipient's confidence in the sender.

Not all businesspeople have the ability to express themselves clearly and well in the letters they send to business colleagues. This is often best accomplished by people with good secretarial skills. It is not always feasible, however, for small businesses to maintain full-time secretarial staffs. Many growing business organizations can increase their productivity and profits by using independent secretarial services to handle their business correspondence on a fee-for-service basis.

GETTING STARTED

If you are or have been a secretary or are willing to take some shorthand, typing, and English composition courses, this profession can be practiced on a self-employment basis directly from your home or office. There are many good secretarial books that offer guidelines to good business letter writing. One such book is *The Modern Business Letter Writer's Manual,* by Marjane Cloke and Robert Wallace, published by Doubleday/Dolphin Books.

A good secretarial service operator stores the client's business stationery for the typing of correspondence dictated over the telephone. A professional typewriter such as the IBM Selectric, or a similar instrument offering a variety of type styles, is desirable. A typewriter of this caliber generally sells for approximately $1000 or rents for about $50 per month.

A good cassette recorder can be purchased for approximately $100 with a telephone attachment for an additional $1.50. When the client calls in, the pertinent information is taken down in shorthand; but it is also a good idea to record the conversation as a back-up and reference procedure. When feasible, the client can also transmit into your recorder via the phone while you are busy typing other correspondence. This can provide for a more efficient utilization of time. Once the letter or letters are typed, deliver the originals plus addressed envelopes to your client for signing and mailing, and keep duplicates for your files.

You might also want to install a telephone answering machine to record dictation and messages while you are away. In this manner you can offer a 24-hour service.

FINANCIAL REWARDS

The rate for secretarial services is from $15 to $30 an hour, depending on how much structuring of the letter you have to do yourself.

ACQUIRING CLIENTS

In announcing your service, place small ads in the business section of newspapers and in local business publications. Your librarian can assist you in selecting the proper publications. A direct mail or newspaper ad might read as follows:

> MR. OR MS. BUSINESS PERSON: Is your business mail bogging you down? Spend your time on promoting your business and not in the back room writing letters. Let us take care of all your business letter writing needs while you go out and make money. There is no need to pay for a full-time secretary; we are a phone call away. Call us only when you need us. Tell us what you want to say and to whom. Our expert staff will compose an effective, well-written, to-the-point letter that will give you a professional communication with your customers, associates, suppliers, etc. We will put your business in its best light with effective communication. Call or write. . . .

If you have a background in legal secretarial work or are willing to become familiar with this specialty, you might want to include legal secretarial services for attorneys. There are many lawyers, especially those just starting out in practice, who find it most economical to utilize independent services. Announce your services in the local publications representing attorneys or address law firms directly by phone or personal letter.

An additional source of work is businesspeople who come from out of town to conduct business in your locality. If you desire this type of client, distribute your business cards to the major hotels where businesspeople stay, particularly all the hotels in the vicinity of your local airport. In addition, many airlines publish their own magazines which they distribute to their passengers. It is relatively inexpensive to advertise in these publications and a good way to attract businesspeople on their way to your area.

When serving a businessperson from out of town, you most

likely will be required to travel to his or her hotel and take dictation either from the individual client or at a small business conference conducted by him or her. Your client may require the dictation to be typed up immediately on the premises. In this type of situation, it is advisable to carry a small portable electric typewriter. This type of personal service commands a fee of $30 per hour and includes travel time to and from the client's location.

FUTURE GAINS

There will always be a demand to meet the written communication needs of a continually growing and increasingly complex business world. After you attain a large volume of business, you may want to consider the purchase or rental of a word processing system, discussed in this book under "Word Processing Service." Eventually you can hire other secretaries to work for you, paying them a percentage of your client fee for the work they perform.

With some imagination and planning, a small secretarial service can grow into a major service enterprise.

Sales Letter Writing

WHY

Every business has something for sale, be it service or a product. The potential customer might be the individual consumer or another business organization. One of the most popular ways for an organization to get its sales message delivered is through well-organized and convincing letters.

GETTING STARTED

As already discussed, businesspeople are not always the best writers. A lot of money goes into the printing and mailing of sales letters. They must be written as well as possible. An effective letter is direct, to the point, and not flowery, and is written in good English.

You may already possess a knack for this type of communication. If desired, there are ways to learn. Many colleges teach "sales letter writing" through their extension divisions. Consult your librarian regarding books on this subject.

FINANCIAL REWARDS

A good sales letter can command a price of $100 and up.

ACQUIRING CLIENTS

People who send sales letters in their businesses usually use mailing list brokers to purchase lists of likely buyers for their products and also mailing services (discussed later in this book) for the actual addressing and mailing of the letters. Quite often the operators of these two types of business services can be influential in recommending your services to their clients. Look them up in the telephone book yellow pages.

Frequently, the composing of sales letters is the responsibility of a firm's advertising agency. Contact all advertising agencies in your area about subcontracting this type of work for them. Practically all advertising executives read *Adweek* magazine. Place a small ad in this publication to make agencies aware of your specialty. You can even work with agencies all over the country via mail and telephone.

And most important, contact as many business organizations as possible to make them aware of your specialty. When calling a firm, ask to speak to either the vice president of marketing, sales manager, product manager, or advertising director. The people in these positions are most likely to have the authority to give you an assignment. In the beginning, you might have to work "on spec." This requires your having to write the letter first with a purchase only if they are pleased with your work. As your reputation grows however, this practice can be eliminated, replaced by a direct promise of payment after the completed work is delivered.

FUTURE GAINS

As previously mentioned, this skill can be practiced as part of a full-service secretarial service. Or, you can expand your talents to do all types of advertising writing as discussed in the chapter "Advertising Copywriting."

Complaint Letter Writing

WHY

Each year, millions of consumers get stuck with inferior products and services. It is not always easy for them to receive proper compensation through an exchange or refund. Unfortunately, not all businesses are as considerate as they should be when dealing with consumers. And to complicate things, it is often impractical to effect legal proceedings against the supplier of inferior merchandise. The lawyer's fees can easily offset any financial justice later received. Nevertheless, many vendors will offer compensation to a mistreated customer if they feel the customer can create an embarrassing situation for them resulting in financial losses greater than the purchase price of the product under contention. Most people, however, do not know how to assert themselves in getting compensated for poor products. They don't know how to write an effective "complaint letter" that will get results, nor do they know where to send such a letter. *They need you to do it for them.*

Please note: In no way are you selling legal advice to your clients. You are just helping them articulate and communicate their feelings effectively.

GETTING STARTED

To get started in this field you need a clear and forceful writing style and some information on where to send complaints. The first place to address a complaint is the store or organization where the product was originally purchased. If this proves ineffective, write a letter to the main office of the retail outlet where the product was purchased, if the store is part of a chain. Or, send a letter to the president of the company which manufactured the product.

Your library offers two important sources of getting to the right people: *Poor's Register of Corporations* and the *Thomas Register of American Manufacturers.* These directories list the addresses of national companies and the names of the principal officers. Usually, contacting the president will be most effective.

Another method is to write to the Better Business Bureau in your client's community, advising them of the situation. Call the information operator for names and addresses of local and state consumer protection agencies who can put some thunder into the inner circles of the offending organization.

If all this fails, write:

U.S. Office of Consumer Affairs
330 Independence Avenue, S.W.
Washington, D.C. 20201.

Usually, however, just writing a letter to the parent company is sufficient. But don't worry; if one source fails you, one of the other groups mentioned can get on their backs. After all, it is easier and cheaper for a company to correct an injustice than to go through the turmoil and expense of having government agencies involved in the situation.

To prepare yourself to become an effective fighter for your clients, here are some books worth reading:

A Consumer's Arsenal, and
by John Dorfman,
Praeger Publishers;

How I Turn Ordinary
Complaints into Thousands
Angry Buyer's Complaint *of Dollars,*
Directory, by Ralph Charell,
by Joseph Rosenbloom, Stein & Day Publishers.
Macmillan;

When handling a client's complaints, make sure you get all the facts down on paper. Then use your own ingenuity and the guidelines offered by the professional books mentioned above to write an effective letter. The following illustrates one style that can be used:

September 11, 1981

Jane Doe
221 Smith St.
Washington, D.C. 20001

Manager
Gray's Department Store
300 Anyplace St.
Chicago, Illinois 60005

Dear Sir:

I recently purchased a vacuum cleaner from your West Washington store and I feel very strongly that I have been cheated by the inferior quality of this product.

Immediately upon using the vacuum, I was distressed by the apparent lack of suction power and returned it to your service department for inspection and/or repair or replacement. I was treated rudely and obtained absolutely no satisfaction whatever. The vacuum was supposedly repaired, but when I returned home to use it, it was still unsatisfactory.

I have informed your local store and have had no reply to my letter, nor have any of my phone calls been returned.

Since you are the manager of your store chain, I am sure you will want to take care of this matter personally and quickly to save both of us the time and trouble of my having to take the situation to your superiors or the courtroom.

I have enclosed a copy of my sales slip as proof of purchase.

Sincerely,

Mrs. Jane Doe

As with all business letters, make a copy of the complaint letter for your files, and send the original with an addressed envelope to your client for signing and mailing.

If your client receives no satisfaction within a two-week period, prepare a follow-up letter to the president of the company that manufactured the product, or the president of the chain store where it was purchased. This letter might read as follows:

October 7, 1981

Jane Doe
221 Smith Street
Washington, D.C. 20001

Mr. Frank Smith, President
Vacuum Cleaner Company, Inc.
1233 North Independence Ave.
Los Angeles, California 90024

Dear Mr. Smith:

I feel I have been defrauded by Vacuum Cleaner Company, Inc., in having received a defective product manufactured by your company.

I purchased one of your vacuum cleaners at Gray's Department Store on August 21st. The vacuum did not work properly. I took it first to the repair department of Gray's West Washington Store where I was treated rudely and obtained absolutely no satisfaction whatsoever. The vacuum cleaner was supposedly repaired, but when I returned home to use it, it still didn't work. I then wrote to the manager of Gray's. He never answered my letter.

Others may just want to put in a 9:00 a.m. to 5:00 p.m. day getting as little involved as possible, but I am sure that you, as a professional overseer of a large company, will take enough pride in yourself and your company to correct this problem quickly. I would appreciate your cooperation in order to avoid the necessity of our both having to go to court to settle this issue or the need for getting various government consumer agencies involved.

I look forward to your response.

Sincerely,

Mrs. Jane Doe

FINANCIAL REWARDS

A good complaint letter should be no longer than one page. A fee of $15 to $20 for the first letter and $10 to $15 for any follow-up letters that might be required is quite reasonable. If your letter can achieve satisfaction on an item costing $100 or more, the money spent by your client is well worth it.

ACQUIRING CLIENTS

Advertising this type of service can be very inexpensive. Community bulletin boards in supermarkets and Laundromats are a good place to start placing your announcements. Advertisements in the newsletters published by church and civic organizations and in local shopping newspapers can also be effective.

This being a unique service, local radio and television talk shows might welcome you on as a guest to discuss the steps a consumer can take to achieve compensation after purchasing faulty merchandise. The publicity from these shows can result in business for you. As the word from satisfied clients starts to circulate in the community, your business can accelerate at a rapid rate.

FUTURE GAINS

You could become so involved in and achieve so much satisfaction from this type of business, you might even decide to go on to law school to represent people with more complicated problems. In fact, you might even be able to work your way through school practicing "complaint letter writing."

PRIZE CONTESTS

WHY

Manufacturers of consumer products frequently find prize contests a valuable marketing tool. The sponsoring of contests is good public relations. It keeps the name of a product constantly in the minds of the public, which often results in increased sales. Additionally, a slogan or jingle a contestant thinks up can sometimes be effectively used in a sales campaign, again increasing sales. Or a prize-winning recipe utilizing a manufacturer's product can result in hundreds of thousands of dollars in increased sales of that product.

GETTING STARTED

These contests usually entail the writing of a short slogan or jingle, such as 25 words or less on why you like a particular product. Are you creative in cooking? Very often the manufacturer of food items will award large sums of money to people who can come up with tasty original recipes utilizing their product.

There are a number of publications available which will introduce you to the skill of winning prize contests in addition to announcing the names, addresses, rules, and prizes available in the many contests sponsored throughout the country. Some of these publications are:

Golden Chances
P.O. Box 655
South Pasadena, California
91030

Prizewinner Magazine
291 28th St. North
St. Petersberg, Florida
33713

Glasser Guide
241 Dahill Road
Brooklyn, New York 11218

Fell's Official Guide to Prize Contests and How to Win Them
By Allen and Selma Glasser
published by Frederick Fell Publishers

In 25 Words or Less
By Gloria Rosenthal
published by Fireside Books/Simon and Schuster.

FINANCIAL REWARDS

Of course, you cannot depend on a steady income entering contests. Nevertheless, there is the definite possibility of receiving a windfall of money from such endeavors. Every year, hundreds of manufacturers of consumer products sponsor contests in which anywhere from $100 to $50,000 is awarded to the winners and runner-ups.

ACQUIRING CLIENTS

Obviously, there are no clients to solicit in this type of business. The sources for sponsors of these contests, however, are mentioned under the heading "Getting Started."

FUTURE GAINS

There is an old saying: "Nothing succeeds like success." The entering and winning of a contest, no matter how small the reward, can inspire you with the entrepreneurial spirit to enter and succeed in other business ventures—and often the necessary capital as well.

PUBLISHING

WHY

You've heard of "how to" books? Well, there is also a big market for "where to" books. For example, where to go for free entertainment such as museums, outdoor concerts, zoos, amusement parks, historical sights, etc. Where to go for good food at reasonable prices, such as the best pizza stands, hamburger stands, ice cream parlors, etc. When televisions, automobiles, cameras, stereo equipment, etc., break down or malfunction, where to go for quality repair services at reasonable prices.

GETTING STARTED

The "where to" possibilities are almost infinite. You can gain a lot of experience and have a lot of fun researching and compiling this information. Your telephone book can provide you with many sources of information for a variety of different publications. Look in the white pages under the headings of local, county, state, and federal government agencies and services. You are most likely to come upon numerous government services that the average citizen would find it advantageous to know about.

Browsing the yellow pages can provide you with hundreds of idea for unique services and products that would benefit people's lives.

FINANCIAL REWARDS

These types of books don't have to be fancy—just informative. Any offset printing shop can make them up for you for approximately 75¢ each. They can then be wholesaled for $1.50 to $1.75 each for eventual resale at $3.95. This leaves you a profit of from $.75 to $1.00 per book. Your wholesale prices can be adjusted according to quantities purchased by your customers.

ACQUIRING CLIENTS

"Where to" books are best sold when placed at the checkout counters of bookstores, variety shops, record shops, grocery and liquor stores, school supply stores, and the like. Call on the owners or managers of these establishments. In the beginning you might have to sell on consignment, which means placing your books in a store free of any initial charge. The owner or manager signs an invoice showing the number of books left in the store. Then, at the end of a reasonable period of time, you return to the store to receive payment for the amount sold. The remaining books can be taken back by you or left for further sale. As you build a reputation for the popularity of your books, you can then bill your clients in the conventional manner: everything received must be paid for.

FUTURE GAINS

As mentioned, you can write and produce as many books as you can think up. This endeavor can be developed into a full-scale publishing business. On this level, you would solicit writers to write different types of books for you. Your main responsibility would be to see to the printing, publicizing, and distribution of such books. Publishing is very competitive. Nevertheless, there are a number of conscientious individuals who profit handsomely from year to year operating on a small scale.

If your business continues to grow and you produce a book that receives a lot of attention, and you are able to publicize it on radio and television talk shows, it is possible to have it professionally printed and distributed by a major publishing house. In this situation, a 50,000-word book will cost you approximately $2 to have each copy printed. A major publisher will charge you anywhere from 15 to 25 percent of the wholesale price to place your book in their catalog and sell and ship it for you. They will also require you to place a large quantity of inventory with them to have on hand in their warehouse. In addition, some publishers will also require an advance of about $5,000 against commissions. If you do produce a book that receives a lot of attention, you can then contact major publishers to work out a mutually profitable deal.

2

SERVICES REQUIRING SPECIAL VEHICLES

LOCAL MOVING— LIGHT

WHY

We are now living in the age of compact and subcompact cars, where transporting anything over two bags of groceries presents a problem. People are always encountering situations where they are in need of transporting something light but bulky. It might be a room divider, shelving, or wall paneling from a hardware store, maybe a large painting from an art gallery or an old spinning wheel from an antique auction, or a bookcase from a furniture store, or maybe some items that have to be taken to the local dump. Whatever it is, people are usually stumped when these situations arise. You can be their solution.

GETTING STARTED

Do you own a van, large station wagon, or pickup truck? If so, you are already prepared to operate a small local moving business. If not but you are considering the purchase of a new car, you might want to consider the purchase of one of those new compact pickup trucks with a "crew" cab. These trucks are economical to operate, possess a suitable load capacity, and have room for a family of four in the cab. Because the items you will be hauling will be fairly light, you most likely will not need a helper. However, because it is always possible to accidentally damage your cargo, it would be a good idea to obtain liability insurance to protect your client's valuables. This is classified in the insurance industry as an "inland marine policy." You can cover yourself for $20,000 worth of possible damage for approximately $310 per year.

FINANCIAL REWARDS

The general fee for light hauling is $15 for the first hour and $12 for each additional hour of work involved, plus 15¢ a mile (optional) to cover your gasoline expenses.

ACQUIRING CLIENTS

Obtaining moving business can be rather easy. Go to hardware and building supply stores, art galleries, antique shops and auctions, furniture stores, and home and garden shops and inform the operators of the services available to their customers. They will be glad to know about you. Because of the high cost of doing business these days, many of these establishments are not able to offer their own delivery service to accommodate their customers. If they can recommend you, it will increase their "good will" and quite often turn a possible sale into a definite sale. Leave your business card with every establishment you visit. Better yet, leave a poster for their customers to see.

Periodically, everyone gives his home or apartment a thorough cleaning and ends up with many worn-out and useless items to be thrown away. The problem is: How do you get everything to the local dump? And where is the local dump? By inquiring at your city hall, you can find the location of public dumping areas and offer another valuable service to an important segment of the community.

Advertise your services in local newspapers, inexpensive shopping guides and throwaways and on community bulletin boards. In fact, put a sign on your vehicle such as: "MIKE'S LOCAL MOVING SERVICE—Phone 000-0000."

FUTURE GAINS

In addition to light moving services, you can also offer a local courier service as part of your business. In this segment of your operation, you would also pick up and deliver light packages and important documents that needed to be transported from one business or professional organization to another quickly.

LOCAL MOVING— HEAVY

WHY

People are constantly changing residences in the same community. In addition, commercial firms frequently find it necessary to change the location of a retail store or office within their community. It is often hard for people to find reliable movers who are courteous and careful of their belongings. If you are generally healthy and strong, there are opportunities to fill this need.

GETTING STARTED

Obviously, a large truck is needed for this venture. Unless you definitely decide to do this on a full-time commercial basis, it would be silly for you to make such a purchase. However, there are many truck rental facilities that can rent you an appropriate vehicle on an hourly or daily basis.

An 18-foot enclosed bobtail truck with an electric tailgate lift can be rented for approximately $40 a day, plus a mileage charge of 18¢ a mile. In addition, these large trucks customarily get 5 miles per gallon of gas. At $1.50 per gallon, this computes to an additional 30¢ per mile or a total of 48¢ per mile traveled.

In addition, you will also need a strong helper to assist you with the loading and unloading of your cargo. A reasonable fee for such a helper is $10 per hour. In the introduction of this book we discussed the importance of obtaining Workmen's Compensation Insurance to cover any injuries incurred by a helper. As mentioned, most premiums are very small. However, the rate for moving people is approximately $16 per 100 paid an employee, or an extra 16 percent of gross salary. Therefore, if you pay a helper $10 an hour, add another $1.60 per hour to arrive at a total of $11.60 representing your actual hourly payout.

As discussed in the chapter on light local moving, you can protect yourself from any liability claims resulting from damaged cargo by obtaining an "inland marine policy." For approximately $310 a year, you can cover yourself for up to $20,000 damage.

After you locate a resource for a good truck and insure yourself properly, you are ready to start business.

FINANCIAL REWARDS

Local commercial moving rates average out to approximately $45 per hour for a truck and a two-person crew. It takes approximately four hours to move a typical two-bedroom home or apartment. This covers just the physical moving of the furniture from the old residence to the truck and from the truck to the new location. The time spent driving between locations is additional.

If you receive an assignment to move a two-bedroom apartment to a location approximately 30 miles away, this will require approximately one hour of driving time. This could easily add up to a five-hour assignment. At $45 per hour, this comes to a total fee of $225. Your total expenses, including your helper, truck rental, and gasoline, would come to a total of approximately $125, leaving you a profit of $100. If you are able to obtain two moving assignments within the same day, your net profit per hour would increase since your truck rental fee would remain the same.

ACQUIRING CLIENTS

Ads in the real estate section of local newspapers and the yellow pages of the telephone directory are an effective way to start an advertising campaign. In addition, advise all real estate agents in your area of your service. After all, every time they sell a house, someone moves away and someone else move in. If these moves are all within the same community, there is a lot of business for you to obtain. Call on the managers of apartment and office buildings. They too know who is moving out and coming in, and can be of value in recommending you. After a while, you can depend on referrals from satisfied customers.

FUTURE GAINS

There is a lot of business to be had just on the local level. If desired, however, you can expand your business on a county, state, or nationwide basis. For a larger operation, you can use leased trucks. However, for your business to remain profitable, it is desirable to obtain additional assignments on return trips.

DOOR-TO-DOOR ADVERTISING DISTRIBUTION SERVICE

WHY

Newspapers, magazines, radio, television, and billboards are the primary vehicles for advertising messages. Direct mail advertising is used to reach a certain specific segment of the population having similar interests or certain things in common, although the recipients may live in widely scattered areas. Quite often, however, an advertiser wants to reach just the people in the vicinity of his operation. The announcement of a special service or product is usually the reason. Special prices on these goods and services are announced not only to sell these particular commodities, but also to bring people into the establishments in hopes of inducing them to purchase other goods or services.

Direct mail advertising, even when bulk-mailed, costs approximately 10¢ per mailing. However, the door-to-door distribution of circulars can be accomplished for under 4¢ per circular. This can represent quite a savings to the advertiser and also a profit opportunity for you.

GETTING STARTED

To operate this type of business, you need a van or pickup truck and from six to ten helpers. Your helpers can be recruited from high schools and colleges. The minimum wage of approximately $3.50 per hour is all that is usually required to retain these people. Workmen's compensation premiums will add approximately another 35¢ to this figure, bringing it to a total of $3.85.

For a distribution campaign to be effective, at least 10,000 circulars have to be distributed to residents in the area. In fact, this is the minimum amount most distributors will accept.

Ten helpers working from one truck can distribute 10,000 pieces of literature in approximately six hours. If many of the residents live in one location such as a large apartment house, less time will be required. The total labor expense for a six-hour run will come to approximately $231. Gasoline will account for another $9 of expense.

After receiving a distribution contract, your job is to coordinate and supervise the entire project. Each of your workers can meet you at the particular location he or she will serve to receive the required number of handouts. Point out to your workers that they should slip the handouts inside or under each door—*not* in the mailbox. It's illegal to put anything besides mail in a mailbox. You may desire to offer your helpers transportation to and from their locations. This is strictly dependent on what is most ideal for each situation.

FINANCIAL REWARDS

The customary rate for door-to-door advertising distribution is approximately $33 per 1000, resulting in a fee of $330 for the above-mentioned 10,000 circular run. If expenses run consistently, your profit would be $330 minus $240, or $90 for a typical six-hour run. If your helpers are dependable and can travel by themselves to their locations, your actual time spent on the run can be considerably less than six hours. This can allow you to spend your time soliciting and supervising additional runs in other parts of the city. In addition, it is often permissible to distribute for more than one client in the same area at the same time, providing they do not compete with each other. Two circulars can be passed out almost as easily as one, thereby increasing your profits.

ACQUIRING CLIENTS

Sometimes small advertising agencies create for their clients circulars designed for door-to-door distribution. Contact advertising agencies in your area to contract for these distribution assignments. Call on every retail store and neighborhood shopping center in a given community. If they are not already advertising via door-to-door circulars, tell them how beneficial it would be for them to do so and how you could make sure their circulars were properly distributed.

FUTURE GAINS

After you develop a satisfactory system for operating this type of business, you can add more trucks and helpers to offer your service on a citywide basis. In addition, if you are also creative in producing good advertising copy, you can extend your service to the creating and producing of the circulars. This endeavor is discussed in this book under "Direct Advertising Production."

DRY CLEANING
SERVICE ROUTE

WHY

All you van owners, here is another opportunity to make some money with your vehicle. With the busy career and social life that single people lead, coupled with the fact that more and more wives are working, people don't have the time to take care of many of their routine chores—such as dry cleaning. Think about it: They have to carry the clothes to their car, drive through traffic, find a parking space, haul the clothes out of the car, and then stand in line to be waited on. This process has to be repeated when their clothes are ready. And, if they forget to pick up their garments before a holiday or important trip—they've had it! You can relieve them of this burden in the form of your own pick-up and delivery dry cleaning service.

GETTING STARTED

It is unnecessary to wonder where you can learn about dry cleaning or how you can afford all the necessary equipment. The dry cleaning stores you see on the street—do you think they actually do their own cleaning? Some do, but most send out their customers' clothes to independent cleaning plants for the actual cleaning process. The plant charges the store a wholesale price for each garment and the store in turn charges the customer a retail price. These same dry cleaning plants will be glad to have you as a client. With the permission of your customers, the managers of condominiums and apartment houses can let you into each unit to pick up the clothes for cleaning, and again to return the clothes when finished. In this manner, your customers don't even have to be home to be serviced—another attractive aspect for them to consider. You can bill them once a month.

Note: You would be wise to obtain a bond, if you're thinking of entering this business. Clients will want proof of your trustworthiness, before giving you permission to enter their buildings. See pp. xi-xii for instructions on becoming bonded.

FINANCIAL GAINS

Retail dry cleaning stores generally work on a mark-up of from 50 percent to 65 percent. A typical plant will charge about $1.25 for a pair of slacks, $1.50 for a sport jacket, and approximately $1.00 for a skirt. Retail stores will then double this figure to arrive at their price. Because you are offering a very personalized service, you can generally charge approximately 30 percent to 50 percent more than the retail establishments.

ACQUIRING CLIENTS

When soliciting customers, concentrate your efforts in high-density areas such as large apartment houses and condominium complexes. In this manner, you can service a lot of customers with just one stop. As you develop a beginning clientele in a building, the word of your fine service will spread until you achieve a sizable business in each building. Also, call on individual homes in wealthy areas. Your client's domestic staff can let you in.

Because of security problems in today's society, you will have to establish yourself as a reputable and honest person. One way to do this is to become bonded through a bonding agency. The details of this are explained in the introduction of this book. Being bonded contributes to your image of integrity.

FUTURE GAINS

A successful dry cleaning route can be supplemented with the building of one or several retail dry cleaning establishments.

3

AUTOMOTIVE SERVICES

MOBILE CAR WAXING SERVICE

WHY

In today's economy, people might have to keep their cars a long time, but they want to keep them looking like new. One of the best ways to keep a showroom finish on a car is to give it periodic washings and waxings.

If you can make things easier for people, you've got yourself a business. Typically, when people need wax jobs for their cars they have to drive to a car wash, wait for the car to be washed, leave it to be waxed (usually a four-hour wait when there are cars ahead of them), find transportation back to their home or office, return again to pick up their car, and then drive home through heavy traffic. You can alleviate this whole problem with a mobile waxing and polishing service operated out of the trunk of your car.

GETTING STARTED

The necessary materials and equipment are minimal. Your biggest expense will be a good heavy-duty buffing machine with separate cleaning and buffing pads available at most hardware stores for about $150. This buffing machine can be powered by your car's engine via a small electrical adapter which attaches to your car's alternator. When the engine is idling, the adapter converts 12 volt direct current generated by your engine to 110 volt alternating current needed to operate electrical appliances. Just plug the cord of the buffer into the adapter and you're in business. This type of adapter can be purchased at any auto or recreational vehicle supply store for about $35 to $50.

If for any reason your car's engine cannot generate enough power to operate the buffer, there are individual gasoline-operated generators available that can do the job just fine. They are very small and can be purchased used or new for about $100 to $350. (Honda Motors makes a fine one which sells for about $350. Many Honda motorcycle dealers carry them.) Whether you use your car's engine or a portable generator, very little gas is required to propel the buffer.

The only other materials required for your mobile car waxing service are a container of liquid cleaning solution, a good commercial liquid wax, and some applicator cloths. Then *presto!* You're in business.

One important word of caution before you start: In order to avoid streaking, a car's surface should be cool before any wax is applied. Therefore, it is advisable to work on cars parked indoors. However, your service can also be performed outside, providing the temperature is no more than 70 degrees or the car is protected from direct sunlight by use of a canopy.

The actual waxing process is quite simple. Have your client give you the keys to his car and then drive it to the nearest commercial car wash for a preliminary washing. This will cost approximately $4. It should not take very long, since most commercial car washes are not usually very busy on weekdays when most people are at work. This step can be avoided, however, if by chance you also supply a mobile car washing service (discussed in next chapter).

After the preliminary washing, apply the cleaning solution with an applicator cloth and work it in with your buffer. This process removes deeply inbedded dirt and oxidation products from the paint. This alone enhances the car's finish and prepares it for a better wax job. Next, apply the liquid wax with another applicator cloth and buff it to a high gloss. Be sure to use separate pads on your buffer for the cleaning and waxing steps.

FINANCIAL REWARDS

The complete waxing process should take about 45 minutes to an hour to complete. You can easily charge $30 to $35 for this service. The cost of the cleaning and waxing solutions will come to about 50¢ per car. Only a very small amount of gasoline is required to operate the engine of your car or portable generator. Thus, your fee will represent approximately 90 percent profit. If you do five cars in the same location per day, this will allow you approximately $150 to $170 profit for a day's work.

ACQUIRING CLIENTS

Every car owner is a potential customer of yours. However, to make the best use of your time, concentrate on high density areas—apartment dwellers on weekends and office workers during the business week. Their cars are usually parked in subterranean or enclosed parking structures enabling you to conveniently go from one car to another, avoiding the need for time-consuming street travel. People living in an apartment building or working in an office complex would appreciate having their cars waxed while they are relaxing or working.

The best way to solicit these people as customers is through direct mail advertising, putting fliers on the windshields of cars, and—best of all—a personal visit to large apartment and office building complexes. This may be easier than you think. Once you are working on a car in a parking garage, many of the personnel and inhabitants of the building will stop out of curiosity to watch you for a few moments. This will give you an opportunity to quickly inform them of your services and pass out your business card or flier.

FUTURE GAINS

In addition to a mobile waxing service, you can also secure locations on the premises of commercial car washes providing waxing services to their clients. You can accomplish a lot of business via a combination of stationary and mobile operations.

MOBILE CAR WASHING SERVICE

WHY

With today's high prices, taking care of a car's exterior is of great importance to automobile owners. The appeal of mobility in a car waxing service is also true of washing—you perform a service on the customer's premises, leaving him or her free to do other things. You will have an even broader range of customers to choose from in mobile car washing, for you will not be restricted to enclosed parking garages. And due to the fact that each car can be washed in about five minutes, a great number of people who normally do not have their cars washed frequently will become more inclined to do so.

GETTING STARTED

This type of business does require one rather expensive piece of equipment: a portable high-pressure de-ionized-water washing machine. These machines sell for about $1500, but they can make you a small fortune. And let's face it, $1500 is about the price of a conventional stereo system.

The machine operates on the following principle: Water is fed into the unit via a garden hose attached to a conventional outdoor faucet. It first passes through a de-ionizing chamber to remove the minerals. From there it is mixed with a premeasured amount of soap (the manufacturer of your machine can recommend a mild soap to use). The soapy water is then sprayed out at tremendous force through an applicator wand which is guided over the car about three feet away from the surface. This easily removes all the ground-in dirt and grime. The applicator wand has a dial on it with which the operator can regulate the water pressure, adjust the soap concentration, and then finally allow for only clear rinse water to come out. The whole process takes only five minutes to complete. De-ionized water evaporates very quickly leaving no residue or streaking, thus eliminating the need to hand-dry the car.

This washing machine can easily be transported in a station wagon, pickup truck, van, or small trailer attached to a conventional automobile. Suppliers of this type of machine can be found in the yellow pages of your phone book or in the *Thomas Register of American Manufacturers* under the heading "Car Washing Equipment," "Automobile Washing Equipment," or "Washing Equipment."

Obviously, a water tap must be available to perform this work. If by chance you run into a situation where a water supply is unavailable, there is a solution, providing you have a pickup truck with heavy-duty springs. It takes approximately 5 to 10 gallons of water to wash each car. It is possible to have a 300-gallon water tank installed on your truck for about $300 plus an extra $100 for a water pump. This will allow you to do from 30 to 60 vehicles with just one filling. You can then drive to the nearest gas station to fill up with more water for another run of cars. Look in the telephone book yellow pages under "Tanks" to find people who can supply you with the tank.

The water-washing system runs on electricity and can be powered from the engine of your truck via a $35 to $50 adapter attached to the alternator of your vehicle or a small, individual gasoline-operated generator. See page 40 of the Mobile Car Waxing Service chapter for further information about this equipment.

FINANCIAL REWARDS

You can easily charge $3.00 for a five-minute car wash. After all, the commercial stationary car washes charge around $5.00 and there you have to wait in line. If you do 12 cars per hour, this adds up to $36 per hour in income. The soap and de-ionizing material averages out to 15¢ per car. Therefore, your actual net profit for 12 cars is $34.20. You can also travel to truck stops and trucking companies for washing assignments. A 20-minute job on a trailer truck brings in about $25 in revenue.

ACQUIRING CLIENTS

You can take your service to a number of facilities where large numbers of vehicles are found. Shopping center parking lots are filled with dirty cars and busy shoppers. With approval from the management, you can approach people as they get into or out of their cars. To find out the name of the managing company and its location either look on the shopping center's directory of tenants, or inquire at one of the stores.

New and used car sales lots are also prime sources for your services. They depend on clean-looking cars to attract customers. You can offer to do these cars on a contract basis: once a week for $1.50 per car. This computes to $18 per hour less $1.44 overhead, leaving you with $16.50 per hour net profit. The average sales lot has at least 50 cars on it. That's about $69 net income for just one stop. This same type of contract service can be offered to office building and apartment house tenants: once a week on the same day, in the same parking lot.

As mentioned above, commercial trucks require periodic cleaning. Contact trucking companies and companies operating a fleet of trucks for the delivery of goods. Large baking companies are a prime example. Cab companies and police departments are also an excellent source of business.

When selling your services to potential customers, there are some important points to mention, whether in a sales letter, flier, or verbal discussion:

1. Your service uses mild soap in the machine, thus preventing damage to the car's paint.
2. Your service uses de-ionized water, preventing mineral deposits from adhering to the car.

3. Your service eliminates the hassle of traveling to and from and waiting at commercial car washes.
4. Commercial car washes drag or push a car through a metal gully, creating the possibility of throwing the front end out of alignment. With your service, the car remains stationary.
5. A commercial car wash costs almost $5.00. Your charge is $3.00.
6. In snow areas, it is important to wash road salt off a car frequently to prevent corrosion.

FUTURE GAINS

This type of business can be operated in conjunction with a mobile car waxing service, discussed in the previous chapter. You can also arrange to lease a small amount of space from numerous gas station operators to offer their customers a car washing service. By using the gas station's water and electrical supply, you can eliminate the need for a water tank and pump. In this manner, the washing equipment for each operation will only cost you $1,500. You can then hire young people to work for you for an hourly rate or a percentage of the income they produce. The more gas stations you solicit, the more money you make.

A gas station will usually charge 10 percent of your volume as rent. You can easily do 6 cars an hour at a gas station, earning a gross income of $18 per hour. (You can actually handle more, but you will not be busy all the time.) Your rent will be $1.80 for the hour, and overhead expenses per car compute to 15¢ each or 90¢ for the six cars. Your expenses now come to $2.70 for the hour, leaving a gross income per hour of $15.30. If you pay your help a respectable $5.00 per hour and then compute an extra 50¢ for workers compensation, this computes to $9.80 per hour net profit for you. And remember, you are not doing the actual work. Therefore, if you operate several successful locations, the net profits per hour can add up. Of course this is an average; some locations will not do as well and others will do better. Nevertheless, a good car wash facility helps the gas station do more business in gas. One function supports the other.

MOBILE LUBE AND OIL-CHANGING SERVICE

WHY

Here's another opportunity to take advantage of the mobility principle in the car care world. The engine and chassis are composed of numerous metal parts, many of which are required to rub against each other creating friction. This friction can wear out and damage the metal parts, reducing the car's performance level and longevity. Proper lubrication prevents this. A fine grade of oil is used in the engine to lubricate the moving parts. An oil filter is used to filter dirt particles from the oil as it circulates through the engine. In addition, a heavier lubricant (grease) is used to lubricate the suspension system, ball joints, and other important parts making up the underside (chassis) of the car.

Engine oil and grease eventually become dirty, break down, and dissipate. Automotive authorities agree that if a car's engine oil and filter are changed every 2000 and 4000 miles respectively, and the chassis lubricated every 2000 miles, the average car can operate at top performance for well over 100,000 miles. And with today's car prices, this is a matter of great concern to drivers. A car's engine also requires the intake of clean air for maximum performance. It is advisable to change the air filter every 7,000 miles.

In addition to paying $25 to $33 for the above-mentioned services, the customer at a garage, automobile dealership, or service station sometimes has to wait for long periods of time for the job to be done if there are other cars ahead or the dealer is short of employees. You can eliminate this by entering this field on a mobile and discount basis.

GETTING STARTED

Here is what you will need to get started in this business:

Permanent Equipment:
A portable hydraulic jack	$80.00
A grease gun to lubricate the chassis. (NOTE: A grease cartridge for the gun costs 85¢ and can service ten cars. This cost is so negligible, we will not include it.)	5.00
A shallow pan for collecting the old oil	6.00
A funnel to aid in pouring the oil from the can into the engine opening	3.00

46

A 30-gallon plastic or metal drum to store discarded engine oil in. (NOTE: It is illegal to dump this in the sewer.)	15.00
TOTAL ONE-TIME INVESTMENT:	$109.00

Consumable Materials per Car

5 quarts of engine oil at $.90 each	$4.50
Oil filter	3.00
Air filter	3.00

Total: $7.50 per car without air filter change
$10.50 per car with air filter change

It is best to have a van or small pick-up truck to transport your equipment. However, a small trailer attached to your car will work out fine. The whole process takes approximately 20 minutes to perform and is conducted as follows:

1. The portable hydraulic jack is placed under the front end of the car to elevate it.

2. Place the drain pan under the engine and open the oil drain, allowing the oil to run out into the pan.

3. While the old oil is draining out, lubricate the chassis at the designated "lube" points. They are almost the same for every car.

4. Remove the old oil filter and replace it with a new one.

5. Replace the drain cap on the underside of the engine and dump the old oil into the oil barrel on your truck, van, or trailer. (Remember! It is illegal to dump it in a sewer.)

6. Lower the front end and remove the hydraulic jack. Add the fresh oil to the engine.

7. If necessary, install a new air filter—every 10,000 miles.

You do not need much mechanical ability to perform these steps. However, if you do have trouble in the beginning, you can consult *Chilton's Auto Repair Manual* published annually by Chilton Book Company. Or, you can pay a garage mechanic a few dollars to show you how.

Regarding the discarded oil: Gasoline stations have large tanks to store old drain oil. This oil is recyclable and companies specializing in this process send special pump trucks to pump the old oil out of the storage tanks. Some firms pay the gas station owner a small fee for the old oil. Therefore, it should be easy to make arrangements with a gas station to dump your old drain oil from your storage barrel into their tank.

FINANCIAL REWARDS

As mentioned, conventional garages, auto dealerships, and service stations generally charge $25 for the lubrication and oil and filter change of a car and $33 when a new air filter is also installed. At materials' costs of $7.50 without and $10.50 with an air filter, this allows you a profit of from $17.50 to $22.50 for approximately 20 minutes' work. You can maintain these fees or reduce them to become competitive and still profitable.

ACQUIRING CLIENTS

The same high-density-area customers are open to you as in mobile car waxing and washing: apartment house dwellers and office building employees. You can also make arrangements to set up discount lube and oil concessions at self-service gas stations where these services are customarily not available. In addition, you can contract with taxi services, auto leasing and rental companies, sales fleets, and police departments to service their vehicles on a periodic basis.

FUTURE GAINS

Because the equipment needed in this type of service is inexpensive, you can develop a wide-scale operation. As you acquire new accounts and locations, you can add extra help to carry out the manual chores of your enterprise. Your employees can be paid on an hourly and/or commission basis. In fact, you can even hire additional salespeople to solicit new business and locations in discount self-service gasoline stations. This will allow you to initiate and supervise the setting up of new territories in other cities.

THEFT-PROOFING CARS

WHY

Car theft has always been popular with both amateur and professional crooks. With increasing inflation, the stealing of automobiles is even more popular—especially those gas-saving compacts. To date, the most common method of discouraging car thieves has been the installation of complex alarm systems activated by the driver by setting an outside switch with a special key. If a thief opens a car door, an electrical circuit is completed and the alarm goes off. The thief is then supposed to take off in fear. Let's face it, if these guys were the type to get scared, they wouldn't be thieves in the first place. All a crook has to do is insert a special instrument into the keyhole of the outside switch and then the alarm is inactivated and the car is his. If this special switch is somehow hidden from view and the alarm does go off, the alarm system's wires can be easily found and cut before a police officer arrives. What is even worse, many of these alarm systems cost the owner about $50 to purchase and install.

There is one thing, however, that can be done to a car to make it difficult and discouraging for a thief to steal it—the installation of a "kill switch." The installation of such a switch is not only simple, but also inexpensive.

GETTING STARTED

A car's engine is started by an initial boost of energy supplied by the starting motor. The starting motor in turn is powered by a short burst of electricity supplied by the car's battery. The ignition switch lies in circuit between the battery and starting motor. When the ignition switch is turned on by the car keys, the electrical circuit is completed and the engine starts.

If the electrical circuit is interrupted by another switch in addition to the all-familiar key-operated ignition switch, then this switch has to be activated in addition to the ignition switch in order to complete the electrical circuitry necessary for starting the car. If this additional switch (the kill switch) is hidden somewhere in the car, a spot known only to the car's owner, it presents a real problem for any potential thief.

Normally when a car thief breaks into a car, he crosses the ignition wires located near the steering column, thus bypassing the key-operated ignition switch. The car starts immediately and the owner takes a cab. However, if there is another switch needed to complete the electrical circuit and the thief cannot readily locate it within a short period of time, he will usually take off. The extra switch (usually a simple toggle switch) can be hidden under the dash, in the ashtray or glove compartment, under the seat, in the door handle, or even in the back seat. When the car's owner goes to start the car, he or she will first engage this secret switch and then turn the ignition key, completing the electrical circuit needed to start the engine.

The actual mechanics of the installation process can be learned in a couple of hours from any qualified automotive repair instructor. There are also many manuals dealing with automobile electrical circuitry. One such book is *Chilton's Auto Repair Manual* published by the Chilton Book Company.

The fundamental procedure, however, is as follows: The wires used should be the same color as one of the existing wires. In this manner they are indistinguishable from the rest of the car. The wires are run along the existing wires making it even harder for a thief to know which wire is which. If he disconnects the wrong one, then the car will be inoperative. You can wrap a sheath around the entire wiring system so that the thief surely cannot trace any wires. The anti-theft kill switch wires are run through the fire-wall and into the passenger area underneath the carpeting for concealment. As stated above they can be attached to the switch anywhere that is well covered and convenient. This spot can be under the dash or even somewhere in the back seat area. Naturally this will make it a little more inconvenient for the driver to start his or her car each time, but a thief surely won't find it in the back seat area.

FINANCIAL REWARDS

The installation of this switch requires about $3 worth of equipment and approximately 20 minutes of your time. If the installation of a conventional burglar alarm costs $50 and more, and it is almost useless, you can certainly charge at least $20 to $25 for a system which is effective.

ACQUIRING CLIENTS

Practically every car owner is a potential customer. Some good places to start advertising your services are to apartment dwellers and office building employees who keep their cars in unattended parking lots. The installation can be done right on the premises.

Place small ads in the travel section of newspapers—people who utilize airplanes, ships, and busses on their vacations, like to know their car is safe while they are away. Print up fliers which can be placed on the windshields of parked cars. The flier could read: "Your car could have been stolen while you were away. Protect it with Mike's Anti-theft System. Phone number: 000-0000. It's the only thing that discourages thieves."

In addition, call on all automobile insurance agencies advising them of the service you can render their clients. They would be glad to recommend you. After all, the fewer cars that are stolen, the less money insurance companies have to pay out.

FUTURE GAINS

As your knowledge of working with automobile electronics increases, you can expand your services to include the installation of car stereo systems.

4

MANUAL AND MECHANICAL SERVICES

PAINTING AND PAPERHANGING

WHY

A well coordinated and skillfully applied paint or wallpaper job can turn a drab room into an attractive and exciting place to be in. Wall decorating is a major industry. Apartment house, office building, and hotel and motel owners continually upgrade the internal appearance of their properties in order to solicit higher revenues. Homeowners upgrade their interior living quarters to improve the quality of their lives and to increase property values.

GETTING STARTED

There are many trade schools and community colleges offering night classes in color and design coordination plus the proper application of paint and wallpaper. Make sure the course you take includes instruction on how to prepare a wall for painting or papering, which is a skill in itself.

Obviously, as in the other endeavors mentioned in this book, your goal in this field is to become an independent operator. In most states, however, to do this type of work on your own you need an "Independent Contractor's License." Four years of on-the-job experience are required in order to qualify for the exam. However, there are ways to get around this requirement and eventually still get your license.

If your client signs for and pays for the wallpaper or paint, you in effect are being hired as a handyman to do some work around the house (quite legal). You can actually select and arrange for the purchase of the materials; all the customer has to do is make the actual purchase. Or you can work under the auspices of an already licensed contractor. This is known as being a Responsible Management Employee (RME). Under this arrangement, a small fee of approximately 10 percent of your fee is turned over to the licensed contractor you are working under. In either case, the time you put in working at your craft counts as work credits for qualifying to take the exam.

Another method of securing independent assignments is to work through a licensed painting and paperhanging contractor or a general contractor as an associate. He or she can sign for and take legal responsibility for the jobs you solicit and perform on your own. Many contractors who become familiar with and have confidence in the quality of the work of an unlicensed individual, will often let that person work under their license for a token fee of approximately 10 percent of the money taken in on the job. In addition to the token fee they receive, it is also to their advantage to form these relationships to help them with assignments they solicit in the operation of their own business. The 10 percent you pay the general contractor is well worth the opportunity to make a good income and still stay within the law.

Keep in mind that all the work you put in as either a handyman or a contractor's associate is credited to the earning of your own contractor's license.

FINANCIAL REWARDS

Good paperhanging contractors charge by the roll, as follows: $15 for paper and vinyl wall coverings and $30 for metallic wall coverings. This is because metallic paper is harder to work with. Necessary tools such as razors to remove old paper, and various brushes cost approximately $10. But this is a fixed one-time expense. The materials needed to remove the old wallpaper, prepare the wall, and then apply the new covering average out to approximately $1.67 per roll used. Therefore, your net fee per roll is $13.33 for paper and vinyl and $28.33 for metallic wallpaper.

It takes a good craftsperson approximately 30 minutes to apply either paper and vinyl or the metallic covering. Thus, the net earnings per hour can amount to between $26.66 and $56.66. If you have people helping you, their beginning wage should be $7 to $8 per hour. And once they are experienced, they should earn from $10 to $15 per hour. As you can see, once you expand your operation and have several people working under you, there is a lot of money to be made.

ACQUIRING CLIENTS

There are many sources for finding wallpapering or painting opportunities. In fact, people are always looking for you. As mentioned, apartment and office building owners frequently remodel vacated units in order to rerent them for higher fees. Contact all apartment house owner's or office building owner's associations in your area to advise the members of your services. Also call on individual owners and managers. Contact all real estate management companies, which often take care of the maintenance requirements for commercial or co-op properties. They need you to help them serve their clients properly.

Interior decorators are another group of professionals to call on. They need the services of good painters and paperhangers to apply the wall coverings they select for their clients.

Whenever someone puts his house up for sale, the investing of several hundred or even several thousand dollars on cosmetics and repairs can increase the sale price by a multiple of two to three or more than the money paid to the contractor. Contact all real estate agents advising them of how you can help their clients increase the sale price of their homes. They will be only too happy to recommend your services.

Contact all real estate investment groups. There are people who purchase all kinds of buildings for improvement and eventual resale at a much higher price. Your services are of great importance to them.

General building contractors and owners of remodeling companies generally subcontract the wall covering assignments of their projects to independent operators. Therefore, contact all building contractors in your area for subcontract assignments in wall covering.

With today's high inflation, many homeowners who normally would have traded up to more elaborate houses are electing to improve the quality of their present residences. Place small ads in the real estate and home decorating sections of your local newspapers advising homeowners of your services. If there is a homeowner's association in your area, attend some meetings and advertise in their bulletins to make the members aware of your services.

FUTURE GAINS

Decorating will always play a prominent role in improving our living environment. From an individual craftsperson, it is possible to develop a large contracting business employing many workers and soliciting the patronage not only of the aforementioned individual clients, but also that of government agencies and other big businesses when they require the decorating of buildings under their domain.

CUSTOM PICTURE FRAMING

WHY

There is a great deal more to picture framing than merely putting four strips of wood around a picture. A properly chosen and constructed frame can complement a piece of artwork, showing it off to its best advantage and often enhancing its value. For example, a picture costing $50, when properly coordinated with a frame costing $30, can often sell for $200, a substantial increase in value not to mention the extra aesthetic pleasure it gives its viewers. People in the art world are aware of this and place a great deal of importance on finding a good framer. This presents an opportunity you can capitalize on.

GETTING STARTED

A good framer must get a feeling for the art piece to be framed and then pick out the proper molding and matting materials so that the picture and frame appear as one integral unit. For instance, you would not put an ornate gold-leaf molding around a simple pencil drawing, nor would you put a plain thin-line molding around a Van Gogh.

Many night school programs in high schools, community colleges, and trade schools offer excellent training programs in this field that require relatively short periods of time to complete. A good training course will teach you how to handle both wet and dry mountings, mat cutting, the covering of mats with fabric, how to select and measure molding, cutting and fitting techniques, glass cutting, the use of color in framing, how to stretch canvas and fabrics, how to frame with metal and plastic as well as wood, the making of shadow-box frames, how to repair and restore old frames, and how to do "creative" framing that might involve the use of such crafts as decoupage.

When starting a framing business you will need approximately $100 worth of tools. You will not have to start out carrying a complete inventory of the various types of moldings you will be working with. It will be sufficient to carry a sample cornering of each type of molding offered to your customers. As orders come in, the complete molding can then be purchased from your wholesaler. Later on, when a substantial amount of profit is accumulated, you can start inventorying the most popular types of moldings.

FINANCIAL REWARDS

Wood molding wholesales anywhere from $1.50 to $8.00 a linear foot. Aluminum molding, very suitable for modern artwork and posters, wholesales for about $3.00 a linear foot. Glass wholesales for approximately $2.60 a square foot and matting (the back support of a picture), $1.00 a square foot.

When determining the retail price for a custom frame, most framers calculate the wholesale cost of the materials used and then multiply by either two or three. They may or may not add a labor charge ranging from $10 to $20. The multiple charged usually depends upon the locale and type of clientele served.

One common size frame is approximately $24'' \times 30''$. If glass is to be used (here, 5 square feet) and the molding wholesales for $3 per linear foot, this represents a wholesale cost of $45. When multiplied by either two or three, this comes to $90 or $135, representing a profit of from $45 to $90 for approximately one hour of work.

ACQUIRING CLIENTS

When soliciting business, you have a wide range of potential customers to choose from. Among them are art galleries and dealers, art supply stores, poster shops, decorating departments of department stores, museums, and antique shops.

Many people who travel to Europe often return with dozens of pictures purchased not only from prominent European art galleries, but also from talented but struggling artists. The first thing they think of when they get back is framing their new possessions. It is a good idea to place small ads in the travel sections of your local newspapers, in travel magazines, or in brochures distributed by travel agencies. You can also advertise inexpensively in the newsletters and bulletins of religious, fraternal, and civic organizations. Pick the ones in the wealthier neighborhoods—it is their members who most likely travel to Europe often and purchase these paintings.

Ask the owners and managers of small photography shops if they'll display posters advertising your skills. Very often when their customers take good pictures that have a lot of personal significance, they like to have them framed. You can even work out a deal with a shop's owner to do the framing with him or her acting as your agent and sharing in a portion of the profit. Recent college graduates and professionals receiving certificates and licenses are another prime source of customers. Advertise in college newspapers and professional journals.

FUTURE GAINS
Some really big payoffs come when you tap commercial and institutional accounts such as offices, hotels, art galleries, retail stores, churches, hospitals, schools, banks, and other kinds of public accounts. All of these facilities use artwork to decorate their walls. Some framers deal with such volume accounts exclusively and forego individual jobs entirely. When serving this type of clientele, however, you will not be able to triple your money on each job. A 50 percent mark-up based on cost, plus a $15 labor fee will probably be the most you can charge. However, when you consider you will be framing in mass volume, the net profit figure can rise to a very lucrative annual income.

KEY DUPLICATING SERVICE

WHY
Happiness is finding your keys when they are lost! The next best thing is to have a duplicate set. People also need to have duplicate sets of keys made for use by other members of their household or business. However, many people find it inconvenient to take the time to have keys duplicated due to personal impatience and the fact that most key duplicating stands are located in inconspicuous places. If you can make yourself obvious and convenient, many people will order on impulse.

GETTING STARTED
A key duplicating machine can be purchased for about $500 from a wholesale locksmith supply company. These firms are listed in the yellow pages of your phone book under Locksmith Supply, Wholesale. The blanks from which the keys are made cost from 20¢ to 25¢ each. There are six basic types of blanks used to accommodate the different contours of all the different types of keys. You could start out your service with 20 blanks each, of the six

different types—a total of 120 blanks. At 20¢ to 25¢ each, this investment comes to around $24 to $30.

Key duplicating machines are very small and light, occupying an area of approximately one square foot. The blanks fit into a small tool box. You can set up a small stand almost anywhere that there is a source of electricity.

The actual duplication of the key is quite simple: The original key is placed in a viselike bracket in the machine. A blank with the same general contour is placed in another bracket next to it. The machine is then started. The original key is moved in a pattern following the little ridges on it. This causes the key blank next to it to move in the same exact pattern along a cutting edge, thereby having the same ridges cut into it, thus creating a duplicate. The whole process takes about 30 seconds to complete.

FINANCIAL REWARDS

The finished key sells anywhere from $.85 to $1.50, representing a profit of from $.65 to $1.25 per key.

ACQUIRING CLIENTS

With permission of the management, you might set up shop in a college cafeteria, bookstore, or student union. Or find a busy gas station and ask the owner or manager if you can set up shop there on weekends and other periods when you have free time. He should be very agreeable to this, especially if you offer him 10 percent of your gross as rent. This still represents a very reasonable fee for you to pay when you consider the business that this type of location can attract. Most gas stations are located on corners, and if you operate on the corner of the lot, this will give you maximum exposure to attract business. As people drive in for gas, offer to duplicate their keys while they wait. At 30 seconds to process a key, you can have their keys ready before their tank is filled.

Airport lobbies are another place you can derive much business. How many people waiting to leave on a plane suddenly realize that if they were to lose their keys somewhere on their journey they would encounter numerous problems on their return home? Contact the airport management to arrange a small concession for yourself.

You might be able to set up shop in the parking lot of a large shopping center, duplicating keys for people while they shop. If an electrical source is not handy, you can operate your duplicating machine via a gas-driven generator. As discussed in the chapters on mobile car washing and waxing (see page 40), such a generator can be purchased for about $350. For this type of operation, it will be necessary to obtain a city permit. One can usually be obtained from your local city hall for about $65. In addition, you must also obtain permission from the management of the shopping center. (To find the location of the management office, look on the shopping center's directory of tenants.)

Contact managers of apartment houses to make an appointment to drive there at a designated time to take care of all the key needs of the tenants. Drive to large office buildings. Your duplicating machine can be easily transported from office to office via a lightweight narrow table with wheels. Just by going to each office, you should be able to solicit a lot of business, not only for the needs of the office, but also for the personal needs of each individual office employee. Be sure to leave your card for repeat business.

FUTURE GAINS

You can set up a chain of permanent stands in retail stores, gas stations, airports, and shopping center parking lots. Retired people make excellent employees for operating these stands. They can be paid on an hourly and/or commission basis.

If desired, you can receive further training in a good trade school to become a licensed locksmith. In this capacity, you would learn how to install locks wherever security is needed. By working with real estate developers, brokers, builders, and management companies, you could receive contract orders to install or replace locks in large commercial developments such as apartment houses, office buildings, shopping centers, schools, factories, etc.—*quite lucrative.*

RUBBER STAMP MANUFACTURING

WHY

The demand for rubber stamps is vast and continuous. The commercial and personal applications of rubber stamps is extensive. They can be used as return address labels, to identify a particular department in a large organization, to endorse checks, to give special mailing instructions on a letter or package (Special Handling, Third Class, Fragile, etc.), to show acknowledgment or approval of a business report, to give simple verification of a particular procedure or act (Approved by Accounting, etc.)—the list of possibilities is endless. As businesses grow and procedures become more involved and complicated, more and more innovative uses for rubber stamps will be discovered.

GETTING STARTED

To initiate this endeavor, a small table-top vulcanizing press is required plus an extensive array of metal letters to set up the necessary "type" formats. This will require an investment of $350 to $500 for the press and necessary type. Once this equipment is obtained, however, a stamp can be manufactured in about 15 minutes for about $.50 to $1.00 worth of material, depending on whether or not self-inking capabilities are to be incorporated into the stamp.

The manufacturing principle is rather simple. The metal type is arranged and set in a frame, or "case" as it is known in the industry. The type is then placed against a bakelite material and placed in the press. Heat and pressure are applied to form a negative mold in the bakelite material. A piece of stamp gum is then placed next to the bakelite mold. Both are then placed in the machine. Heat and pressure are applied forcing the gum into the negative type impression in the bakelite to produce a rubber "positive" which is the final stamp. This rubber positive is then mounted on an applicator frame for handling by the customer. Each press manufacturer will supply a detailed description on the proper use of his or her particular machine. To find sources for these machines, look in the yellow pages of your phone book or in the *Thomas Register of American Manufacturers* in your library under the heading "Rubber Stamp Equipment."

FINANCIAL REWARDS

A typical three-to-five-line stamp can sell for approximately $3.95 to $6.95 at retail. The cost to you is from $.50 to $1.00. This represents a profit of from $3.45 to $5.95 for 15 minutes of work.

ACQUIRING CLIENTS

Ads placed in the business section of newspapers and magazines are valuable aids in promoting your business. However, one of the best ways to promote yourself would be to utilize independent sales agents to call on stores and offices to solicit orders. Very often an organization is in need of a new stamp which it has neglected to order. You can split the profit 50–50 between you and your sales agents and still be left with a high margin of profit, not to mention volume. Be sure to give your sales agents a copy of the various type styles you offer. In addition, call on office supply stores, stationery stores, and instant print shops. They too can act as agents for you. Banks customarily supply their commercial customers with "endorsement stamps" to process their checks for deposit. Contact all banks in your area. This could add substantially to your business. In fact, it could even make up your entire business.

FUTURE GAINS

This type of operation can be conducted nationally on a mail order basis with ads going into newspapers and magazines under the heading "Business Services." In addition, because individual consumers like to have return address stamps when sending out their personal mail, advertise under "Personal Services."

STENCILING HOUSE NUMBERS ON CURBS

WHY

Most homes are set back a considerable distance from the street, and the house number is hard to see. It is important for home dwellers to have their house numbers prominently displayed for cab drivers, police and firemen, dinner guests, dates, and delivery people. Who would want to get a pizza delivered cold simply because the delivery person had a hard time finding the house?

This problem can be easily remedied by stenciling house numbers on the curbs. And here you come to the rescue, Sir Galahad with the white paint.

GETTING STARTED

You can purchase a stencil numbering kit with interlocking and rearrangeable numerals for about $10 at a hardware or sign making supply store. A spray can of white weather-resistant paint costs about $3.98 at paint and hardware stores and will last for about 100 homes. The process is quite simple. Arrange the numerals in the proper order for each address, place the stencil against the curb, spray the paint, and remove the stencil. Presto! You have just neatly numbered the curb in about 30 seconds and for about 4¢ worth of paint.

FINANCIAL REWARDS

It is typical and reasonable to charge anywhere from $1 to $5 per house for this service. You can make yourself several hundred dollars just doing both sides of a large city block.

ACQUIRING CLIENTS

People usually subscribe to this type of service on impulse. Take a good black and white picture of one of your jobs and use it as an example to show potential customers. The best way to solicit business is to go from door to door explaining and showing to homeowners what you can do. Remind them you can do the whole thing in the next few moments. For the low cost to them, it will be worth getting the job done once and for all.

FUTURE GAINS

Because proper identification of a residence is so important in police and medical emergencies, it might even be feasible to contract with local governments to number the curbs of every home, apartment, and office building in a city. When large orders are solicited, you can hire crews of high school and college students to do the actual work while you supervise.

ANTIQUE RESTORATION AND FURNITURE REFINISHING

WHY

Antique restoration and furniture refinishing is swiftly becoming a major enterprise. The high cost of purchasing new furniture is causing people to upgrade their worn and faded furniture instead of replacing it. Also, an increased interest in antique collecting has created a need for people who can refinish antique pieces to bring out and enhance their original beauty.

GETTING STARTED

Wood refinishing is the main method of restoring antiques and furniture. There is no one easy procedure for learning this craft. Nevertheless, there are some general guidelines one can follow in becoming skilled and successful in this field. Above all, a refinisher must be an artist, a chemist, possess manual dexterity, and be a problem solver. As you read further, you will see why.

Wood has a personality all its own depending on its type, age, and the wear it has withstood. The chemistry of the old finish can be complex. All of this must be taken into consideration when deciding what procedures to follow in refinishing the wood. You must decide whether or not the finish has to be removed. There are various chemicals that can be used to rejuvenate the finish without removing it. There is a process known as reamalgamation which consists of removing the old finish and then reapplying it. If the preceding is not advisable, then the old finish has to be removed. Which chemicals to use depends upon the chemistry of the finish and the type of wood lying underneath. Once the proper chemicals are selected for the finish removal, you must choose the correct grades of sandpaper and steel wool to insure complete removal but safety to the underlying wood. After the finish is removed, flaws that are in the wood have to be corrected. Various chemical compounds and manipulation are usually called for. The underlying wood must then be prepared to accept the new finish. When preparing the wood, you must be careful not to remove the natural patina in the wood. The patina is an attractive darkening of the wood surface brought on by changes in the atmosphere and by the aging process. It gives certain types of wood an especially impressive look.

The most suitable type of new finish has to be selected. It may be a stain, a clear finish, or both. There are few times when an enamel might possibly be used. The type and age of underlying wood determines what type of finish is best. After the finish is applied and allowed to dry, it must be hand rubbed with other compounds to bring it to it's maximum appearance.

While the preceding responsibilities may seem perplexing, they can also be exciting. You are a doctor deciding which procedures to use to bring the patient back to life. And when you do, it's a tremendous accomplishment and financially rewarding.

One book that can offer you guidelines is: *Furniture Finishing and Refinishing*, a Sunset Book, published by Lane Publishing Co. There are night school programs offered in the curricula of many high schools and colleges conducted by knowledgeable instructors. The manufacturers of wood finishes and removers might help you acquire skills. Formulations are constantly changing and improving. Keeping up with new manufacturing developments can increase your expertise. A six-month course in a good night school program, consisting of four hours a week for six months can prepare an interested person to practice professionally.

As a point of information, there is a course conducted by John Stair, the head of the restoration department at Sotheby-Parke-Bernet, in New York City: a four-day seminar on the fundamentals of fine wood refinishing. The course costs approximately $100 a day. Mr. Stair invites the highly talented participants from the course to join the apprentice program in wood restoration at Sotheby-Parke-Bernet. This program is full time and runs anywhere from three to six months. A beginner starts out as a volunteer. But if he or she is good, he or she will gradually work up to $6 to $8 per hour. And what an education one receives! For more information on this program, write:

Mr. John Stair
Sotheby-Parke-Bernet
Restoration Dept.
440 E. 91st St.
New York, N.Y. 10028.

FINANCIAL REWARDS

It is customary to charge for your work by the job. However, most commercial wood refinishers calculate their time at about $30 to $60 per hour plus the cost of the remover and stain, which incidentally is almost negligible.

ACQUIRING CLIENTS

To solicit business, advertize in the yellow pages of the phone book, neighborhood newspapers, and appropriate trade magazines. Have business cards made up and distribute them to used furniture stores and antique shops. Their customers will welcome knowing about your services.

Another fruitful means of soliciting business is to go to as many antique auctions as possible. They are listed in the yellow pages of your phone book and in a special "Auction" section of most newspapers. Approach people who have bid on and purchased antiques as they leave the auction. Present your business card and give them a brief sales talk on your expertise.

FUTURE GAINS

You can eventually hire other people to assist in the manual requirements of this business. If you pay your employees $10 to $15 an hour for their labors, this allows you a gross profit of from $20 to $25 an hour per employee and the opportunity to go out and solicit more accounts.

5

CLEANING SERVICES

GENERAL JANITORIAL WORK

WHY

With competition as keen as it is in the commercial world, image is everything. The cleanliness of an office or store reflects upon the quality of goods or services it provides. Thus, the availability of a good janitorial service is of paramount importance in today's society. As the operator of a janitorial service, you can either perform all types of cleaning assignments required by a facility or specialize in just one area, such as window washing, rug and upholstery cleaning, or the cleaning and waxing of floors.

GETTING STARTED

A good janitorial equipment company, listed in the yellow pages of your phone book, will not only tell you what type of equipment you will need to perform cleaning jobs effectively, but will also instruct you on the proper use of equipment and supplies. There is a proper way to mop and wax a floor, dust furniture, clean windows, etc. Many reputable janitorial equipment companies hold regular classes and seminars to instruct their janitorial customers on the latest and most effective cleaning procedures. They have a good reason for doing so: The more successful you are, the more successful they will be. After all, their success depends on your coming back to them for more supplies and to purchase or rent various types of cleaning machines.

For the relatively small investment of approximately $200 you can purchase the beginning necessities: a vacuum cleaner, a few mops, brooms, dust cloths, sponges, pails, mop wringers, and some cleaning and waxing solutions.

There are, of course, various types of electrically operated machines which strip, clean, and wax floors or shampoo carpets and upholstery. These machines can allow you to clean large areas not only with little physical effort, but also in a relatively short period of time, thus increasing your hourly average earnings. These sophisticated machines sell for anywhere from $500 to $5000. They can also be rented very reasonably on a daily, weekly, or monthly basis until your business warrants outright purchase. (See chapters on Rug Cleaning and Upholstery Cleaning.)

FINANCIAL REWARDS

There is no simple formula when submitting a bid to secure a job. Some janitorial firms charge by the square foot. There are variables to this, however, depending on how many objects such as desks, tables, waste baskets, etc., occupy the cleaning area. When determining what you should charge for a particular building or store, call on the manager or owner of a similar facility to find out what he or she is paying for services. Your competition's fees can act as a guideline for what you can charge. As a general rule, however, general cleaning such as sweeping, mopping, and vacuuming should bring in about $15 an hour for your services, with your help receiving approximately $5 to $8 per hour for their labors. When expensive machines are used to strip a floor of wax and apply a new layer, approximately $20 to $25 an hour is charged.

ACQUIRING CLIENTS

Call on the managers and/or owners of the commercial facilities in your area. In the beginning it would probably be best to call on the owners and managers of small apartment houses, office buildings, and stores. These facilities can be easily handled by just you and a helper. When you are ready to increase the size of your staff you can contract to handle larger facilities. In addition, call on real estate management companies. It is their business function to provide all types of services to allow for the efficient operation of their clients' commercial properties, which include apartment house and condominium complexes as well as office buildings. The providing of janitorial maintenance to these properties is one of the most important functions they are responsible for, and they usually subcontract it to a reliable janitorial service firm.

FUTURE GAINS

A janitorial business can be expanded to service as many small and large accounts as you can handle. As you grow, it would be a good idea to hire (or promote from within) certain individuals to act as supervisors and take responsibility for different accounts and locations of your business. They can be paid an hourly salary plus a percentage of the profits. In this manner, you can hold a firm control on your enterprise as you grow. If desired, you can even start your own real estate management company. After all, you will already control one of the most important functions of such a company—the janitorial service.

RUG CLEANING

WHY

Carpeting is the most common type of floor covering for homes, apartments, offices, and institutions such as banks, theaters, hospitals, retail stores and other types of facilities that wish to project a sophisticated image. Periodic cleaning restores the original appearance to a carpet and the room it decorates. Rug cleaning can be combined as part of a regular janitorial service or practiced as an individual specialty.

GETTING STARTED

There are two basic machines used to shampoo rugs: the first is a rotary brush unit; the second is a steam-cleaning unit. The rotary brush unit can work in two ways: First shampoo can be applied directly to the floor by the operator or it can be applied through a dispenser attached to the rotary brush. In either case, the rotary brush grinds the shampoo into the carpet fibers where it emulsifies the dirt. The rotary action subsequently brushes the emulsified dirt and shampoo mixture to the surface where it is later vacuumed up. The steam unit has an applicator wand which when pushed forward along the rug propels out a mist of steam that has cleaning and conditioning agents suspended in it. This mist, along with its suspended ingredients, penetrates deep into the pile of the rug. On the back stroke of the wand, the steam and suspended dirt particles are vacuumed up into a receptacle tank. Each type of machine has its individual advantages. You will have to use both in order to decide which you prefer. For large jobs involving rugs that are badly soiled, you may want to use the rotary brush machine followed by the steam unit to perform a superior job.

The rotary brush machine retails for approximately $600 and a good steam unit sells for approximately $1000. Nevertheless, they can both be rented from your supplier on a daily, weekly, or monthly basis until outright purchase is practical.

FINANCIAL REWARDS

Rug cleaning is one of the more lucrative specialties in the cleaning field. There are several methods used to calculate fees. When cleaning a rug covering a wide surface area with obstacles, such as in a bank, theater lobby, art gallery, etc., a fee of from 6¢ to 12¢ per square foot is usual. As a general rule of thumb, the larger the surface area with fewer obstacles to clean around, the less you charge per square foot.

A one-bedroom apartment will usually return the operator approximately $60 for an hour and a half of work. A three-bedroom home or apartment brings in approximately $80 for two hours and a half of work. With good management, you can earn approximately $30 an hour in this endeavor.

ACQUIRING CLIENTS

Any facility with carpeting on its floors is a potential client of yours. As in so many other maintenance projects, contact real estate management firms responsible for the maintenance of their clients' floors, and janitorial firms who do not offer rug cleaning services but would like to do so with you as the subcontractor. Homes with well-groomed carpets can command a higher price when put on the market. Contact all real estate agents to advise them of the services you can render them and their clients in increasing the value and saleability of their properties. There is a great deal of evidence showing that shoppers prefer to patronize stores with a clean image. Contact all retail stores that have carpeted floors. Each new client you acquire is also a candidate for repeat business as its rugs again become soiled.

FUTURE GAINS

Rug cleaning can be developed into a major enterprise. As you acquire new clients, you can add new equipment to your inventory and hire supervisors to assist you in completing the assignments you solicit. In fact, you can even start hiring salespeople on a commission basis, to help you solicit new accounts.

UPHOLSTERY CLEANING

WHY

Every piece of furniture that is covered with fabric, whether it be a chair, sofa, or couch, will eventually become soiled. It is often difficult and impractical to remove these objects for cleaning. This creates a demand for people willing to come and clean them directly on the premises.

GETTING STARTED

There are a host of portable foam and dry cleaning machines designed to clean upholstery. They are available on a purchase or rental basis from janitorial supply firms and companies specializing in the manufacture of such machines. Look in the telephone yellow pages under "Janitorial Supplies" and "Upholstery Cleaning Equipment." These firms will also instruct you in the proper use of their equipment.

FINANCIAL REWARDS

Upholstery cleaning fees range from $20 to $30 per hour depending on the locale and the number of pieces requiring cleaning. If you solicit a job requiring at least eight hours of work, you can drop your fee slightly to compensate for the large volume of work.

ACQUIRING CLIENTS

The clients mentioned in all the other types of cleaning services are fair game for this type of business. In addition, give special attention to hotels, motels, and restaurants. Because of the nature of their businesses, these establishments have many pieces of furniture which frequently get soiled.

FUTURE GAINS

Upholstery cleaning can be practiced separately or in conjunction with a rug cleaning service (discussed in the previous chapter). As in rug cleaning, growth is almost unlimited. It is determined by how many new accounts you can attract and the number of people who work under you on either a part-time or full-time basis to carry out the assignments you solicit.

STAIN REMOVAL SERVICE

WHY

Very often, someone spills something on a perfectly clean carpet or upholstery fabric. It is impractical to have a whole carpet or piece of furniture cleaned just to remove one stain. This provides you with the opportunity to offer a special stain removal service.

GETTING STARTED

Most janitorial supply houses sell special stain removal kits containing special solutions for each type of stain. These kits sell for approximately $5 and come with instructions for their use.

FINANCIAL REWARDS

In this type of business, you are not necessarily charging for your labors as much as your technical knowledge and traveling time to and from the job. Because of this, you can easily charge $20 to $50 for a stain that takes only 15 minutes to remove. It is worth it for someone to pay this lesser amount in contrast to paying up to $200 for a complete shampooing.

ACQUIRING CLIENTS

The resources listed under janitorial, rug cleaning, and upholstery cleaning services also apply to a stain removal service.

FUTURE GAINS

This endeavor is best practiced as a valuable adjunct to the aforementioned rug cleaning and upholstery cleaning services. It not only puts extra money in your pocket, but the people who use you will be likely candidates for complete rug and upholstery cleaning chores when needed.

WINDOW WASHING

WHY

Housewives don't like to clean windows. In fact, nobody likes to do them. Remember the saying, "Fools rush in where wise men fear to tread?" Well, wise men probably don't like to do windows either. You can therefore make good money doing what no one else wants to do. Clean windows can make a big difference in the appearance of a home or apartment. Sparkling panes highlight the merchandise in a retail store window. Clean windows help a commercial or professional office maintain an aura of dignity and sophistication. The need is there.

GETTING STARTED

A cup of vinegar and three gallons of water plus a sponge squee-gee and you are in business. There are special commercial clean-ing preparations on the market. However, people in the business tell me that this simple vinegar solution works the best.

Note: For your service to be complete, you will want to be able to clean the outsides of windows as well as the insides. This auto-matically limits your clientele to the owners of small buildings whose windows are either on ground level or are low enough to be cleaned easily and safely from the inside or with the help of a sturdy ladder. You will not want to do buildings of more than two stories. Leave the high rises to the professionally trained window washers.

FINANCIAL REWARDS

This service can be offered to homeowners, apartment house dwellers, retail store operators, and commercial offices. The fees can vary according to window size, the volume of work located in one area, and the time required to do a good job. A typical 4 foot by 3 foot pane should go for at least 35¢. A sliding glass door can bring at least 60¢. A large store front window easily commands $1.25; a glass door, approximately 60¢. In general, most window cleaners base their fees on $10 to $15 per hour.

ACQUIRING CLIENTS

The secret to success in this endeavor is to build up a steady and permanent clientele whom you service on a weekly basis. If your customers are in close proximity to each other, you can accom-plish a great deal of work in a short period of time, thereby earn-ing a large sum of money per hour. Therefore, concentrate your efforts in areas where you can work in a large group of homes, apartment houses, and retail stores on the same street, in the same shopping center, or some downtown business area.

To secure the business of retail stores, it is best to go from store to store, talking to each owner or manager and passing out your business card. For apartment house dwellers, call on the man-agers of each building, informing them of the services you can render their tenants. A one-page flier about your services would be a good idea. These fliers can be produced at any instant print shop for about 3¢ each. After talking to an apartment house manager, leave a flier in front of each tenant's door. To secure the business of residential homeowners, pass out your fliers "door to door" and advertise in the local newspapers and shopping guides. Again, as in all other cleaning endeavors, contact the operators of real estate management companies.

FUTURE GAINS

As soon as you obtain all the business you can handle personally, you can hire other cleaners to handle your assignments while you go on and secure more accounts. In this manner you can build up a city-wide window cleaning service.

INDUSTRIAL CLEANING

WHY

Almost all cleaning is done for aesthetic and hygienic reasons— rugs, floors, walls, windows, upholstery, streets, sidewalks, etc. However, there are many types of industrial equipment that collect hugh amounts of dirt and grime which, if not removed properly, can affect the operating efficiency of these expensive pieces of machinery. Furthermore, when a piece of machinery breaks down because of accumulated dirt, not only is it expensive to repair the apparatus, but there is also an accompanying expense when the process which it serves is delayed.

In industrial plants, dirt can clog ventilating and air conditioning systems, foul power generators, slow down materials-handling equipment, corrode wiring, make floors slippery, hide defects in tools, begrime washrooms, and bring complicated electrical systems to a halt. In the construction industry, dirt can clog cooling systems, foul engines, slow down hydraulic cylinders, and hide cracked blocks and hydraulic leaks. In the trucking industry, dirt can also clog radiators, foul engines, slow down hydraulic cylinders, corrode wiring, destroy components, and hide cracked blocks and hydraulic leaks causing expensive delays in transporting important goods. Industrial dirt can be expensive; removing it can be profitable.

GETTING STARTED

There is no special skill required for this business. One special type of machine is very effective, however, in removing heavy sludge, grease, and grime from all kinds of equipment and surfaces. It heats water to very high temperatures and sprays it out under very high pressure onto the intended surface via an applicator hose. Various types of detergents can be added to the water tank to aid the cleaning process. Several companies manufacture this type of high-pressure hot water machine. Each company has a wide range of models to provide for light-, medium-, and heavy-duty cleaning and all will quickly instruct you in the use of their machines. One such company is the *Hotsy Corporation, headquartered at 6757 South Emporia, Englewood, Colorado 80110.* They have dealers throughout the country with whom they can put you in touch. One of their heavier-duty machines that can handle a wide variety of jobs sells for approximately $3500. This unit will heat water to 210°F and emit it at a pressure of 1100 pounds per square inch. To this instrument you can add a generator and trailer for another $1500 ($5000 total) to achieve complete portability. The unit can then be attached to your car or pickup truck for transportation to your business assignments. There are also rental and lease arrangements available for this equipment. Look in the yellow pages of your telephone directory under "Steam Cleaning Equipment."

FINANCIAL REWARDS

The general fee for heavy-duty industrial cleaning of this type is from $40 to $50 per hour. You might reduce this fee by 10 to 15 percent on long-term cleaning contracts for your clients.

ACQUIRING CLIENTS

Contact every factory in your area. Ask what type of manufacturing they do and what type of equipment they use. Inquire if they ever have mechanical breakdowns. After all, who doesn't? Ask if you can go over their equipment with them to see if you can prevent costly breakdowns and accidents through your high-pressure hot water process. Call on trucking companies to clean not only the mechanical parts of their vehicles for operating efficiency, but also the outside of their cabs and trailers for aesthetic purposes. Call on all construction companies, especially those involved with digging and grading. Do not forget to call on companies that rent out trucking and construction equipment. After the equipment is returned to their headquarters, it usually requires extensive cleaning. The pumps in oil wells are also subject to the accumulation of tremendous amounts of unwanted grease and grime. If there are some pumping facilities in your area, you have a possibility for another group of clients.

High-pressure hot water cleaning is also very effective in cleaning farm equipment and cleaning and sanitizing barns and other structures that house animals. If you live near a farming community, here is another client source for you.

This process is also effective in removing grease, grime, and oil slicks from streets, sidewalks, and parking areas. Contact real estate management companies periodically to clean the unsightly and dangerous oil slicks that accumulate in the parking areas of the buildings they service. Almost every community has several private airports serving it. The management of these airports like to clean accumulated ground-in rubber and oil from the runways periodically. Restaurants can also use your service periodically to clean and sanitize their kitchen areas. As you can see, the possibilities are numerous for providing this kind of service.

FUTURE GAINS

You have seen some of the possibilities in this business. If you are aggressive and industrious, you may soon develop more business than you can handle. You can then purchase or lease more equipment and hire other people to take care of the cleaning assignments you develop. A reasonable compensation arrangement is to split your fees equally with your workers. As mentioned, a unit with generator and trailer can be purchased for approximately $5000 or leased for about $750 per month. If you establish contract cleaning assignments at 10 percent to 15 percent off the regular hourly fees, this amounts to $34 to $45 an hour for your services. Split evenly, this allows anywhere from $17.00 to $22.50 per hour for both you and your workers. If a worker works 160 hours a month, this allows both you and him or her from $2720 to $3600 each. When the $750 leasing fee is deducted, this allows you a gross monthly profit of from $1970 to $2850 per unit operated. With each 160 hours a month of work accumulated, you can add another unit and another worker. After you develop sufficient experience in managing this type of operation, you can eventually expand your operation to serve and profit from many communities.

6

CREATIVE AND ARTISTIC ENDEAVORS

PERSONAL CATERING

WHY

Can you prepare a cold scallop mousse, galantine of turkey, or maybe veal scallopine? Would you like to learn? There is a great deal of money to be made preparing elegant dinner parties in people's homes or apartments. It might involve a romantic repast for two, dinner for the entire family, or an elegant dinner party for some important business and professional associates of the host.

This is the era of the two-income family. It is typical for husband and wife to each be involved in exciting but demanding careers. There is a lot of income being produced, but who does the cooking? Fast-food stands, coffee shops, and conventional restaurants can become very mundane. Many people are now enjoying the luxury of having elegant meals prepared for them in the privacy and comfort of their own homes—not every night, of course, but just often enough to make life interesting. This phenomenon has given rise to exciting opportunities for amateur chefs who would like to capitalize on their culinary talents.

GETTING STARTED

You may already have a number of unique dishes in your repertoire which you are now competent in preparing. Or you might want to supplement your skills through gourmet cooking classes in a local high school or college night school program. In fact, at this point, you may not even cook at all but still be intrigued with the prospect of being the talk of the town in personal catering. Well, why not enroll in a culinary program at one of the educational institutions in your community? If you have the basic talents and instinct for this craft, you could even rely on just reading several gourmet cooking books. And then, with a little practice, hang up your shingle.

Basically, the only equipment you will need is your own skills. The food is purchased after a catering assignment is acquired. However, it might be a good idea to invest in some basic cooking utensils as well as a set of fine dishes and serving utensils to add to the elegance of your service. This would be just a one-time investment. Or, in the beginning, you could rent the necessary utensils. Just look in the yellow pages of the phone book under "Catering Supplies."

FINANCIAL REWARDS

Most caterers compute the cost of ingredients and then multiply by five to arrive at the fee charged the client. So you see, the profit potential is there. Typically, the bill will come out to $20 to $40 per person, although there have been many instances where a lavish dinner accompanied by an assortment of vintage wines has produced tabs of $200 per person. Affairs like this are often given by up-and-coming executives who want to secure favorable relationships with their peers. When a young insurance salesperson who hosted such an affair was asked why he didn't just take his corporate clients to a good restaurant, he explained: "When it's done in your home, it's done in style. A restaurant chef cooks for everyone. A personal caterer cooks just for you and your chosen guests."

ACQUIRING CLIENTS

After becoming adept at preparing a variety of menus, you are ready to market your services. The best place to advertise is in publications frequently read by affluent people. Local professional and executive business journals are an excellent way of reaching people who like to entertain on a high plateau. Call on the corporate offices of all prominent business concerns in your community. After all, mightn't the manager of a local bank want to have some of his or her senior associates over to dinner now and then? Or an advertising executive want to secure an account he or she has been working on? Or an ambitious insurance salesperson want to sell a group life insurance program to the head of a large business concern? Theater-goers might desire an elegantly prepared dinner after a performance. Advertise your services in the magazine or program that is handed out upon admission. The possibilities are almost endless. And once you establish a good reputation, future clients will then seek you out.

FUTURE GAINS

When ready, you can expand your operation to also include large affairs such as weddings, bar-mitzvas, corporate parties, etc. This is accomplished through the establishment of your own central catering facility complete with ovens, refrigerators, coolers, warmers, and other utensils necessary for the preparation and delivery of elegant meals. The hiring of more cooks and servers can allow you to cater a large number of affairs on the same day at the same time. As each banquet is ready for delivery, it is put on a special catering truck containing equipment that can keep each delicacy at it's optimum temperature and flavor for a period of four hours. This allows you to cater events considerable distances away from your base of operations. Freelance servers can be hired on an hourly basis to meet the truck at the banquet location and serve the guests.

A well-equipped catering facility with several ovens for multiple parties will cost you approximately $20,000 to furnish. The catering trucks can be rented on an hourly or daily basis. The financial rewards can be tremendous. Just one party of 50 people can furnish you a net profit of $500.

SANDWICH
AND SALAD
BUSINESS

WHY

Sandwiches and salads make up an important part of the American diet. They provide a convenient way of obtaining a quick, nourishing meal, which is most important to millions of workers on their lunch hour. A good sandwich or salad is not always easy to obtain. The sandwiches served in most luncheonettes and cafeterias or from catering trucks are either very expensive, poor in quality, or both. It is not feasible or economical for most households to purchase and store a large assortment of foodstuffs in the refrigerator to make an interesting bag lunch every day. This provides a tremendous opportunity for you to create nutritious and appetizing sandwiches and salads for the working person. They can be made by you and sold in large quantities to grocery stores, supermarkets, and sometimes even gasoline stations for resale to people on their way to work.

GETTING STARTED

Before you can prepare sandwiches and salads for commercial purposes, you must get a license (about $65) and your facilities must be approved by your local board of health. Some communities will allow you to operate out of your own household kitchen if it meets local requirements. In other localities, you will have to operate out of a specialized catering facility that meets department of health standards. The cost of renting space in a catering facility is negotiable, but before you go investing in a specialized catering facility, see if you can make arrangements with a restaurant to use a small space in their kitchen to make your sandwiches and salads. The fact that the restaurant is in operation means that the kitchen facility must be approved for food preparation. If your sandwich business does not compete with the restaurant's main cuisine, and especially if that restaurant's daytime business is slow, there is a good chance of developing this type of arrangement. The rent you pay for this privilege can help the restaurant offset some of its daily operating expenses. A reasonable rental fee might be 5 to 10 percent of your gross revenues.

When your business builds up, you can then open your own sandwich preparation facility. The equipment required in establishing such a facility consists mainly of refrigeration and cooling equipment plus counters, sinks, plumbing, and storage cabinets or shelves. This investment comes to approximately $4000 plus the rental fee for the space. The facility does not have to be large, just enough room to prepare the sandwiches and salads. Because your products will be shipped out to other localities for resale, you can rent space in a low-rent area.

WHAT KIND OF SANDWICHES AND SALADS SHOULD YOU PREPARE?

Sandwiches and salads are limited only to the imagination of the preparer. There is always a better way to make a tasty and nutritious egg, tuna, chicken, meat, or ham salad. There are different types of relishes, herbs, and condiments that can be added to sandwiches to turn them into gourmet delights. And don't forget the hero sandwich. When you use the best delicatessen meats, onions, tomatoes, peppers, herb dressings, and other ingredients, you can create a sandwich which is a meal in itself. This is also true with a good "chef's salad."

A variety of fresh lettuce leaves can provide the base for a good salad. To this, almost any combination of vegetables or other foods (e.g., cheese, meat, fruit, legumes, sprouts) can be added to create a mouth-watering delight. The salads can be dispensed in disposable Styrofoam containers covered with cellophane or plastic wrap for easy inspection. You can make up your own variety of special homemade dressings which can be stored in single-serving containers and dispensed with each salad sale.

There are a variety of special breads and rolls that can be used to make sure your sandwiches stand out. They can be purchased from a wholesale bakery. Later, you can even have a commercial bakery bake a special type of roll exclusively to house your creations. This alone can give your business that special identity that encourages a large patronage.

After you develop a format for your products, the next step is to see that they are properly marketed. There are two avenues you can take. As mentioned, grocery stores, supermarkets, and gasoline stations can increase their sales by selling your products. Call on the owners and operators of these facilities. In addition, there is a big market for delicious sandwiches and salads delivered right to the door of the workplace. Housewives and college students can work for you as independent sales agents. They can purchase your products at a wholesale price and travel to office buildings, stores, and factories to sell them to the employees. Whenever a large number of sandwiches and salads can be sold in one stop, there will be tremendous profit opportunities for your independent sales agents. To assist your salespeople (and of course your business), you can make up a simple menu sheet listing all of your products and their retail prices. This menu can be inexpensively duplicated in large numbers at any instant print shop. Your sales agents can pass out the menu sheets to their customers. They in turn can check off their selections for the following day or days. This encourages repeat business and allows your sales agents to maintain a good control over their inventory.

FINANCIAL REWARDS

The beautiful part of this business is that you can probably produce better sandwiches and salads and sell them for a lower retail price than most restaurants and luncheonettes. Most of these facilities have to pay extremely high rents which in turn have to be included in the price of their products. By operating from a small facility in a low-rent district, you can avoid this problem.

As the manufacturer, you should allow yourself a profit of at least $.75 to $1.50 per sandwich or salad. Your retail clients and independent sales agents should also be able to make a similar profit. Because you will be purchasing your ingredients in large quantities from your wholesale food suppliers, your own ingredient costs can be kept to a minimum.

There are several methods of determining wholesale and retail prices: You can calculate your actual cost for each sandwich or salad and then add $.75 to $1.50 per item. The same fees can be added to the resultant wholesale price to determine the retail price. Another method is to mark up the cost of ingredients by 50 to 100 percent. The resultant wholesale price can then be marked up by a similar percentage to arrive at the final retail price. These figures can be adjusted slightly so that the retail price of each sandwich is competitive with restaurant prices and you, your sales agents, and your store clients all end up with a suitable profit.

ACQUIRING CLIENTS

Any business with refrigeration equipment is a potential customer of yours. Many gasoline stations offer convenience foods to supplement their gasoline sales. We've already mentioned grocery stores (e.g., 7-Eleven food stores) and supermarkets. How nice it would be for people to be able to stop in these facilities on their way to work, pick up a delicious sandwich or salad, and continue on their way again.

Another possible source of clients are the cafeterias in factories, schools, offices, etc. Instead of making their own sandwiches, workers or students could purchase them already prepared from you.

To solicit independent sales agents to sell directly to the consumer, place ads in college newspapers and in your local newspaper in the "Personal" or "Business Opportunity" section.

If you sell your sandwiches to gasoline stations, grocery stores, cafeterias, and independent sales agents, there might be a slight overlap in distribution. But don't worry, there is enough business for everyone.

FUTURE GAINS

Your sandwich and salad business can be expanded to cover an entire city. The whole operation can be conducted from just one location, or if more convenient and economical, from several food preparation facilities strategically located in your city. Eventually you could even hire production and sales managers to help you expand your operation to other cities. Your key employees could be paid a salary plus a portion of the profits of new business created.

CALLIGRAPHY

WHY

Did you ever see an invitation or announcement that just seemed to stand out with a certain extra personal touch, where even the address on the envelope possessed a warm but sophisticated style which seemed to say: "This contains a special message for a special person"? This effect is usually accomplished through the art of calligraphy, or fine penmanship. This special writing will usually follow variations of Roman, Greek, Gothic, and Old English script styles. It is decorative, distinctive, and artistic. It is used by people who want to send an invitation or announcement of special significance.

GETTING STARTED

Provided you possess artistic ability and manual dexterity, this specialty—usually taught in a high school or college night school curriculum—can be learned in approximately 60 to 70 hours of training. The main tool is a special calligrapher's pen with approximately eight different points (or "nibs" as they are called professionally). The total price of this outfit is no more than $20. You can supplement it with a drafting table (c.$80), drafting lamp (c.$35), drafting stool (c.$20), ink (c.$7), and paper samples (c.$15). The paper samples are to show your customers the various types of paper they can have their work printed on. After an order is received, you can then go to a printing supply shop to purchase the necessary stock to complete the order. As you can see, you can start up this business with approximately $177 of capital.

A good teaching program will instruct you in the freestyle development of letter forms and their application in design projects. Calligraphy emphasizes freely written expression rather than mechanical lettering.

FINANCIAL REWARDS

It is quite common for calligraphers to charge $30 to $50 an hour or more for their services. I interviewed many calligraphers who charged up to $75 just to execute a 50-word invitation or announcement, which takes an experienced person only an hour to do.

A typical invitation or announcement assignment would proceed as follows: You would lay out and write the main body of the announcement (charging at least $30 an hour for your time) and then take it to a professional printer who would take a picture of your artwork and make a printing plate from the negative. He or she would then insert the plate in an offset press and run off the desired number of invitations. You would pay him or her for this, then pass this expense on to your client. Quite often, you can make some profit on the production work done by the printer, since most printers allow calligraphers a professional trade discount.

In most cases, your client will want you to hand-address each envelope. A three-line custom-written address will usually take five minutes to construct. A typical charge for this is $3 per envelope ($36 per hour). Thus, a simple 50-unit order will take you approximately one hour for the body of the announcement ($30) and four hours to address the envelopes ($144), to yield you a total of $174 in fees plus any profit derived from the printer.

ACQUIRING CLIENTS

Almost anyone requiring decorative handwriting can use your service—printers who require special freehand printing effects that cannot be produced by conventional typesetting machines; advertising agencies creating ads requiring special graphics; professional people announcing their services to an elite clientele; people desiring unique and distinctive wedding, bar-mitzva, confirmation, or other types of invitations; organizations requiring the production of special certificates signifying special accomplishments of its members.

Colleges and state licensing boards usually require the services of calligraphers to inscribe the recipients' names on diplomas and professional licenses. Just the inscription of a person's name will pay up to $2 and should only take a couple of minutes to complete.

When advertising your business, take out an ad in the yellow pages of your phone book under "Wedding Announcements" and "Business Announcements." Take out classified ads in the newspaper under "Business Services." Independently employed professional people who desire to cater to an elite clientele are prime customer sources, so you should advertise in all professional journals such as those of the medical, legal, accounting, and architectural professions. For a list of these publications, consult *Ulrich's*

International Periodicals Directory, obtainable in your local library.

FUTURE GAINS

A calligraphy service can be developed to encompass a complete graphic arts service designing entire layouts for individual advertising agencies and advertising departments of large companies.

SIGN MAKING

WHY

A picture is worth a thousand words. Likewise, a simple but well-designed, hand-lettered sign can create an image or transmit a message. It might announce an event or call attention to merchandise on sale. Retail stores require signs to help sell merchandise. Office buildings require signs to identify tenants on their office doors or post restrictions such as "No Smoking." Wherever you go, signs are in abundant use.

GETTING STARTED

Although sign making can be self-taught through books and supplemented through high school and community college night school programs, one should possess some artistic talent before engaging in this type of endeavor. Artists' supply and sign making supply stores can offer you valuable assistance by making you aware of materials and instruments that can enhance your talents. An interesting source of information and opportunities in the sign business can be found in the magazine *Signs of the Times,* published monthly by the Signs of the Times Publishing Company in Cincinnati, Ohio. It might be found in your local library, or you can send away for a copy.

All signs are different and can offer the craftsperson the chance for creative self-expression. There are as many types of signs as there are things to announce or items to identify—the name of a store, office, or building, merchandise, a special event, etc. The most popular type of sign in this category is the "point of sale" sign found in retail stores. These signs announce and call attention to items on sale and take approximately from 30 minutes to an hour to create. With the addition of new merchandise and price changes, these signs have to be changed constantly, thereby offering you the opportunity for a great deal of repeat business.

FINANCIAL REWARDS

Approximately $10 to $15 an hour is charged for a rough freehand sign. These signs are usually found in retail stores to announce a special sale for a particular type of merchandise. For signs requiring a lot more care, such as lettering on an office door, or commercial outdoor signs, $40 and more per hour is customarily charged.

ACQUIRING CLIENTS

To attract a sizable and steady clientele, go to every retail establishment in an area, informing each owner or manager of your talents and services. To attract their interest and inspire them to order from you, make up some sample signs to impress them with the quality of your work. Look around their stores at the merchandise they have for sale and suggest signs you might create for them that would stimulate sales. You may find yourself selling to people who never even considered having signs made before.

Call on the management of office buildings. Every time they rent office space, the name of the new tenant usually has to be inscribed on the door. Read the real estate section of your newspaper. Watch for new office buildings that are planned for construction. Contact the developer or leasing agent to handle the door lettering assignments for all the incoming tenants.

Truck lettering is another type of sign making. Most businesses that use trucks and vans in their operation want to have their name, address, phone number, and a commercial business message on their vehicles. Contact the dealers who sell and lease trucks. They can be instrumental in referring their customers to you.

Many outdoor electric sign manufacturing companies subcontract out their design requirements to independent artists. Contact these companies to advise them of your talents and skills.

FUTURE GAINS

You can operate a full-time business specializing in just one or several of the sign-making opportunities discussed in this chapter. For example, designing and lettering signs for outdoor electric sign manufacturers can become a lucrative business in itself. In fact, you can even develop your own outdoor electric sign company. After you solicit an account and design the lettering, you can subcontract out the actual manufacturing process to another company. Even though that company might be a competitor of yours, it is customary for sign companies to cooperate with each other, giving trade discounts for the work they subcontract for. In this manner, you not only make money on the designing and lettering of the sign, but you also share in some of the manufacturing profits.

JEWELRY MANUFACTURING

WHY

Jewelry is an important accessory in the fashion world. The proper piece of jewelry can enhance the appearance of any type of wearing apparel, from a simple denim outfit to elaborate dinner clothes. Tasteful jewelry might be made with simple, natural products such as seashells or coconut shells, or turquoise and various precious stones, or metals such as gold and silver. Other less expensive metals such as copper can also be expertly crafted to produce attractive ornaments.

GETTING STARTED

Many people who started out making jewelry in their basements or spare rooms now have businesses of factory-sized proportions. To supplement your natural talents for jewelry making, it would be advisable to take jewelry making courses to learn such specialized skills as silver and copper smithing, the proper crafting of other metals, and the selection and mounting of stones.

FINANCIAL REWARDS

The price that can be obtained for a piece of jewelry depends upon the market value of any precious stones or metals used in its manufacture and the manner in which the materials are styled and crafted together. Quite often, an attractive piece of jewelry crafted from an intricate and tasteful blending of both expensive and inexpensive components can command a substantial price. In fact, a well-designed ornament created from a tasteful, original blending of inexpensive materials can often command a higher price than a dull, unimaginative piece of jewelry made of expensive materials. All this means one thing: If you are creative with both your mind and hands, you can produce jewelry of great value.

In this type of business, even if it is only small scale, it is not uncommon to receive anywhere from $16 to $200 for a silver pendant and from $60 to $2000 for a gold one. Mark-ups on well-crafted items can range up to 200 percent and more.

ACQUIRING CLIENTS

In the beginning, you may want to sell each piece yourself. The sales prospects are many. Very often, a high class boutique, department store, or retail jewelry store may desire to buy up almost everything you can produce. If you do not wish to become involved in direct sales, there are many opportunities to sell wholesale to individual sales representatives who in turn will resell your products to either the retail jewelry community or private consumers. The option is yours.

FUTURE GAINS

If you decide to expand your business, you may desire to solicit independent representatives to purchase and show samples of your work to buyers from jewelry, boutique, and department stores for the solicitation of large orders which would then be shipped out and billed by you, with a sales commission paid to your sales representatives.

MAKEUP/EYELASH/ NAIL ARTIST

WHY

The beauty world is intricate and involved. Cosmetics is a billion dollar industry catering to women. There are several important specialties which can be learned in a short period of time and can provide the operator with a substantial income. One such specialty is the professional application of eyelashes and makeup. Another is the manicuring of nails and the building and sculpting of artificial nails.

GETTING STARTED AND FINANCIAL REWARDS

Note: Because there are so many individual procedures in this business, each with its own professional fee, we will combine the financial rewards with the steps in getting started.

There are relatively short training programs available in many community colleges and trade schools for learning beauty skills. Quite often, they can also be learned through books or by having an experienced operator teach you personally. In any event, artistic aptitude, manual dexterity, and patience are essential. In fact, they are the prime prerequisites for success. Some states require a simple oral or written exam for licensing in this field. Contact your local state bureau of licensing for information concerning any special requirements.

Considerable sums of money can be made in this endeavor. The overhead is usually low. All of your supplies can be purchased from commercial beauty supply stores.

EYELASHES

There are two basic eyelash procedures: the application of individual lashes, and the application of the entire strip at one time. The application of each lash individually requires approximately 30 to 45 minutes to complete. The box of lashes and glue cost approximately $3. The typical charge for this procedure is $15 to $25. The application of the complete eyelash strip naturally takes far less time—approximately five minutes. A good eyelash strip will cost you anywhere from $1 to $5 and the typical charge for the procedure is from $5 to $15.

MAKEUP

Facial makeup is used to enhance the natural beauty, and also to create different moods and appearances by different color selections and application techniques. The typical charge for this process is at least $20 to $30.

A typical makeup procedure is as follows: Cleansing and moisturizing creams are applied to the skin. After the skin is thoroughly cleansed, the foundation or base is applied. Next, the proper color of mascara is skillfully applied. Various eye shadow combinations are applied to accent the eyes. The eyebrows are highlighted by use of colored eyebrow pencils, and finally the proper shade of lipstick and lip gloss are applied to the lips.

There are essentially two different makeup programs. First there is the so-called party makeup application, where the artist/ technician just does a complete makeup process. This procedure requires from 30 to 45 minutes to complete and usually the cost is from $20 to $25. Next, there is the makeup lesson. In this procedure, the artist not only applies the makeup, but also gives the client a detailed lesson on the proper application of makeup. This combination makeup application and individual lesson takes an hour to complete and the customary fee is $30. In addition, the artist has the opportunity to sell the client makeup for self-application at home. The typical mark-up on this makeup is double to triple the cost to the artist.

NAILS

The handling of finger and toenails is altogether another type of procedure. It might be conducted by the same artist in conjunction with an eyelash and makeup business, or conducted entirely as an independent business, depending on the desires of the operator.

Fingernails may just require a simple manicure, which takes approximately 30 minutes and brings a fee of from $7 to $10. Damaged nails or nails that don't grow well require the application or "sculpting" of artificial nails custom designed and contoured for the individual customer. In this process, porcelain or acrylic is applied to and built up on the nail with the aid of a form. After the application is completed, the form is removed and the hardened acrylic or porcelain is trimmed and filed down, and a coat of polish applied, dried, and buffed until a natural-looking nail results. The process takes approximately one and a half hours to complete and the charge is anywhere from $35 to $50.

Sometimes, instead of applying and designing artificial nails, the client's own nails are strengthened by the repeated application of special papers or liquified nylon fibers applied in the form of a polish. The application of special papers is known as the "Juliet Manicure," takes approximately one hour to complete, and brings a fee of approximately $15 to $20.

Pedicures take 30 to 45 minutes to complete and customarily bring a fee of from $12 to $18. The massaging of the feet, application of moisturizing creams, and some partial callous scraping usually accompanies a well-done pedicure.

ACQUIRING CLIENTS

These skills can be practiced as a concession in a professional beauty salon, in your own private office, or even in your home or apartment. Newspaper ads are the best way to announce your services to the public.

FUTURE GAINS

You may want to proceed further into the beauty business by hiring other operators to work for you in your shop, office, or concession on a percentage basis. A typical split is 60 percent of the fee going to the individual artist/technician and 40 percent to the shop owner. You can also expand your operation to include hair styling, which allows you even greater profit margins. If desired, you can just add the necessary equipment for hair styling to your shop and hire experienced hair stylists to work for you on the conventional 60–40 arrangement instead of learning the skill yourself.

CHILD PHOTOGRAPHY

WHY

Commercial photography is very competitive. However, child photography offers certain money-making advantages over other forms. Have you ever known a parent who could resist photographs of his or her child, especially those taken in situations which are spontaneous and capture the personality and various moods of the child?

GETTING STARTED

Do you have a good 35mm camera and some proficiency in using it? If the answer to any one or both of these questions is no, but if you would like to get into this field, a good automatic 35mm single lens reflex (SLR) camera can be obtained for approximately $350. Being a good child photographer does not depend as much on technical ability as it does on a certain artistic sensitivity and intuition in recognizing scenes that will turn out to make a good picture. Many schools and colleges offer excellent extension programs in photography. Do not worry about doing your own developing and printing; there are many fine photographic laboratories that can handle your processing requirements.

FINANCIAL REWARDS

An 8″ × 10″ black and white print costs the photographer about $1 to have processed and can sell for as much as $10 to $25 each. You can offer special rates when more than one print is ordered.

ACQUIRING CLIENTS

A child photographer does not necessarily have to solicit work assignments in advance. You can take freelance shots of children at amusement parks, playgrounds, ice skating rinks, or any place where children are most apt to "be themselves" and project the greatest self-expression. After the shots have been taken, you can give your card to the parent, inviting him or her to look at the picture proofs of the child at a later date.

It is a good idea to pass out fliers or place announcements in neighborhood newspapers advising parents of your service and announcing where you will be on a given day. This will help induce interested parents to accompany their children to the play areas where you will be located. After you build up a reputation in your area for good child photography, many parents will want to bring their children to your studio to have special portrait shots taken of them or will hire you to come to their house to take impromptu shots at a birthday party or similar event.

FUTURE GAINS

This part-time endeavor may inspire you to enter other areas of professional photography. Or you may want to pursue a professional career just specializing in and perfecting your techniques in child photography. There are many child photographers who make $50,000 a year and more in this one specialty alone.

SELLING AND MAINTAINING INDOOR PLANTS

WHY

The selling and maintenance of ornamental plants is a multimillion dollar industry. There is opportunity for you to become a part of this industry in your spare time and at a very good profit.

Indoor plants provide an effective and creative way to decorate the interiors of homes, apartments, and offices. They add a new dimension of beauty and warmth to any interior. They make the lobby of a building more inviting and provide offices with a more pleasing atmosphere to conduct business in. They can brighten up a hospital room to encourage and promote a patient's recovery, or complement the merchandise in a department store.

Many people and institutions appreciate plants and would like to have them on their premises, but there are two problems that often arise: First of all, many offices are too busy to take the time to go out and shop for plants. Secondly, they become lackadaisical when it comes to caring for the plants. You can solve both problems with your own door-to-door plant service.

GETTING STARTED

Wholesale nurseries in your area are not only the prime source for your plants, but in addition, they will be glad to provide you with tips on what plants to purchase and how to take care of them. Some can even provide you with good books on proper plant selection and care. Two particularly good books in this field are *The Sunset Garden Book*, published by Lane Publishing Co., and Thalossa Cruso's *Making Things Grow*, published by Alfred A. Knopf.

Select hardy but decorative plants that require minimal care. There are a great many around that with proper care will last for years.

Decorating plants range in height from one foot to ten feet and wholesale from $3.00 to $20 each. They can be sold directly from your car, van, or truck. However, to save yourself the time of lugging large plants from office to office for sales presentations, you can show pictures of suitable plants at full growth and take orders based on these pictures. Your wholesale florists can help you obtain these pictures.

When selling your plants, the larger ones should be featured for building lobbies, the medium-sized ones for waiting and reception areas in offices, and the smaller ones for individual office areas.

Plants can be sold to individual home owners at county fairs, garden parties, and flea markets. Whenever civic groups have their meetings, you can display and take orders for plants and give a percentage to the sponsoring organization. Also, you can have someone sponsor a house party for plants, giving the sponsor a part of the action.

FINANCIAL REWARDS

The mark-up on individually sold and delivered plants is from three to five times the wholesale price. The actual amount of mark-up you charge will depend on the volume of each order.

Many of your office building customers will want you to maintain the plants you sell them. The average fee charged for taking care of just one plant, just once a month, is $1.50 per month. This includes trimming, polishing, application of insect repellent, fertilizing, and watering the plant. These simple skills can be learned from your wholesale florist or in any night school horticulture class.

Often retail stores such as grocery, drug, and small department stores may desire to purchase an assortment of plants from you for resale to their customers. When an arrangement such as this is made, the average mark-up to your retail store customers is approximately 30 percent. It is worth it for them to allow you this mark-up rather than take the time to travel to the wholesale nurseries to select and bring back the plants themselves.

ACQUIRING CLIENTS

Every office in every office building is a potential client of yours. In addition, call on the management of all office and apartment buildings. Large attractive plants can dress up the lobbies of these buildings and increase rentals. Banks, hospitals, and hotels are also likely candidates for your services.

To stimulate sales of your plants, it might be a good idea to offer a one-year guarantee on each plant, if a maintenance contract is purchased along with it. Money from increased sales plus money from maintenance contracts equals *success!* With proper maintenance, it is easy for any plant to survive a year. The few that might die can easily be replaced by you at your wholesale price. The increased sales potential made possible by your guarantee will easily offset a few possible losses.

FUTURE GAINS

You can supplement your door-to-door business with one or several retail stores of your own. You can supply your retail stores from your wholesale nursery sources. From your retail stores, you can sell to individual shoppers in addition to supplying your commercial clients.

If desired, you can even start your own interior landscape design business, designing and installing plant arrangements for large office buildings, hospitals, schools, department stores, banks, hotels, shopping centers, and other businesses and institutions. It is quite possible to build a business grossing over a million dollars a year in this specialty field.

MURAL PAINTING

WHY

Today, there is considerable interest in the use of murals to decorate the walls of office and apartment buildings, banks, restaurants, etc. It is a very pleasant experience to dine in a restaurant surrounded by a tranquil scene. Pediatricians like to have child-oriented murals painted on their waiting room walls. Cheerful scenes painted on the walls of hospital hallways soften the clinical atmosphere by giving patients something pleasant to focus on. A wall mural is really nothing more than a large picture painted on a wall. If you are capable of painting conventional canvasses, this same concept can be applied to walls, and quite often, more profitably.

GETTING STARTED

Obviously, you need artistic ability. Your present talents can be supplemented with some night school art courses. A good art supply store can furnish you with all the materials needed plus a few helpful hints. If possible, get some practice in working in large scale by applying your artistry to those homely wooden structures surrounding construction sites.

FINANCIAL REWARDS

A wall 15 feet long and 8 feet high can easily bring you $400 to $500. As your reputation for good work grows, these figures can be raised significantly.

ACQUIRING CLIENTS

When starting out, take some sample pictures to the owners and managers of places where your skills could be utilized. Banks, restaurants, hotels, hospitals, churches, and public buildings are likely candidates. Inform these people how dull interiors could be brightened with your work. They may want to choose scenes from the sample pictures you show them or they might have their own ideas of what they would like illustrated. Whatever is decided, do your best work.

After a job is completed, be sure to sign your name and phone number in a fairly prominent spot on the picture. This will inform onlookers, who are also potential clients, where to locate you. Be sure to call on interior decorators, especially those specializing in commercial structures. They may be already looking for someone like you to enable them to do more creative decorating for their clients.

FUTURE GAINS

As your expertise and reputation grows, you could develop a lucrative full-time practice applying your artistry to prominent buildings not only in your local community, but also on a state and even nationwide level. If desired, you could even venture into a full-scale interior decorating business with mural painting as one of your specialties.

MOSAIC MURAL MAKING

WHY

Another medium for decorating the walls of commercial buildings and institutions is mosaic murals. A mosaic is a picture or design created by the interlaying of small pieces of colored stone, glass, or tile on an adhesive surface. A good mosaic is literally "striking" in appearance. Find a building with one and you will see what I mean. It gives an aura of elegance to any building lobby or office waiting room. Real estate developers and office or apartment building owners can increase the value of their properties through artistic and well-planned mosaics. In addition, office building tenants can impress their business and professional clients with tasteful mosaics in their waiting rooms. There is a large business potential to be developed in this area. It can be yours if you think you might have a talent for this type of work.

GETTING STARTED

Artistic talent and a sense of style are prime prerequisites for this business. For commercial wall mosaics, glass tile squares approximately three-fourths of an inch square are usually used. We will refer to this glass as "mosaic tile" in our discussion. Mosaic tile squares come in every color imaginable, offering a great deal of latitude in designing colorful creations. Usually, squares of one color are attached next to each other on an adhesive paper backing and sold commercially in one-square-foot sheets for approximately $3 a square foot. An entire square-foot sheet of tiles can be attached directly to the wall in a few moments via an adhesive applied to the wall, or the same tiles can be removed from the sheet and attached individually in patterns with tiles of different colors.

There are three basic types of wall mosaics that can be created for commercial use. First of all, there is the "true-to-life" picture created by the careful placing of individual tiles to create lifelike images with color. This by far is the most difficult, the most time-consuming, and thus the most expensive. It would be advisable not to get involved in this type of intricate, detailed work unless you eventually practice this endeavor on a full-time basis.

The second type of wall mosaic design is the artist's simplified interpretation of a picture in which only the general outline of each object is depicted with the tiles. In this manner, a true-to-life

94

painting can be reduced to its basic essentials and fairly easily reproduced.

The third type of wall mosaic (and the easiest to make) consists simply of an arrangement of nonrepresentational geometric designs. This style can be executed by the proper placement of whole one-square-foot sheets of tile interlaced with partial sheets and individual tiles to create the desired geometric schemes. When starting your practice, I suggest you concentrate your efforts in this area. Not only is it easier and faster, but the results can be simply magnificent.

When starting a project, allow yourself time to work accurately and comfortably. First, draw a scaled-down version of the finished design on graph paper, with each square on the paper representing a specific number of inches on the wall. Color each area of the graph paper with the color that will be close to the one used on the finished wall. Use a thin water color that will allow the squares on the paper to show through. Then the graph paper can be used as a guide for arranging the tiles.

It is not necessary that a wall mosaic cover the entire wall. Wall mosaics are more vivid and dramatic than painted murals. Keep this in mind when you determine the size of your mosaic, and just try to scale it to the proportions and needs of the room.

To find a source for your materials, look in the yellow pages of your phone book under "Tile Distributors." To protect yourself, have the client pay for the tiles in advance and sign an agreement to pay for your artistry and labor immediately after the job is completed.

FINANCIAL REWARDS

As mentioned, your tiles will cost you approximately $3 a square foot. Thus, a typical 80-square-foot mosaic will cost you $240, plus $5 for the adhesive compound. Naturally, you don't order the tile until a job order is secured. Therefore, your pre-investment expense is almost zero. A reasonable fee for the design and execution of a good mosaic is easily $400 to $1000. An 80-square-foot mosaic featuring a geometric design can be completed in a weekend.

ACQUIRING CLIENTS

Modern builders like to include mosaics in their buildings. Go to as many architectural and building firms as possible informing them of your talents. They may include you in their original plans for a building project. Apartment house owners are prime targets for your skills. A fine mosaic in the lobby can often bring an extra $20 to $50 in rent per month for each apartment or add to the price of the building when the owner wishes to sell. The same goes for office buildings. Don't forget banks. They have plenty of money to spend for improving their interiors and projecting the high class image their success is often based upon. Also, remember interior decorators, especially those involved in commercial decorating.

When approaching potential clients, show them some pictures and designs that would look good on their walls. This can be done simply by going to your local library and obtaining books on mosaic designs, architecture, and interior decorating, and bringing the books along with you on your calls. Often, just the presentation of some of the possibilities can inspire a contract.

FUTURE GAINS

After your reputation grows, you can increase your fees considerably. As your proficiency increases, you can contract to apply your skills to the walls of churches, museums, and other public structures such as state and federal office buildings.

TYPESETTING

WHY

Printed matter is one of the main vehicles for communication in today's society. Whether it be a small sales brochure, a magazine, or a 500-page book, the production of all printed material is an involved process requiring the performance of several procedures. Fundamentally these procedures are as follows: The text must first be created by an author or authors. Next a type style and format have to be selected. The material then has to be typeset and the resulting proof "pasted-up" for proper arrangement on the page. A picture is taken of the paste-up with a special copy camera and finally a printing plate is made using the negative. The plates are then inserted into the printing machine for the final printing.

Most printers prefer not to get involved with the actual typesetting procedure. They like to have the finished typeset proof handed over to them ready for the platemaking and printing steps. When people do hand over raw manuscript material for printing, the printer usually subcontracts this work to specialized typesetting firms or private individuals working as independent contractors. Book and magazine publishers and advertising agencies frequently subcontract typesetting requirements to independent typesetters. This can provide a lucrative opportunity for you to provide this service.

GETTING STARTED

There are many types of machines available for setting type which can easily fit into a den, garage, basement or attic. Some are operated by hand, some are semiautomatic; but the easiest and most modern method of typesetting is through the use of computerized phototypesetting machines. In these instruments, rays of light pass through a stencil of the desired letter or number to be printed. The ray of light, which conforms itself to the outline of the stencil, then strikes a photosensitive paper behind the stencil. The image of the letter or number is then imposed upon the photosensitive paper which when further processed yields "camera ready" copy with the image permanently inscribed upon it. Before the ray of light passes through the stencil of the letter or number, it first passes through a series of lenses which adjust the size of each letter or number inscribed upon the paper.

The operation of these phototypesetting machines is relatively easy. If you can already type and follow manuscript typesetting instructions, you can learn to operate these machines with approximately one week of training. Most manufacturers will teach their customers the proper operation of their equipment. There are several fine phototypesetting machines on the market. One excellent machine is the Quadritek, manufactured by the Itek Corporation. It provides the owner with a wide variety of features. The Quadritek accommodates four different type styles at one time. If desired, there are almost 1000 additional type styles that can be easily inserted into the machine in a matter of seconds. The size of each type style can easily be adjusted to provide heights from 5.5 points to 74 points. (A point is a printing term for size. One point is $1/72$ of an inch. Therefore, 5.5 points to 74 points means a range of from 0.076 inches in height to 1.02 inches in height.) If a larger size is needed for a headline or banner, the 74 point size can be used and then later blown up via the camera used to make the printing plates. The Quadritek possesses a computerized keyboard which the operator uses to manipulate the style, size, and length of each line. By pressing the proper keys, the operator can center each line, make columns, and arrange even margins on both sides of a column of print.

Everything typed appears on a screen for easy viewing. In addition, the typeset text goes into a memory and is further recorded onto a magnetic tape or disk. Because of this feature, if there is a mistake, or if the author of the material desires to make changes later, the entire copy does not have to be retyped. All the typesetter has to do is program the machine to find the part of the text to be corrected or changed (this will appear on the viewing screen) and then type in the correction or new copy. The electronic pulses typed onto the magnetic tape or disk cues the machine to inscribe the images on the photosensitive paper. When the final comes out on the paper, it is run through a photoprocessor which fixes the paper to provide camera-ready copy. Because the operator can adjust the width of each line on the Quadritek, there is no need for his or her client to do much additional paste-up—a savings in time and money.

The Quadritek comes in four models, each with additional features. The prices range from $13,000 to $15,000. Now don't get excited by these prices. These machines can be purchased for approximately 10 percent down with monthly payments ranging from $350 to $450 per month. This allows you to go into business with a reasonable investment. When you see the earning potential of this endeavor, you will see how reasonable this cost is.

As mentioned, if you can already type, you can learn to operate a typesetting machine in approximately one week. Quadritek offers a 21-hour training program with each unit sold. For more information on the Quadritek, contact

ITEK GRAPHIC SYSTEMS
822 Jefferson Rd.
Rochester, N.Y. 14692

All a typesetter is required to do is "set type" as dictated by the customer. However, typesetting is a competitive business. And, as is illustrated throughout this book, if you can offer your clients something extra, you can beat the competition and obtain a great deal of business. Many clients will have some mistakes in their copy. Others will be unsure as to what layout and type styles to use. If you can assist your customers with proper layout and design in addition to minor spelling or punctuation correction, you will be offering a tremendous service resulting in a lot of business. Furthermore, you can charge additional money for your extra services. To prepare yourself to provide these services, enroll in night school programs in graphic arts and English grammar.

FINANCIAL REWARDS

The fee range for commercial typesetting is from $30 to $50 an hour. If you subcontract a typesetting assignment from a large printing company or advertising agency, you might charge them the lower rate ($30 an hour) and allow them to recharge their client at the rate of $40 to $50 an hour. If printing companies and advertising agencies can profit from your skills, they will be only too willing to assign as much work to you as possible. If you work directly with the client requiring the printing, you can charge your skills out at the rate of $40 to $50 an hour and subcontract the platemaking and printing out to printing shops. In this type of situation, the printing shop will allow you a trade discount on the printing which you can then mark up and charge your client.

I know that the purchase of a typesetting machine represents quite a large investment. If you are considering going into this venture, you may first want to test your ability to solicit business. Make up some business cards advertising yourself as a typesetter. Call on some of the potential clients discussed in *Acquiring Clients* below, and ask if they have any typesetting jobs they want done. Then call on members of the typesetting trade and find out the lowest and highest prices for a particular job. Make a bid slightly higher than the lowest price. See if you can get the job. Then subcontract the work out to the lowest bidder. You will not make much money. Nevertheless, if you can repeat this procedure several times, you will know that you can succeed in this business. The Itek Corporation also has a plan whereby you can rent the machine for 90 days for $2,000. For this rental fee, they will also instruct you in the proper use of the machine. If you are successful enough during those first 90 days to decide that you want to keep the machine, Itek will allow you to apply the rental fee to the cost of the purchase. Either way, your biggest risk is $2,000, whereas your potential earnings are $50,000 a year and up.

ACQUIRING CLIENTS

There are many potential clients to draw upon in operating a typesetting business. As mentioned, printers like to print from camera-ready copy; they don't like to get involved in the intricacies of typesetting. Contact as many printing companies as possible. Advertising agencies produce tremendous amounts of literature for their clients. Contact all advertising agencies in your community. All businesses require some form of printing: catalogues, brochures, instruction pamphlets, labels and tags to accompany products, business forms, and so forth. Athletic and entertainment organizations require tickets to be printed. Contact all of these facilities. Offer to work with them in typesetting or designing their requirements. You can prepare everything for the printer and then subcontract the printing procedure to a good printer instead of the printer's getting the initial business and subcontracting the typesetting procedure out to you. All of this is acceptable in the trade.

Many small book and magazine publishers subcontract their typesetting requirements to independent typesetters and then turn over the camera-ready copy to selected printers. You can obtain additional business by contacting book and magazine publishers not only in your local community but also in surrounding areas. A lot can be accomplished via mail and telephone.

FUTURE GAINS

Once you build up a large business, you can add additional machines and hire other operators to run them. A good typesetter has to be paid anywhere from $10 to $13 an hour. However, if you charge your work out at the rate of $30 to $50 an hour, your profit can accumulate rapidly. As indicated, if you solicit printing clients directly, you can arrange for the artwork and provide the typesetting and then subcontract the actual printing to a commercial printer. In this capacity you would be functioning as a full-scale printing business. As in other endeavors, you can function in as many areas you can handle and profit in. You can even hire salespeople to go out and solicit as much business for you as possible. They can be paid on a commission basis determined by the amount of business they obtain.

SCREEN PRINTING

WHY

There are two basic types of printing—offset printing accomplished through conventional printing presses and screen printing. The offset principle is utilized to print books, magazines, brochures, pamphlets, etc. However, whenever large and colorful letters and designs are required to be inscribed upon paper, cardboard, fabric such as T-shirts or jackets, containers, or metal objects such as instruments and machinery, the screen process is usually used. Screen printing is fast becoming one of the most sophisticated methods of applying designs or words to any type of material regardless of size, shape, or configuration.

Screen printing utilizes the "stencil" principle, in which a coating of ink or paint is applied to a material in a controlled fashion by passing it through a coated screen. The design pattern is produced by removing the coating from portions of the screen. This allows the ink to pass through and affix itself to the underlying material, following the contours of the uncoated portion of the screen. The ink is forced through the uncoated mesh by means of a squeegee.

The applications for screen printing are almost unlimited and so are the profit opportunities. It is possible to start your own business with a few simple machines and gradually increase your business and equipment to handle every type of job.

GETTING STARTED

The principle of screen printing is simple. The proper equipment is the most important prerequisite. The fundamentals of this art can be easily learned in a short trade school or community college adult education program. In addition, there are many manufacturers and distributors who carry screen printing equipment that you can operate from your garage. These companies are only too happy to teach their potential customers the proper use of their equipment. Although it takes some artistic talent and manual dexterity to prepare the screens used in the process, this procedure can always be subcontracted out to specialists in the area. In fact, as you will see later, you can even specialize in this one area alone.

THE SCREEN PRINTING PROCESS

The screens, available as stock items, consist of a fine mesh coated with a nonporous material that does not allow any ink or paint to pass through. The desired outline is fashioned by removing the coating only in the areas where the ink or paint is to pass through. Only one color of ink can be passed through a given screen. Nevertheless, designs in different color combinations can be created by using a separate screen for each color. Each screen is treated (to remove the coating) only in the areas where a configuration of that particular color is desired on the underlying material.

To remove the coating exactly in the designated areas, a guide is made of hand-cut emulsion film. A piece of transparent emulsion-coated film is placed on the artist's original work. Since the film is transparent, the underlying artwork shows through. The desired outline for just one color area is traced. The tracing perforates the emulsion coating which can then be peeled off leaving the desired stencil. This film with the primary stencil cut into it is known as camera-ready artwork, to be used in preparing the final printing screen for that color. It is placed on the screen and the stenciled portion is used as a guide in removing the desired configuration of coating from the mesh, thereby creating the final stencil in the screen. The screen is now ready to have ink passed through it. This process is repeated to make a separate screen for each color required in the design.

An alternate, newer, and more advanced method of preparing the screens is as follows: A picture is taken of each color segment of the original artwork. A negative is produced followed by a correspondent positive on a transparent background. The screen is sprayed with a photosensitive emulsion. The positive on the transparent background is placed on the treated screen. A special light is directed toward the screen which "fixes" the emulsion exposed to the transparent area of the positive but leaves the emulsion covered by the actual design untouched. This untreated area of the emulsion conforms to the contour of the artwork and is washed off leaving the desired stencil. The "fixed" portion of the emulsion remains impervious to the wash water. This method of screen preparation is becoming very popular.

By means of the above method, true-to-life pictures of people, scenes, or objects can also be reproduced on fabrics or other material. Every color in a picture is a composite of four basic colors—red, blue, yellow, and black. In this process, four pictures are taken of the picture (artwork) to be reproduced. In each picture, a different lens—red, blue, yellow, and black—is used in front of the camera lens to extract (separate) that color. As in the previous process, a negative and corresponding positive on a transparent background is made of each color contour, which is then inscribed onto a screen sprayed with photosensitive emulsion. Again, a special light "fixes" all of the emulsion except for the contoured area, which will become the stenciled portion once the emulsion in that area is washed off. Then different colors (red, blue, yellow, and black) are passed through these stencils and superimposed upon each other on the material to be printed to produce an exact likeness of the original picture.

Stock screens sell for approximately $3 each. There are firms that will create the desired design in a screen for approximately $20 per screen, providing you supply them with the camera-ready artwork. Therefore, a four-color design or a picture (which is a composite of four colors) will require $80 worth of screens. However, if the camera-ready artwork also has to be created, the charge will run higher. In other words, if hand-cut emulsion film has to be traced, or pictures taken, colors separated, negatives and positives made, the cost will be higher. But don't worry if you don't care to do this work yourself. The charges are customarily passed on to the customer as artwork or screen preparation charges. In fact, if desired, you can even specialize in this one area yourself, serving just people in the screen processing industry who serve individual clients.

Once the screens are prepared, they are put onto machines holding the material to be printed. The desired ink color is passed through each screen onto the material via a squeegee forming the desired configuration. As mentioned, if an actual picture is being reproduced rather than a design, two or more colors might be passed through the same stencil to reproduce an actual "lifelike" color.

For commercial use, there are machines that handle four screens and corresponding colors at a time. As an example, if T-shirts or similar apparel are to be printed, they are loaded (four at a time) onto the bottom part of the machine. The screens rotate on the top part of the machine on a carousel-type component. The screens rotate, cover each piece of material to be printed, ink is passed through each screen onto the material, and then the screens rotate again to the next piece of material. This basic machine sells for approximately $2000 and can handle 120 four-color shirts or similar material an hour. Once your business builds up, there are more sophisticated machines and accessory items available that will allow you to process up to 840 four-color items an hour. There are machines available, such as the Phase 4 Universal Screen Printer, that will allow you to print on irregularly shaped objects such as containers for baby powder, cosmetics, patent medicines, motor oil, etc.

After the desired material is printed, the ink must be dried in a special cold or hot air dryer. A dryer will cost approximately $3400. All the machines required in the screen printing process can be purchased or leased on a time-payment plan.

To find sources of supply and further orientation into the mechanics of this field, look in the yellow pages of your phone book or the *Thomas Register* (in your library) under "Screen Printing Supplies, Equipment, or Services." In my research, one very fine firm I discovered was:

Advance Process Supply Co.
400 North Noble Street
Chicago, Illinois 60622.

They have twelve branches throughout the United States handling every type of equipment and service required by the industry. In addition, they sometimes hold clinics to assist newcomers and even experienced professionals in the industry.

FINANCIAL REWARDS

Fees in this industry vary depending upon the item and quantity being printed. Irregularly shaped items that are more difficult to print on will obviously require a higher fee. As a guideline, the general industry fees for T-shirts are as follows: one-color design—50¢ per shirt; two-color design—75¢ per shirt; three-color design—$1.00 per shirt; and four-color design—$1.25 per shirt. As previously mentioned, depending on the sophistication of the equipment you use, you can handle from 120 to 840 four-color shirts per hour. This computes to $150 to $1050 in income per hour. The machine that can handle 840 shirts per hour sells for $12,000, however. So, you might want to start off with the smaller investment and financial return. And let's face it, there is nothing wrong with making $150 per hour. You can always work up to the larger investment and income. Once you use a screen, it can be recycled for approximately $8.

If you prefer to specialize in just creating artwork and processing screens for the industry, you can charge your time out at $50 an hour. These skills can be learned in many trade schools and community colleges. Once you become proficient, call on all the screen processing companies in your area and offer to serve them.

ACQUIRING CLIENTS

When it comes to soliciting business, the sky is the limit. When you go into a drugstore or supermarket, notice how many plastic, metal, and glass containers have the labels printed directly on them. This is screen printing, my friends. Contact every manufacturer of consumer products in your area—there can be a lot of business awaiting you.

If your screen printing business becomes successful, and you do decide to take on large orders, you will have to arrange for the shipping of the printed goods. Contact several shipping companies in your area and select the most economical one. The freight cost is passed along to your client.

Practically all instruments and gauges have numbers, words, and lines imprinted upon them. This too is an example of screen printing. Call on all instrument manufacturers in your area. Your local library may have a compendium of all the industries in your area. Contact as many as you can to see if you can serve some or all of their screen printing needs.

Always keep one thing in mind—screen printing allows the application of designs, messages, and slogans to any material regardless of size, shape, or configuration. This allows you to handle jobs that the average printer cannot. Most offset printing presses can only handle paper sizes up to $8^{1}/2'' \times 11''$. In screen printing, you can handle any size material. For orders requiring a large surface area to be printed, visit local printers. Offer them your services on a subcontract basis for assignments that they cannot handle on their conventional printing presses. Naturally, allow them a trade discount so they can profit also. In this manner, you can allow them the opportunity to present a full service image to their clients.

If a person or organization requires one or several signs or posters to be made up, their best and most economical source would be a conventional sign maker also discussed in this book. However, if a large number of the same sign or poster is required, screen printing is definitely the fastest and most economical approach. Contact all sign makers and offer to subcontract for their large-quantity assignments.

Call on all advertising agencies to point out that the announcement and promotion of their clients' products can be greatly assisted by screen printing the product's message and design on T-shirts or other forms of wearing apparel. The T-shirts can be sold for the cost of the shirt itself plus the fee for printing. In effect, the advertiser pays no money to have advertisements of his or her product worn on the chest and backs of thousands of people. Furthermore, it is considered fashionable by many people to wear clothing carrying commercial messages. I once saw a restaurant selling T-shirts with their menu printed on them—clever! Many recording companies have T-shirts imprinted with the picture of their recent recording star or album. If you live in an area where recording studios are located, you have another source of potential clients.

Contact schools and universities. They may want to order large quantities of shirts or jackets with their school name on them for resale to the students. Fraternities and sororities are also prime sources for the sale of personalized T-shirts or other garments. Actually, any business enterprise or social, civic, or religious organization may want some type of garment with their organizational name, message, or insignia imprinted on it, for distribution to their members. If they haven't thought of the idea themselves—suggest it! Every athletic team is a potential customer of yours. Also, go to clothing manufacturers who may want to print humorous or cute messages on garments to promote their sale. Once in this business, you will come across a lot more sources and possibilities to solicit.

FUTURE GAINS

Many people have started in this business with just a $5000 to $6000 investment and have gradually grown into larger operations grossing over a million dollars a year in printing orders. This is a fascinating and creative business with new opportunities being presented at an accelerated rate. Everything produced has to have printing inscribed on it.

DIRECT ADVERTISING PRODUCTION

WHY

We have already discussed the financial opportunities in distributing advertising circulars. As a separate endeavor or as a valuable adjunct to a distributing business, you can also create effective advertising circulars for retailers.

Most retailers, no matter what business they are involved in, are burdened by mounds of annoying and time-consuming red tape required in the daily operations of their businesses. Quite often, they are too busy to take the time to plan and develop effective advertising campaigns. You can use your ingenuity and creative abilities to do this for them.

GETTING STARTED

To assist you in this project, take some art and graphics courses in a high school or college night program curriculum. Meet with your retail clients to help them select effective "sale" merchandise and develop the "message" they want to communicate to their customers.

After a general format is decided upon, the ad must be drawn and laid-out by a graphic artist. If you can do this yourself—all the better. If not, there are many talented graphic artists looking to get a start in this field, who are willing to perform this chore inexpensively. Contact all the schools in your area that teach graphic arts to solicit talented students who would like to get some commercial experience. After the ad is drawn and approved by your client, take it to a printer for final reproduction.

FINANCIAL REWARDS

Because every job will possess different requirements, and because there is a wide variation in prices charged by artists and printers (depending on how much they need business), it is hard to quote an exact fee for this type of service. However, there is a general rule of thumb you can work by: Shop around to find the best price for artistic and printing work. After your production costs for a given job are ascertained, add 5¢ per circular printed to establish your own profit. Thus, for a 10,000-circular run, this would amount to a profit of from $300 to $500 in addition to the $90 made in the actual delivery process.

ACQUIRING CLIENTS

Contact all owners and managers of local retail establishments. Point out that your service represents the most effective and inexpensive form of advertising for them. Furthermore, inform them that you can take complete responsibility for their neighborhood advertising campaigns, allowing them to concentrate their energies on internal store operations.

FUTURE GAINS

This type of operation can be expanded to many neighborhoods. You can make a fine living in this specialty alone, or eventually expand into other types of advertising and develop a highly sophisticated advertising agency.

Or, this type of operation can eventually be expanded by your creating a neighborhood "Shopping Guide," which would list and promote the various retail stores in the area and possibly even contain feature articles about individual shops and/or their owners. To finance the venture, you would contact all of the retailers in a certain neighborhood and have them take out ads in various sections of the publication. To make sure people read the newspaper, the ads can be interspersed with articles of consumer interest such as cooking, home repairs, etc. These articles can be written by yourself or by journalism students from a nearby college for a small fee.

FASHION DESIGN AND MANUFACTURING

WHY

People are constantly on the lookout for new designs in clothing. In fact, with dress and leisure clothes, styles often change with each season. This means that manufacturers constantly require fresh ideas to keep up with or surpass their competition.

Naturally, large manufacturing companies have their own design staffs. Many supplement their staffs with freelance designers. In fact, there are prominent manufacturers who rely solely on the designs created by freelance designers in developing new products. You must first have a number of top money-making designs under your belt before the major manufacturers will even talk to you. Nevertheless, there are many small but aggressive firms that will seriously consider purchasing, either outright or on a royalty basis, new designs created by fresh talents.

GETTING STARTED

Fashion design is an art. You must not only possess innate artistic talent but also have manual dexterity in cutting and sewing in order to make several "sample" models of your creations to show to potential buyers. Your natural talents should be supported by some professional training. A four-year program leading to a degree would be great. There are, however, many successful designers who learned their art by taking night school programs in "apparel design" conducted by qualified people in their local high schools, colleges, and universities. There may even be an accredited design school in your area that offers night school programs in the particular area you are interested in. Please remember! You do not have to start out by designing complete dress outfits. You may have an exciting idea for a blouse, blazer, undergarment, or uniform for a particular trade or profession.

Once you have created a drawing for your idea, as mentioned, you may want to sell it directly to a manufacturer for an outright fee or on a royalty basis. The methods of doing this will be discussed under the section "Acquiring Clients." You may also want to manufacture the garment yourself for the purpose of selling larger quantities to retail stores. A qualified instructor in a good wearing apparel program can offer you excellent advice in doing this. To give you an idea of what the manufacturing process entails, the following description illustrates the various steps you would have to take:

1. You first draw the design on paper.

2. A working pattern is then developed from the sketch. *Note:* A pattern is a scaled drawing of each component of the garment, which when reproduced on fabric and sewn together will create the product that the designer originally conceived in his or her mind.

3. The material for the garment is selected.

4. The material is cut and sewn using the pattern as a guide.

5. You sew up several garments, using your design, to show to prospective store buyers.

6. You take the garments around to clothing purchasers, hoping to get advance orders for large quantities in different sizes. *Note:* You can call on these buyers yourself or retain a salesperson to work on commission.

7. If you have confirmed orders from stores with good credit ratings, it is often possible to borrow the necessary funds for large-scale manufacturing from banks. *Note:* It is only fair to warn you that if your customer does not have a credit rating high enough to obtain a bank loan based on his or her order, you had better obtain a downpayment or be prepared for legal action in case you are not paid.

8. Once you receive bona fide orders for your creations the large-scale production then begins, as follows:

9. Your patterns are taken to a professional pattern maker who will produce a durable pattern of each component of your garment and then reproduce these components in different sizes so that the final garment can be produced in different commercial sizes.

10. You purchase quantities of fabric. The patterns and fabric are then given to a cutting company who will use the patterns as a guide in cutting out large quantities of each component in different sizes.

11. The components are kept separate according to design and size and then sent to a commercial sewing company for final assembly and ironing.

The preceding is the general format used to produce wearing apparel items. In many cases, you may be able to find companies that will take care of making sample garments and subsequent large-scale commercial production all under one roof. Or, a private contractor may be able to properly select good subcontractors, give them their assignments, and then collect the finished product for delivery to you. You will have to find out what your net costs are using both methods of production. If the cost of assigning all the responsibilities to one manufacturing company or a general contractor who will take care of all the subcontracting assignments is only slightly more than selecting and coordinating everyone yourself, it may be wise to use this method and devote your energies to the promotion of your products.

It should also be noted that even before you show your sample garments to potential buyers, you will have to get some accurate quotes on the entire manufacturing process so that you can determine what your costs and subsequent price quotes to customers will be.

Also, make sure the subcontractors or even general contractor or full-scale manufacturing company are reputable and dependable and will turn out high-quality goods within the time period agreed upon. If they deliver late, causing you to deliver late, you may find yourself with a lot of cancellations. When selecting manufacturing facilities, check with people in the trade for referrals to good manufacturing contractors. And then when selecting these contractors, ask for further references. If possible, have them put up a bond to guarantee proper delivery. A bond is an insurance policy issued to a manufacturing company that will assure their clients financial reimbursement if they are caused financial hardships as a result of late delivery or substandard goods.

Where do you find good manufacturers and subcontractors? If you live in a large metropolitan area like New York City or Los Angeles, you will have no trouble. Just look in the telephone Yellow Pages under "Apparel or Clothing Manufacturers." They will all be listed. In fact, most of them are located in one general area of town. If there are no manufacturing facilities in your community, you will have to look at nearby communities. Go to a large library and ask to see all the trade journals dealing with the apparel industry. If there are none, ask to see the reference book *Standard Rate and Data*. As mentioned in the beginning of this book under "How To Use This Book," *Standard Rate and Data* lists major publications in all industries. Look for the names of the professional magazines and trade journals for the apparel industry. Write to the magazines and ask for a sample copy. Look for ads placed by manufacturers and contact those companies. Also, if you see one or several journals that are of value to you, you might consider subscribing to them to help with future ideas and decisions.

FINANCIAL REWARDS

The financial possibilities in this field are vast. If you are unsuccessful in selling a design to a manufacturer or in taking production orders from a retail buyer, all you have lost is your time and maybe several hundred dollars in cloth and sewing time in preparing some samples. No one ever became devastated from this. However, if you do go into the production phase, and do receive a lot of orders, your financial future can go either way. If your subcontractors do not meet your deadlines and quality standards, your customers may cancel their orders and you could be ruined. If your subcontractors do meet all their obligations but your retail store accounts do not pay their bills, you could also be headed for a financial bloodbath. Always keep in touch with a good business lawyer to guide you through all your negotiations to prevent or at least handle big troubles if they should arise.

The preceding paragraph pointed out the negative possibilities. Now let's look at the positive. If everyone meets his obligations, you could end up making thousands, hundreds of thousands, and even millions of dollars in this industry. It all depends on the quality of work you can create and how well you can sell it—as will be discussed under "Acquiring Clients."

When you sell a design to a manufacturer you may be paid one lump sum or you may be paid on a royalty basis per wholesale dollar taken in on your design. The outright purchase price for a design may be anywhere from $200 to $1,000. This fee usually gives the purchaser exclusive rights to your design. You may also be able to make an arrangement to be paid a percentage of the wholesale dollar received by the manufacturer for your design. This percentage generally ranges from 2% to 7%. Therefore, if the wholesale price of a dress is $100, your royalty figure may vary from $2 to $7 per dress sold. If your creation "catches on" and if 100,000 units are sold, you can calculate the rest. Some of your top name designers receive royalty incomes that amount to millions of dollars a year. By the way, it is not possible to copyright or patent a design. If someone steals it, while you are trying to sell it, you could be out of luck. However, don't panic! It is the general consensus in the industry that although one manufacturer might try to duplicate the success of preceding designs, a manufacturer will not try to steal the ideas of a new idea presented to him or her. It would ruin their reputation in the industry and good designers would no longer work for them. And without good designers, one no longer has a business. If someone wants to use your creation, it is cheaper for him or her to work out a financial arrangement with you.

When manufacturing for yourself, you first compute your manufacturing costs through bids from contractors and subcontractors. This figure is generally marked up from 40% to 100%. Therefore, if your manufacturing cost per garment is $100, you might wholesale it anywhere from $140 to $200 per garment. The reason for this vast range is because just like a painting or piece of sculpture, you are dealing with a "work of art." The price you receive is what someone else is willing to pay you based on what he or she thinks the item can be resold for to his or her customers. From this profit, you must pay your salespeople (usually on commission), your interest rates on the production money borrowed, clerical help (you may want to use an independent bookkeeping service such as the type mentioned in this book), and factoring expenses. *Note:* Sometimes when a manufacturer is owed money by an account with a good credit rating, instead of waiting 30 to 60 days for one's money, the debt is sold to a "factoring" organization at a discount. The factoring organization gives a percentage of the accounts receivable due from a retail store immediately to the manufacturer, so that he or she has immediate cash to conduct and expand the business. The factoring organization then collects the money from the retail store account at the end of the prescribed time period and pockets the difference between the entire debt and what it was sold for. All of these expenses will generally take an extra 30% out of the profit margin. Therefore, the net profit on an order may amount to 10% to 70% of the manufacturing cost. On a dress costing $100 to manufacture, your net profit may vary from $10 to $70. If 100,000 are sold, that amounts to $1,000,000 to $7,000,000.

ACQUIRING CLIENTS

As you can see from the preceding discussions, there are two types of client groups for you to solicit business from. The first is the clothing manufacturer to whom you would like to sell your creation, whether for a straight buy-out price or on a royalty basis. Let's explore all the avenues.

You might try hiring an agent to represent you. There may be an aggressive person around who would just love to develop a lucrative career representing up-and-coming creative people in the fashion industry. As a matter of fact, the profession of "Agent" is discussed in this book on page 141. But suppose you are not able to locate this aggressive and brilliant person? You've probably got more going for you than you realize. So, let's look at the possibilities.

As mentioned, there is no official compendium listing all the manufacturers of wearing apparel. Here is one very simple and effective method you might try. Go to a good-quality clothing store carrying the type of merchandise you want to design. Ask the sales clerk or resident buyer which manufacturers are prominent in that area. All the clerk or buyer has to do is check an old invoice or representative's business card for the name and phone number of the home office. With this information you simply call the company and ask for the president's name and then ask to speak with him or her. Afraid the president won't talk to you? In most cases he or she will. The president probably rose to his or her high position by having an open mind. If the president's secretary will not put you through, find out the name of the head buyer of a large department store who carries their line and contact him. Describe your concept to the buyer, and ask for an opinion. If you are tactful, this can lead to a conversation and a personal referral to a particular manufacturing executive and permission to use the buyer's name. Now you can call a manufacturer using the name of an important client as a reference. Once you are on the phone with the president, approach him or her from the position of wanting to help with a design that can be a "winner" for them. Inform the president that you are aware of the company's fine products and ask for what time would be convenient for him or her to see you. If you do this tactfully, even if that individual normally does not see new designers, you might just be able to wangle an invitation from this chief executive. Another course of action would be to ask if he or she would look at your design for the purpose of directing you to an associate who might be in the market for your type of creations. Not everyone will agree to see you. But remember! It only takes one or two yesses to get an association going and then develop your business further.

Read the trade magazines (suggested by your librarian) plus business publications like the *Wall Street Journal, Business Week, Forbes*, etc., and scan the pages for mention of apparel manufacturers who are having trouble with sales. Their problem might just be poor designs. Call these firms immediately. The president may just be worried enough about his or her future to consider what you have to offer to possibly turn profits back up. A knowledgeable stock brokerage firm or bank that caters to the apparel industry may be able to give you immediate information on manufacturers in trouble. If someone needs saving, you might as well be their savior. How do you think the designers making millions a year in royalties got their start?

If you decide to manufacture your products yourself you can hire an independent sales representative to take on your line on a commission basis. In the beginning it will be very difficult to get a good salesperson to represent you. So again, you are on your own. But don't worry, there are pathways you can take.

The first pathway is to just call up the buyer of an individual store or small chain and invite him to lunch. You might have several items that interest him which you can discuss during lunch, and then make an official appointment to present it later.

If you can't get a lunch date, don't worry. Just be persistent. Call once a week or every other week. Sooner or later they will have to admire your persistence and figure that if you are that persistent in your sales calls, you are probably that persistent in the exactness of your designs and high production standards. Pretty soon you will be invited to show your wares. If they are good, you will sell them.

FUTURE GAINS

Every year consumers look for new and exciting things to wear, and every year new people like yourself make it big. The more designs you sell, the more your reputation will grow, and so will the opportunities that present themselves to you. Pretty soon, large companies will approach you to design and put your name on their products. This can lead to hundreds of thousands of dollars and sometimes even millions of dollars a year in royalties.

If you decide to manufacture, you may eventually choose to stop using subcontractors and build your own plant with your own hand-picked staff to carry out every phase of the manufacturing operation. Or, you can still subcontract out your requirements, but now be able to have top subcontractors serve your needs exclusively. In other words, no shipping delays. You can grow as fast as your design, manufacturing, sales, and advertising force grows. But don't grow too fast; make sure you have solid footing under you before you take the next step up. It's slower but safer—and more lucrative in the long run.

If by chance, you would like to expand your education in design and wish to know of some fine institutions that can assist in your career development, contact any of the following:

The Alumane Advisory
Center, Inc.
Box AC 541 Madison
Avenue
New York, New York
10022

The Fashion Institute of
Technology
227 W. 27th Street
New York, New York
10001

The International
Association of Clothing
Designers
12 South 12th Street
Philadelphia, Pennsylvania
19107

The Otis Art Institute of
Parson's School of Design
2401 Wilshire Blvd.
Los Angeles, Calif. 90057

Pratt Institute
215 Ryerson Street
Brooklyn, New York 11025

Check with a high school or college guidance counselor in your
community for other qualified institutions in your area.

7

CLERICAL
SERVICES

TAX PREPARATION
SERVICE

WHY

An unpleasant time of the year for many people is income tax time. Not only do people dislike paying money to the government, but the complicated process required to do so can be very confusing and irritating. Even the so-called short form used by the average wage earner is very complex. Having the form prepared by someone qualified to do so takes a tremendous weight off the taxpayer's shoulders. This is especially true if the preparer is adept not only at processing the forms, but also in advising the taxpayer of the many allowable deductions he or she may be unaware of.

This once-a-year activity starts January 1 and ends April 15—providing the opportunity for three and a half months of work and a substantial income for yourself. If you are conscientious and ambitious, the skill of tax preparation can be learned in a relatively short period of time. This does not mean that a tax preparer can always take the place of a certified public accountant. However, after some experience preparing taxes for wage earners, especially those with outside income sources, a tax preparer can eventually handle many complex situations.

GETTING STARTED

As a tax preparer, you can work on an independent subcontract basis for one of the large income tax preparation services (frequently advertised on television), preparing the tax forms of their customers on a fee-for-service basis. Or, you can strike out on your own, soliciting your own clients and keeping the total fee. Both avenues have their advantages and will be discussed in this chapter.

116

There are two basic methods of learning this skill: First, many of the national tax preparation firms offer candidates for employment a 13-to-15 week tax preparation course. These courses usually have two three-hour sessions a week and many provide college credits. The tuition for such a program is approximately $100. After completion of the course, the students with satisfactory grades and attitudes are hired for the three and a half month tax season and assigned a variety of tax preparation assignments which they complete from beginning to end. However, if you wish, instead of working for the firm you could go into private practice, working out of your home or small office.

Many colleges offer the same basic type of course as the commercial firms do. These courses usually come under the title "Fundamentals of Tax Preparation" in the college catalog. To find out where tax courses are taught in your area, contact the public information officer of your local branch of the Internal Revenue Service.

When preparing the tax forms as an independent practitioner, you can take advantage of the various tax computer services available to professional accountants and tax preparers. When utilizing a computer service, the client is interviewed for the pertinent information. During the interview, the client's answers are recorded on a computer "input" sheet. The input sheet is then sent to the computer service. The personnel at the computer firm code and feed your information into a computer programmed to accurately prepare and "print out" the completed federal and state forms for you to turn over to your client. The typical fee charged by most computer firms is approximately $15 for both forms.

As simple as this might sound, do not think for one moment that the tax preparation courses can be eliminated. You still need a working knowledge of tax preparation procedures to intelligently conduct the preliminary interview and accurately record the information on the input sheet. You will also have to be able to advise your clients on what items and how much of each are deductible. In addition, some clients may ask you to explain the results of their computer printout.

To find computerized tax preparation firms catering to the profession, consult the following publications for advertisements: *Journal of Taxation, National Public Accountant,* and *Journal of Accounting.* If you cannot find any of them in your library, consult *Ulrich's International Periodicals Directory,* almost always available in a library. Write to the editorial or advertising

117

department of one of the journals asking for the names and addresses of the tax computer firms who usually advertise with them. The computer service firm does not have to be in your area; everything can be done by mail.

FINANCIAL REWARDS

When working as a subcontractor for a commercial tax preparation service, you can earn approximately $6000 working about 40 hours a week for the three and a half month tax term. This averages out to about $9.75 an hour.

When self-employed, the financial rewards are much greater, although of course you will have to solicit your own clients. The client interview will require approximately 45 to 60 minutes of your time. The computer firm will charge you approximately $10 for both forms. You can justifiably charge $50 to $75 for your services, allowing you a gross profit of from $40 to $65 for your efforts.

ACQUIRING CLIENTS

There are many ways to develop a large clientele. Place notices of your service on the bulletin boards of factories and offices in your community. Supermarket bulletin boards are also a good place to advertise, to attract both the customers and the employees. Advertise in company newsletters and local professional and trade journals such as those for teachers, policemen, firemen, state or federal workers, carpenters, plumbers, meatcutters, etc. Your librarian may be able to help you select a list of such journals.

Call up social, civic, religious, and fraternal organizations. Offer to give a free speech on such topics as "Overlooked Tax Deductions" at one of their meetings. Have your business cards ready; you will be surprised how many listeners will ask if you have time to prepare their returns. After you solicit a following, your clients will quite often recommend you to their friends. Each year your previous clients will automatically contact you to do their taxes again. This can all add up to a lucrative practice.

FUTURE GAINS

This type of business might inspire you to study for an accounting degree, eventually applying for credentials as a certified public accountant (CPA). Your business can then be expanded to include a high level corporate practice. In this profession, the sky is the limit. Many self-employed CPAs earn over $100,000 annually.

BOOKKEEPING SERVICE

WHY

The proper maintenance of financial records is essential to the smooth functioning of any business or professional practice. Although large firms usually maintain their own full-time bookkeeping staffs, it is not always profitable for small organizations to retain full-time bookkeepers.

Through proper systemization and organization, what might take a business operator a whole week to complete, can be facilitated with even more accuracy by you in just a few hours. Because of this, it is often more economical for an independent business or professional person to use your service than to maintain a part-time or full-time employee who may not possess your expertise and organizational skills. This opens up vast opportunities for providing independent bookkeeping services to the small business and professional community.

GETTING STARTED

A quality bookkeeping service can be easily started in your own home and later moved to a small office. Bookkeeping courses are taught in most high school and community college adult education programs. Some of the functions performed for a client by a bookkeeping service are:

1. Examine invoices for accuracy and if there are any discrepancies, contact the vendors.
2. Match invoices to the monthly bills submitted by the vendors and write checks to pay the bills.
3. Enter changes on customers' charge account cards, compute and send out monthly bills, and later record payments.
4. Compute employee salaries and make up payroll checks.
5. Prepare records for client's accountant.
6. Maintain inventory records of client's merchandise.

Most of these functions can be performed by you. As your business grows, you can hire additional employees to perform some of the routine functions on a mass volume, assembly-line type of operation. You might even purchase or lease a computer or subscribe to a computer service to further increase productivity and profitability per employee.

FINANCIAL REWARDS

A professional fee of at least $20 an hour per client is quite reasonable. If you pay your help approximately $5 to $7 per hour and develop a large clientele, your profit picture can escalate considerably.

ACQUIRING CLIENTS

Your prime prospects are small retail stores; small manufacturing companies; service organizations such as independent plumbers, electricians, and all types of repair people; professional practitioners such as doctors, dentists, and lawyers; and small businesses such as small advertising agencies. You can even specialize in one type of service. For instance, apartment house owners can easily become overwhelmed with the bookkeeping procedures necessary to keep track of rent payments, deposits, and maintenance expenditures. Real estate bookkeeping is a recognized specialty in the business world.

Do not overlook the opportunity to receive referrals from accountants. Many accountants encourage their clients to utilize the services of professional bookkeeping organizations. It allows them to communicate the bookkeeping format they desire for their client to someone who can comprehend and carry out their requests. In addition, they can be sure of all financial records being in order when it comes time to prepare taxes and process important business reports.

FUTURE GAINS

You can increase the size of your business in proportion to the number of new clients you keep adding. In addition, you can also include a tax preparation service (discussed in the preceding chapter) during the tax season. And if desired, you can pursue an accounting degree and turn your business service into a full-scale accounting firm.

COLLATING AND BINDING SERVICE

WHY

In the preparation of printed material such as pamphlets and catalogs, many printers like to be involved only in the actual printing operation. They often prefer to subcontract the other steps such as typesetting, collating, and binding. In a typical printing operation, each page of a pamphlet or book is run off individually and placed in separate stacks. These pages then have to be arranged in proper numerical sequence, ready for binding. This arranging process is know as "collating." You can perform this service. Very little skill or training is required.

GETTING STARTED AND FINANCIAL REWARDS

Most printers pay anywhere from $3 to $4 per thousand for pages to be collated. With a little practice, the average person can collate approximately 4000 pages an hour, by hand. This can amount to $12 to $16 an hour for you. The task can be aided by a cardboard collating kit which sells for about $35. The kit is basically a stand consisting of 20 separation partitions or sections. Stacks of the same page are put into the sections in sequence. The operator, aided by a rubber finger cot or specialized finger wax, collects and stacks the pages in proper sequence. After pages 1 to 20 are collated, the next 20 pages are put into the partitions and also collated. Each subsequent collation is added (married) to the preceding until the text is complete.

To further illustrate: let us say you receive an assignment for 500 copies of a 200-page booklet. This amounts to 100,000 pages to be collated. At the rate of $3 to $4 per thousand, this represents $300 to $400 in income for the job. At a working rate of 4000 pages per hour, the job would take 25 hours to complete. This represents just one weekend of work.

It should be mentioned, however, that there are machines available that can automatically collate up to 40,000 pages an hour. This would represent a profit of from $80 to $120 per hour. When you are ready to expand your operation, these machines can be purchased for approximately $6000 each.

There are also semiautomatic collating machines capable of collating up to 15,000 sheets an hour. Again, at the rate of $3 to $4 per thousand, this can represent a profit of from $45 to $60 per hour.

After a book or pamphlet is collated, it must be bound—another profit opportunity for you. Professional binding equipment is quite expensive, costing anywhere from $300 for a machine that will simple-bind up to 30 sheets, to $700 for a machine capable of simple-binding up to 275 sheets. Machines capable of performing binding procedures more sophisticated than the simple-type bind can cost several thousands of dollars. Naturally, this might be too expensive for your immediate needs. There are professional binding firms, however, to which you can send the collated copies. In most cases, they will offer you a trade discount for the work performed. You can then charge your client a reasonable, but slightly higher, price for the service. Thus, you profit from the binding as well as the collating procedure.

A simple binding for the 200-page book just mentioned, would amount to approximately 20¢ to 25¢ each. You could easily charge your client 35¢ each, realizing a profit of from $50 to $75 for the 500 copies in addition to the $300 to $400 for the collating procedure.

When automatic equipment is desired, look in the yellow pages of your phone book or the *Thomas Register of American Manufacturers* in your library under "Collating Equipment" and "Binding Equipment."

ACQUIRING CLIENTS

When starting out in this type of venture, contact every printing and instant press shop in your area via direct mail, telephone, or a personal visit.

FUTURE GAINS

Once your operation is expanded to accommodate a large volume of business, it will be financially feasible for you to purchase or lease the sophisticated collating and binding equipment mentioned, allowing you to earn from $5 to $120 an hour. In fact, you might eventually want to purchase offset printing equipment and offer businesses, book publishers, advertising agencies, and others, a complete one-stop printing service.

MAILING SERVICE

WHY

Almost every type of organization—business, professional, social, religious, or fraternal—needs to send out periodic mailings to communicate with customers, associates, or members. The staffs of such organizations are often too busy with their other responsibilities to take on these large and time-consuming projects. Therefore, ample opportunity exists for you to rescue people from this necessary, but tedious, chore by providing a commercial mailing service. If operated properly, your mailing service can be very profitable.

GETTING STARTED

The first step is the typing of the address labels. To speed up the process, I suggest you use self-adhesive labels, available in rolls, which can simply be peeled off and placed on the envelope. You then fold and insert the letters into the envelopes, seal and stamp them, and then take everything to the post office. In the beginning, all the steps can be accomplished by your own two hands except for the sealing and stamping of the envelopes. It is much more practical to purchase a metering and sealing machine for this procedure. A new one can be purchased for approximately $3000 and a used one for $1500. Lease arrangements are also possible. A used one can be leased for approximately $225 a month and a new one for $450 per month. If you decide to expand your business, there are machines that can also fold, insert, and apply labels. They will be discussed later under "Future Gains."

FINANCIAL REWARDS

The fee for address labels is $75 per thousand. Approximately 240 can be typed in an hour. This computes to $18 per hour for this task. The folding and inserting of one piece of paper, affixing the label, and sealing and metering the envelope by machine generally commands a price of $60 per thousand. You can do approximately 240 pieces an hour. This computes to $15 an hour for this process. The delivering of the mail to the post office brings another $55 per thousand. A standard business letter can be bulk-mailed for $104 per thousand. This postage fee is paid by you to the post office and then charged the customer. As you can see, a nice income can be derived from a small one-person mailing service. Once you build up a large clientele, you can increase your capacity and earnings tremendously by completely automating your operation. This will be discussed under "Future Gains."

ACQUIRING CLIENTS

Almost any business is a potential client of yours. Just consider all the advertising letters and brochures you receive in your own mail box. A mailing service probably took care of most of this. Go through the entire yellow pages of your telephone directory and pick out all the businesses that might benefit from direct mail advertising of their products or services. Contact these people. You might call on a business just as they are planning a mailing. A lot of business can be obtained spontaneously. Professional people such as doctors have to mail out monthly statements. Advertise your services in the yellow pages of the telephone book under

"Mailing or Letter Services." Advertise in local business and professional journals in your area. Contact all advertising agencies. Frequently, they carry out direct mail campaigns for their clients. Call on all mail-order operators; direct mail is one of the methods they use to create business. If you are consistent in your efforts, you can eventually build up a large clientele who will call on you continually.

FUTURE GAINS

As previously mentioned, when your clientele develops, you can fully automate your operation to increase your profits and decrease the drudgery. For $200, you can purchase a semiautomatic labeler to apply each label to an envelope. As mentioned, a sealing and metering machine can be purchased for $3000 new and $1500 used. A machine to fold and insert one piece of paper into an envelope can be purchased for about $5000 new and $2500 used; for two pieces of paper, $7000 new and $3500 used. (The price keeps going up for each additional piece of paper.) However, it is customary to proportionately increase the price of folding and inserting each additional piece of paper. In general, with your automatic equipment you can completely process approximately 3000 pieces of mail in one hour. At the rate of $60 per thousand, this computes to $180 an hour for you, in addition to the $55 per thousand for taking the mail to the post office. To locate dealers of new and used mailing equipment, look in the yellow pages of the telephone book under "Mailing Equipment" and "Addressing Equipment."

Many of your permanent customers will usually send their literature to the same people each time. Therefore, you would only charge them a one-time charge of $75 per thousand for the actual typing of each address and then store these addresses for future use. This can be done in two ways: You can use the Avery Label System to quickly duplicate labels. In this process, you would type each name and address on a ruled master sheet containing spaces for 33 addresses. You would then insert photosensitive sheets of Avery Self-Adhesive Labels into a Xerox or similar quality photostat machine and photocopy each master sheet onto the labels. The labels are then peeled off for application to the envelopes. These labels sell for approximately $21.00 per thousand (2.1¢ each) and are obtainable at most stationery stores.

The alternative is to purchase a small computer addresser for about $2800. With this machine, you type the names and addresses directly into the computer for permanent storage and

124

retrieval on individual self-adhesive labels. At any time, you can program the machine to add, delete, correct addresses or retrieve portions of the address list. After the data is stored in the computer, you would charge your clients approximately $10 per thousand for retrieving the labels.

To increase the scope of your service, you can also offer to obtain specialized mailing lists for your clients. Every business has a target group of customers most likely to respond to a mailing. For instance, a manufacturer of tennis balls might want to advertise his or her product to people who play tennis. A manufacturer of food processing equipment might want to mail to people who have shown they are prone to purchasing this type of equipment through the mail. A person who advertises and sells record keeping books to self-employed accountants might wish to reach all accountants in private practice. There are companies that compile lists of almost any category of consumer in the United States and rent the lists out to "mail list brokers" for eventual re-rental to individual business clients. If you have a client who desires to reach a certain category of people, you can offer to obtain a list of these people for him or her. In this manner, your mailing service is complete and fully accommodates the needs of business. All your clients have to do is to tell you who they want to reach. You obtain the list, pick up their advertising material, and start the mailing process. Your client can then concentrate his or her efforts on other business matters.

You can rent these lists from master renters for approximately $30 to $35 per thousand addresses, and fairly charge your client $40 to $45 per thousand for their use, allowing you a $10 per thousand profit. Notice we use the word *rent*. These fees do not include permanent possession. Each time a list is reused, even though it may be in your computer, the fee has to be repaid because these lists are copyrighted. It does not pay to cheat and reuse a list without paying. A few of the addresses on each list are monitored by the compiler. If a piece of mail shows up at one of the monitored addresses before the fee is repaid, it constitutes a copyright offense and the penalty is severe. If you explain this tactfully to your clients, you will most likely not receive any requests for any wrongdoing.

WORD PROCESSING

WHY

The term "word processing" appears with increasing frequency in today's business world. Many are unsure just what it means. Quite simply, it means composition and communication with the written word. Letters, pamphlets, documents, newspaper articles, and books are all examples of word processing. In fact, every form of literature is an example of word processing. The reason for the recent coining and popularity of this term is the development of machines that allow the operator to produce the final typed draft in far less time than it would take were he to use a typewriter. One might say that the first word processing machine was the original quill pen. Then came the manual typewriter, electric typewriter, and now the computerized word processing machine.

Practically every form of written material has to be reorganized or edited to transmit the exact message the author wants to convey to the reader. Until now, the author or originator of the written material would look at the original typed draft, write in the necessary word insertions, deletions, rearrangements, and other corrections, and return the manuscript to the typist for a complete retyping. The new word processing machines utilize computer principles to allow the operator to just incorporate the corrections into the main body of the text, without retyping the entire document. This allows the final draft to be produced six to seven times faster than with a conventional electric typewriter. A word processing machine might be considered an editing machine.

GETTING STARTED

Because of the vast commercial benefits of this new technology, word processing technicians are in great demand. If you can already type, word processing can be learned quickly in many day and night programs in the community college system. Many business firms will train applicants for this type of work directly in their own offices. This is done either by trained employees or representatives from the company who manufacture the machines they use.

126

HOW DOES THE MACHINE WORK?
WHAT DOES THE OPERATOR DO?

Although word processing machines and their operation will vary according to manufacturer, the components and the manner in which they are utilized are fundamentally the same. Each processing system consists of a keyboard (similar to that of a typewriter) for transmission of letters and words to a display screen (similar to a television screen) for viewing the typed message, a magnetic card or disk for electronic storage of the written material, and a printer for transcription of everything onto paper.

Display screens have a viewing capacity of one full page. Approximately sixty pages can be stored on one disk or card. As the operator types, the characters appear on the screen and are transmitted to the magnetic card or disk. The text can be simultaneously printed by the printer from the stored electronic data on the magnetic card or disk. The text can also be printed at a later date by reinsertion of the magnetic card or disk into the machine. Mistakes can be corrected simply by typing over them. Words can be inserted or deleted wherever necessary. The operator can alter or completely rearrange any part of the text at any time with the corresponding transmission to the magnetic card or disk.

After a page is completed, the next page appears on the viewing screen. If the operator wants to make some changes on a page not in view, he presses a key that automatically moves the disk forward or backward until the desired page appears. Sometimes the author of a document will dictate directly to the operator of the machine with the printing component working simultaneously. Afterward, the author will look over the printout and insert the necessary corrections and changes by pen. The operator will then look over the changes and program the word processing machine to make the changes on the magnetic card or disk for a second printout.

Most word processing machines can print at the rate of 560 words and more per minute. Many machines have the capabilities of performing a variety of printing functions such as both left-hand and right-hand margin justification, column arrangement, variable line spacing, outline arrangement, automatic page numbering, and a variety of other technical procedures required in the communications industry.

A word processing technician can work as an employee on a full-time, part-time, or freelance basis. If desired, he or she can open up his or her own word processing center subcontracting assignments from small and medium-sized firms. With your own word processing center, executives could call in transcriptions from their offices; after typing, you send back the printed copy for corrections by them and subsequent reprogramming and printing by you. Or, an executive could transcribe to his or her secretary, correct the typewritten sheet, then send it to you for sophisticated and speedy typing. There are numerous possibilities.

FINANCIAL REWARDS

As a full-time word processing technician, your wages would be approximately $10 to $11 per hour. As a part-time or freelance employee, you can earn $15 per hour. A supervisor of a word processing pool for a large organization can expect to earn approximately $20 to $25 per hour.

As the operator of your own independent word processing pool, you can easily charge $20 an hour for your services while paying your employees $10 to $11 per hour. A good word processing system sells for approximately $14,000 and can be leased for $350 a month.

ACQUIRING CLIENTS

Almost any business organization is a potential client of yours. Law offices, medical facilities, banks, retail organizations, and manufacturing firms are but a few of the facilities utilizing word processing, and you should contact these organizations.

FUTURE GAINS

You can incorporate the operation of your own word processing center into the development of a full-scale secretarial service (discussed earlier in this book). Or, since many businesses and professional organizations need word processors sporadically on a part-time basis whenever they have an increased work load, you could offer a Temporary-Help Word Processing Service. As an experienced operator, you will be able to locate and recognize good technicians who only want to work on a freelance basis. Clients can avail themselves of your service by contacting you. You then dispatch one of your standby employees from their home to your client's office. The customary financial arrangement in this type of operation is for you to charge your client $20 an hour for your technician's service, and you in turn to pay your technician from $10 to $15 per hour, the difference, of course, being your profit. After you build up a large service, these profit margins can add up considerably.

INVENTORY SERVICE

WHY

Operators of all types of businesses are realizing that large sales volumes do not always result in large profits. Sophisticated management practices are becoming increasingly recognized as very important in maintaining high profit margins. One of these important management procedures is "inventory control." An inventory is the counting of each piece of merchandise in a business and computing it at either it's wholesale or retail value. Through periodic inventory inspections, businesses, whether on the manufacturing, wholesale, or retail level can determine several important factors necessary for proper management: for instance, whether employees are stealing; whether too many products are being purchased in proportion to sales, therefore tying up valuable money in excess merchandise, or too few products in proportion to sales, thus not taking advantage of quantity discounts from suppliers. If inventories are taken at reasonable intervals— usually four times a year—hidden problems can be brought to the surface and corrected before serious damage is done. However, it is not advisable for business owners to utilize their own employees in conducting inventories. If there has been any theft or mismanagement, company employees could falsify inventory counts to cover up any wrongdoings. This creates business opportunities for you.

GETTING STARTED

Most inventories are conducted by a team of workers, each individual working independently in an assigned area. The workers count each item in a product category and record the monetary values on a ten-key hand-held calculator. The results are later compiled and tabulated by a clerical worker for subsequent presentation to the client.

Conducting an inventory requires no special schooling. An alert and conscientious attitude is probably the most important requirement for success in this endeavor. Also, a familiarity with the products being inventoried is desirable.

Because of the almost infinite number and variety of products that require inventorying, no one person or inventory service can be proficient in every type of inventory requirement. Therefore, it is advisable to specialize in just one business category or a few types of products. For instance, you might specialize in inventories of certain types of stores: clothing or jewelry stores, drugstores, grocery or liquor stores, auto parts stores, or whatever. Being familiar with the merchandise in a particular type of retail operation will enable you also to inventory that same type of merchandise on a wholesale level.

If you desire to become familiar with products involved in manufacturing operations, you could even qualify yourself to conduct inventories for manufacturing companies. For example, familiarity with electronic components could enable you to serve the inventory needs of companies manufacturing computers, radios, televisions, and many types of communication equipment. Familiarity with different types of fabric could enable you to serve the inventory needs of the manufacturers of wearing apparel. The possibilities are almost endless.

Okay! You would like to get into this business but know nothing about it and are not familiar with any type of product line. Don't fret. Everyone has to begin somewhere and there is a place for you to start. Before you start out in business on your own, get a job with an inventory service. The pay won't be much, but at least you will have a chance to get your feet wet and become familiar with the field. Because most inventories are conducted when a store is closed so as not to interfere with normal business hours, many inventories are conducted in the wee hours of the night or morning or on a Sunday. This allows you to gain employment on a part-time basis without interfering with your regular job. You might get a little bleary-eyed, but at least you'll have a chance to learn and earn at the same time. If you are conscientious and positive in your attitude, you should not have much trouble in getting hired by an established inventory service as a part-time trainee. Once you gain some experience, you can become a valuable member of one or several inventory services on either a part-time or full-time basis.

FINANCIAL REWARDS

You will not earn much money as an employee in someone else's operation. Nevertheless, as already mentioned, it's a place to start. As a beginner, you will probably start out at $4 to $5 an hour. However, as your product knowledge increases, so will your speed, and you can then earn from $7 to $8 per hour. And don't worry, after several inventories in one type of product line, you will quickly develop expertise in that merchandise category.

130

However, your goal in this endeavor is to start your own inventory service.

There are many formulas used by inventory services to compute their clients' fees. Many charge an amount based on the total value of the merchandise inventoried. Nevertheless, the general fee to the client breaks down to approximately two to two-and-a-half times the amount paid to the inventory workers handling the assignment. For example, it takes four inventory takers approximately three hours to inventory a medium-sized neighborhood liquor or grocery store. This represents 12 man-hours of labor. If the average pay per employee is $7.00 per hour, this amounts to $84.00 in labor costs. The charge to the client by the owner of the service is approximately $168.00 to $210.00.

For every man-hour of inventory taking, it requires approximately 15 minutes of clerical work to tabulate the results. Therefore, 12 man-hours of inventory taking will require three hours on the part of a clerk to do the final tabulations. The payment of $5.00 per hour is quite acceptable for this clerical work. Therefore, subtract $15.00 ($5.00 per hour times three clerical hours) from the total fee charged to the client to calculate your gross profit.

If the client happens to own a chain of stores and you want to secure a contract to inventory each store in the entire chain four times a year, you might want to drop your fee a little to win this substantial assignment.

ACQUIRING CLIENTS

Call on the company headquarters of all retail chains in your area. They should require each of their stores to be inventoried four times a year. This can result in a lot of business for you. The most important facet in acquiring clients is to show that you can serve their total needs. Your potential client not only wants to know his or her total profit situation, but if there are weaknesses, he or she also wants to know in which areas. If your client carries a wide variety of merchandise, offer to break-down your inventory tabulations into product categories. For instance, if you are trying to obtain the patronage of a small drugstore chain, offer not only to tabulate the cosmetics separately, but also every category of cosmetics. When doing a cosmetic inventory, it takes very little extra work to separately tabulate the amount of eyeliners on hand, or eye shadow, or moisturizing lotions, etc. With this information on hand, management then knows which items are selling best and should be featured. When the inventory is compared to sales reports, and thefts are noticed, management can then rearrange and relocate the merchandise to deter consumer thefts. If employee thefts are involved, management can take appropriate measures in that area.

As you can see, a good inventory gives management more than just numbers. It gives them direction for future profits and growth. When calling on a potential client, first ask what his or her problems are. Offer to sit down with them to go over some of their problems and help formulate solutions. Business executives like people who are there to help them. These people are the ones they eventually reward with contracts.

The most successful retail stores are those that purchase and feature products that are best suited to the needs of the residents in the neighborhoods adjacent to them. Educate your clients. Develop a brochure or sales letter informing management how your service can be the deciding factor in profit or loss for them. When a person or group owns several stores in a product category, they cannot keep constant tabs on the honesty and purchasing skills of all of their employees. If you can communicate to them that by using your service four times a year for each store, you can increase their control over their operation without increasing the number of supervising personnel, you can develop a large and satisfied clientele.

Accountants require accurate inventory records when working on their clients' books. Management consulting firms can often get to the root of their clients' problems through the utilization of accurate inventory records. Make sure you also call on these professionals and show them how referring you to their own clients can help make their jobs easier.

FUTURE GAINS

Once you establish a well-run medium-sized or even small inventory service, you can enlarge your business to encompass a larger geographic area or a greater variety of product categories for inventory. As your business expands, you can appoint supervisors for each city served. You can even hire salespeople to help you acquire new clients. If, in addition to their regular pay, you share some of your profits with your employees, whether they be inventory workers, supervisors, salespeople, or clerks, you can develop and retain a permanent and loyal staff that can aid in increasing your business even further.

If desired, you can even couple your inventory service with a bookkeeping service (discussed previously), enabling you to offer a broad range of important services to the business community.

INSURANCE INVENTORYING

WHY

Almost every apartment, condominium, and home dweller carries a "homeowner's" insurance policy to protect their possessions in case of loss by theft, fire, hurricane, tornado, water, or other damage. With all the crime occurring in today's society, a homeowner's policy is a must for almost everyone. The problem that occurs with most policyholders, however, is that when they do incur a loss, they usually have no record of their possessions and do not know what items and monetary value to declare on their insurance claim. Compiling an insurance inventory of one's belongings and their value is a very tedious and time-consuming task which most people would rather avoid. This creates an opportunity for you to provide this important service.

GETTING STARTED

There are no special skills needed for this business except to be able to pay attention to detail and have a pleasant manner when working with clients. A typical insurance inventory would be conducted as follows: Each item in the household should be photographed with either a 35mm or polaroid camera. After each shot, write down the name of the item, the manufacturer, model name, model or serial number, and approximate dollar value. This can be determined by asking the clients what they paid for each item. If they do not remember (and many won't), the approximate price can be determined either through past sales receipts, or by calling or writing the manufacturer or a retail seller of the item.

After each picture is processed, all of the important information should be recorded on the back of the photograph and on a separate inventory sheet containing the name of the item, manufacturer, model name or number, serial number if any, and the retail price. Furthermore, each room should be completely photographed from different angles to show all of the items in their proper context and further prove that they are definitely possessions of the policyholder.

After a job is completed, a record of everything (including photographs) should be turned over to the client for storage in their safe deposit box and a duplicate set retained by you (also in a secure place) just in case something happens to your client's records. If they are lost, and you can produce a duplicate set, you will be a real hero.

FINANCIAL REWARDS

Because this type of work is so important, it is quite reasonable to charge from $20 to $50 an hour for your services. As a general rule of thumb, you can charge in the lower range for middle-income people and in the higher range for people in the wealthier neighborhoods.

ACQUIRING CLIENTS

Insurance agencies who provide homeowner's policies for people, want to serve their clients as well as possible in case a loss does occur. After all, they may desire to sell them other forms of insurance at a later date—life, accident, auto, etc. In addition, they want to develop excellent relations for referral to other people. Therefore, insurance agencies prefer to see that their clients have a complete record of their belongings to facilitate any claims that may have to be filed. Consequently, call on every insurance agency in your area advising them of your service to their clients. They will be more than happy to recommend you. In addition, place small ads announcing your service in all local magazines and newspapers catering to the affluent residents of your community. This might include professional and business journals, and maybe the program handed out at your local music center or playhouse.

FUTURE GAINS

After you practice for a while, you will eventually become very proficient in calculating the prices of the property you inventory. This will allow you to conduct your inventories in a very professional manner. In addition, as your clients purchase new merchandise, offer to return to their residences for further picture taking and record keeping. This will bring you additional income as well as pleasing your client. As you develop a reputation for dependability and professionalism among home dwellers and insurance agencies, your business will increase accordingly. You may even be retained by insurance companies on a freelance basis to examine and evaluate claims for them.

8

FIELD
WORK

PROCESS SERVING

WHY

When a person is instructed to appear in court, he or she is notified through a subpoena or summons of the appearance required of him or her. The subpoena or summons is a written legal order directing a person to appear in court either to answer charges placed against him by another party or to act as a witness to an involved party of a legal proceeding.

Most people do not like being served papers ordering them to appear in court and will often avoid conventional methods of receiving documents. Therefore, a subpoena is usually delivered by a special individual known as a process server. The process server works on behalf of attorneys and their clients to deliver and present subpoenas to the designated receiver.

In the legal profession, it is frequently necessary for attorneys to exchange legal documents with each other and their clients. These documents are usually too valuable to send through the mail and are also entrusted to process servers to assure delivery.

GETTING STARTED

There is no formal training required in becoming a process server. Being alert and conscientious are the most important assets. As a process server, you are essentially a fee-for-service freelance agent working with process serving agencies who solicit delivery assignments from attorneys. These agencies charge their clients a delivery fee and then subcontract the actual delivery to independent servers. The delivery fee charged the client is then shared with the server making the actual delivery.

For maximum efficiency and profitability, it is customary for an

135

independent agent to serve several agencies at the same time and to specialize in just one delivery area. In this business you are paid per "service" or delivery. If the majority of your deliveries are in the same area, your earnings per hour worked will average out to a higher rate.

FINANCIAL REWARDS

The average fee ranges from $6 to $10 per completed delivery. If a lot of deliveries are in the same area, it is feasible to make five deliveries in one hour, earning you from $30 to $50 in that hour. In other situations it might take you an entire hour to make just one delivery, earning you only $6 to $10 for that hour's work. You are expected to use your own car and pay your own gas in this work. It is therefore beneficial to own a high-mileage automobile. Your auto expenses, however, are tax deductible.

Some people who are expecting the delivery of a subpoena will make a conscious effort to avoid confrontation with the server. In this type of situation a "stakeout" has to be arranged to allow the server to eventually face the individual and present the subpoena. When a stakeout is necessary for a difficult case, special permission is required from the client serving the papers and paying the delivery fee. Once this permission is obtained, the general fee for a stakeout is approximately $15 to $20 an hour.

With everything considered, after paying your gasoline expenses, on a full-time basis you should be able to earn anywhere from $1800 to $2700 a month working through agencies.

ACQUIRING CLIENTS

As mentioned, as an individual server you work primarily through agencies. Most agencies are glad to acquire the services of conscientious and dependable people. The process is simple. Look in the yellow pages of your phone book under "Process Service" or "Subpoena Service" and contact the operators of these agencies to develop working relationships.

FUTURE GAINS

As you become familiar with attorneys and other process servers and learn to develop professional relationships with them, you can eventually start your own service, serving the needs of an entire community utilizing independent servers for each area. In many instances, you will be using the same servers as your competition. However, the secret in this business is personal contact and dependability. Work out delivery schedules with potential servers and then contact the office managers of as many legal offices as you can, leaving your card. An attorney or his or her office manager will generally give a chance to a person who conveys an air of dependability. Support these contacts with ads in local legal journals and in the telephone book yellow pages under "Process Service" or "Subpoena Service."

In general, you charge your clients approximately twice what you pay your servers. Thus, each completed delivery will yield you approximately $12 to $20 with a stakeout bringing you $30 per hour. These fees are then shared evenly with your servers. Obviously, as in all business operations, there is room for negotiation and variation on these fees. The more business you do, however, with as many servers as possible, the greater your gross net profit is going to be.

After you develop a successful service in one community, it is also possible to expand and start offices in other cities with each office run by your own personally selected manager.

MARKET RESEARCH INTERVIEWING

WHY

Today's industrial society can manufacture or provide almost any type of good or service imaginable. The secret is to know the moods and preferences of the buying public to produce goods and services that will be readily accepted and sold. Politicians often like to get a representative sampling of the wishes and attitudes of their constituents, in order to plan effective campaigns. An advertising agency might want to pretest some ad slogans to see which ones elicit the highest responses from the intended market.

The above tasks, and similar ones, are usually placed in the hands of market research organizations. The heads of these firms think up questions that when properly asked, answered, and interpreted, will give their clients the information they need to make proper administrative decisions. When given an assignment, these independent organizations must hire freelance market research interviewers to go out into the field and interview the type of people whose moods, attitudes, and wishes the client needs to know.

The person interviewed might be a doctor answering questions that will help a medical equipment manufacturer decide whether or not to manufacture a particular instrument. She might be a middle class worker whose feelings on a controversial issue a politician wants to know. An interviewer might ask selected teenagers their opinions about a certain scent or the packaging of a new acne medication. A group of executives might be asked about the types of services they feel are most needed by their company. A computer manufacturer may want to know how many functions an industry group may desire on new computers and the price they are willing to pay. A beer manufacturer might want to interview hundreds or even thousands of beer drinkers about their preference for a beer can design. Likewise, soda pop manufacturers desire to know the design preferences for their containers. The assignments are varied and numerous, encompassing almost every aspect of today's lifestyles.

GETTING STARTED AND ACQUIRING CLIENTS
Performing this type of work requires no formal training. It does, however, take a conscientious person to intelligently ask the questions and accurately record the answers for interpretation by their supervisors. This type of work is conducted on a freelance part-time basis. However, if you build up a reputation for dependable work, you should be able to acquire as many assignments as you can handle. In many instances, your interviews can be conducted on the telephone right from your home. Look in the yellow pages of the telephone book under "Market Research." If a market research company handles its own interviewing tasks, they might hire you to work for them directly. If they subcontract their interviewing responsibilities (and many do), they can refer you to a field interviewing service they use to handle their field work.

FINANCIAL REWARDS
Some types of interviewing are easier and consequently lower paying than others. It is rather easy to get a large number of people in a shopping center to stop and quickly give you their opinion of a beverage container. This type of interviewing generally pays from $4 to $5 per hour. However, it takes a very tactful person to solicit the time of and successfully interview a busy business executive as to what he or she desires in a computer or similar device. The interviewing of business executives and professional people such as doctors and lawyers is commonly

referred to as "executive interviewing." This level of interviewing generally pays from $15 to $20 per hour.

FUTURE GAINS
NEW CAREER OPPORTUNITIES

There is a tremendous potential for personal gain in this field. First of all, if you specialize in executive interviewing, you will meet many important and interesting people who represent a wide range of professions and industries. There is always the chance to learn about and then pursue new career opportunities in one of the fields you research. And, after all, in many cases you will be meeting and talking to persons who rank high in their companies.

FIELD INTERVIEWING SERVICE

Many market research firms prefer just to devise the questions and interpret the answers to provide accurate information and direction for their clients. They subcontract the actual field interviewing to field interviewing services. These are firms that specialize in the soliciting of freelance interviewers to handle the actual field interviewing requirements for a market research study. You can eventually start your own field interviewing service with your own hand-picked group of freelance employees.

To obtain business, you would contact the market research departments of businesses and industries in your area and also independent market research firms. Furthermore, industries and market research firms located thousands of miles away from your community still require information on the moods and preferences of consumers and executives in your area. After all, most goods and services are manufactured and provided for national distribution, and everyone's opinion counts. Therefore, you can contact market research firms all over the country to conduct regional interviews in your area. Advertise your services in market research magazines. A list of them can be found by consulting *Standard Rate and Data* or *Ulrich's International Periodicals Directory*, both probably in your library. In addition, announce your services in the business section of your local newspaper and in local business journals.

Operating a field interviewing service can be quite profitable. When charging your clients, it is customary to take the fees you pay your freelance interviewers and mark them up 55 percent. To review: general interviewers receive $4 to $5 per hour; at a 55 percent mark-up, this represents $2.20 to $2.75 an hour for you. Executive interviewers receive $15 to $20 per hour; at a 55 percent mark-up, this represents $8.25 to $11.00 an hour for you. As you can see, if you handle a large number of assignments requiring many hours of interviewing, your cumulative hourly earnings can add up to quite a substantial sum of money over the course of a year.

MARKET RESEARCH FIRM

If you have the background, or are willing to return to school for additional training, you can start your own market research firm. In this capacity you would devise the questions and collect and interpret the answers to help your clients develop products and services that will be readily accepted and sold in the marketplace. A course of study would include business administration, marketing, psychology, statistics, and related subjects. The members of almost any industry, business service, or profession are potential clients of yours. Fees are strictly negotiable. Fundamentally, you would calculate the number and length of interviews required; the fee you will have to pay a field interviewing service (hourly interviewer fee plus 55 percent); the amount of time required to devise the questions and collect and interpret the answers; and other business overhead such as travel, telephone, mailing, secretarial, and other operating expenses. To this you would add a professional fee that reflects your efforts and is agreeable to your client. For more information contact:

American Marketing Association
230 North Michigan Avenue
Chicago, Illinois 60601.

9

SELLING

AGENTING

WHY

Many individuals are quite proficient at producing a product or providing a service, but not adept at going out and selling it. This is nothing to be ashamed of. Our whole business and industrial society is based on different people specializing in what they do best or have time for, and then utilizing the services of other individuals or organizations to supplement and fulfill the other requirements of their business operation.

A person who represents an individual in selling his or her products, skills, techniques, or services is known as an agent. We are all familiar with the theatrical, literary, or sports agent. In the same manner, you can represent artists, wall mural designers, apparel designers, fashion print designers, jewelry designers, screen printers, cabinetmakers, caterers, photographers, and interior decorators.

GETTING STARTED AND ACQUIRING CLIENTS

The one important factor in this field is to specialize in just one category of products or services. If you decide to represent wall mural designers, you would not also represent clothing or jewelry designers. The reason is very simple: When you concentrate all your efforts in one field, your knowledge and expertise quickly increase, and you eventually become recognized and respected in that field. After a while, you are welcome in corridors not open to everyone. This is the prime function of an agent—to save your client tremendous amounts of valuable time in getting to the right people. So, your first task is to choose the area in which you want to specialize.

Of course, the best field to choose is the one that interests you the most. It's up to you to turn your interest into expertise and to develop your ability to judge quality work. If you've decided to represent a certain kind of craftsperson, instructors in your chosen field can give you some pointers on how to recognize fine workmanship and materials. The salespeople in shops that sell these items can tell you how they judge quality merchandise. Also, attend any appropriate trade shows, crafts fairs or conventions. And trust your own instincts as well.

To acquire clients, advertise in the trade journals read by the artists or craftspeople you are trying to reach. If local schools feature training programs in a field, call on the instructors to find out who the most talented people are. Call on the manufacturers of products that serve the industry to get leads on people to represent. Eventually, your name will get around by word-of-mouth, and those who need an agent will seek you out.

GETTING TO SEE
THE RIGHT PERSON AND
SELLING YOUR CLIENT'S TALENTS

After you select the area you want to operate in and acquire one or several clients, the next big thing is to "sell" your client and his or her product or service. The principles and techniques of representation are the same in all areas of endeavor. Let us say you decide to represent freelance clothing (apparel) designers. The following is an illustration of how you might handle the situation. (*Note:* A clothing designer draws designs for prospective garments on paper. He or she desires to sell these designs to manufacturers.)

Many apparel manufacturers do not retain full-time staff designers. They prefer to review the talents and creations of others out in the field. If you do not already have expertise in the fashion field but have the instinct to achieve it, there are several things you can do to gain a working knowledge of this business. Read the trade journals that cater to this field. One such journal is *Women's Wear Daily*. There are a host of others. The names can be found in *Ulrich's International Periodicals Directory* and *Standard Rate and Data*, both probably available in the library. The ads and articles in these publications will allow you to become familiar with the many apparel manufacturers in this country. You will learn about their problems, who is doing well, and who is having difficulty selling their goods. Attend apparel industry trade shows to supplement your knowledge of the field and also have the opportunity to meet important manufacturing executives. To find the time and location of these shows, contact the official trade associations representing the apparel industry.

They are listed in the *Encyclopedia of Associations* under the heading "Trade Associations." The *Thomas Register of American Manufacturers* can give you a listing of all major clothing manufacturers in the United States. Both of these directories can be found in most libraries.

After you decide who would be the most likely candidates for a client's designs, the next big step is to get to see some of them, otherwise known as "getting your foot in the door." If you have already made some personal contact at the trade shows, this will be a big step in setting up appointments with important executives. Companies who are not doing well with their present designs are very likely to accept a phone call and arrange an appointment with you if you promise some hope of improving their business. In fact, the executives of the manufacturing companies who are doing well might also readily accept a call from you. After all, they want to keep doing well, and constantly being aware of new designs is one way of doing so.

Find out who the local salespeople and sales managers are for the manufacturers you would like to call on. The receptionist at most concerns will readily give you this information. Give these people a phone call. Although they are not the decision makers, they know who are. They want their company to keep them supplied with exciting creations to further increase sales. If you can convince them that your designer clients can do this, they might be willing to arrange for you to meet the top executives. In many business organizations, a "first name" communication exists between management and sales executives.

Once you arrange an appointment and finally get to see the executive who can purchase your client's designs—*Relax*. Don't try to overwhelm the executive with a "hard-sell" approach. Ask him or her how business is. Be glad for their successes. Be sympathetic for any losses. Show them you care, that you are interested, that you want them to succeed. And then, show them your client's creations. At that point, you have really done all you can. The approval or rejection is up to them. There is nothing wrong with that. After all, if you succeed just 50 percent of the time, you can become a very wealthy person. And don't forget, whether you sell or not, if the executive is pleased with the general quality of your client's designs, you will be welcomed back to present more designs.

FINANCIAL REWARDS

All agents, regardless of what product or service they are representing, work on a commission basis. A fee of 10 percent to 20 percent of the revenues you obtain for your client is quite acceptable. Now then, how is the price of your client's creations determined? There is no set formula. Get as much as you can. This is another important function of your job. In the case of your hypothetical fashion designer client, you might arrange for your client to receive a flat fee for his or her design. It might be $5,000. If it is successful in the marketplace, you could receive $10,000 or more for your client's next creation. This can create a commission of from $500 to $2000 for you. In many instances (and the most preferable) you can arrange for your client to receive a percentage of the dollar volume brought in from the sale of the product created by him or her. For example: if the price of a product is $50 and you arrange for a 10 percent commission for your client, this computes to $5 per item. If 50,000 items are sold, this amounts to $250,000 for your client. At 10 percent to 20 percent of your client's earnings for your agent commission, this amounts to $25,000 to $50,000 for you. And this is for just one creation from one client. You might have numerous clients for whom you can achieve the same financial rewards. Does this sound like a preposterous amount of money? It is not. There are fashion design agents who earn $200,000 a year and more year after year.

FUTURE GAINS

Starting out will be slow. However, as your reputation grows, top people in your area will seek you out. Conversely, the top buyers or users of your client's products or services will welcome you into their offices. The rest is gravy.

DIRECT SELLING

WHY

Everything manufactured in our society is done so for one reason: to be sold. Selling is the foundation of and the driving force behind our economy. It can involve the sale of a product manufactured by one industry for use by another, or it may involve the sale of products used directly by the consumer. Consumer sales may be accomplished through the traditional manufacturer to wholesaler to retailer system; or it can be accomplished through independent sales agents who, representing various manufacturers or distributors, sell products directly to the consumer. The latter method is known as direct selling. It comprises a six-billion-dollar-a-year industry.

You might ask yourself why people would want to buy directly from independent sales agents rather than from the conventional retail outlets. The prime reasons are convenience, a wide selection of quality products, and personal service. It offers the young mother a convenient way of shopping that does not require taking the children along or leaving them with a babysitter. Congested highways and crowded stores can be avoided. Direct sellers can often demonstrate the product to the consumer and offer detailed information about the product, a service quickly disappearing from conventional retail outlets. With the high cost of gasoline, direct purchasing offers the consumer a savings on transportation. For those who dislike being rushed, pushed, and pressured, it's a leisurely and relaxed way to shop. In addition, many direct selling companies offer quality products and warranties not offered elsewhere.

GETTING STARTED

The major products sold through the direct selling method of distribution are cosmetics, vacuum cleaners, housewares, home maintenance services, household cleansers, costume jewelry, food supplements, encyclopedias, cookware and cutlery, wearing apparel, decorative accessories, security systems, toys, and hobby crafts. Orders are usually obtained through the displaying of catalogs or samples, provided by the parent company, to the potential end user, or consumer.

Direct selling can be carried out door-to-door, by telephone, and by advance appointment. Another popular approach is the party plan, whereby the seller displays and demonstrates his wares at an informal get-together of friends and neighbors. You can also sell to civic and church groups desiring to raise money for worthwhile causes. In this situation, orders are solicited at a scheduled meeting of a group with a portion of your profits returned to the organization for the attainment of its goals.

In many sales programs, you can use your own ingenuity in promoting a product. Many independent sales representatives use a combination of the door to door, party and civic plans, and the telephone approach. The choice of method is usually left to the discretion of the agent.

When searching for a reputable company to represent, it is generally a good idea to work with organizations that allow you to sell from a catalog or low-cost sample assortment. Some companies will pay you a commission on the orders you solicit for them. Others will have you order your own inventory based on solicited sales, pay for the merchandise at your wholesale price, and then resell the merchandise to your confirmed customers. It is advisable to stay away from companies which require you to purchase considerable amounts of merchandise from them before any sales are solicited and confirmed.

What types of products should I sell? Which company should I represent? These are probably the two basic questions the beginning salesperson asks himself. There are many fine direct selling companies offering a variety of quality products and excellent profit programs to the aggressive salesperson. To get some preliminary direction, contact the Direct Selling Association (DSA). Its 80-plus member companies are pledged to a strict code of ethics in providing quality products and services to the consumer and offering fair and ethical business arrangements to the independent agents representing them. According to the bylaws of the association, those eligible for active membership are persons or firms manufacturing or dealing in merchandise intended ultimately to reach the consumer through person to person contact, as distinguished from retail or mail order sales. An active member must also have a business location in the United States. This does not necessarily mean that a company who is not a member of the Direct Selling Association is not a reputable company to do business with. There are many fine companies not listed with the DSA. The DSA, however, can provide you with a source of firms and organizations that you can feel reasonably sure will deal fairly with you and the people you sell to. For a list of DSA member firms, write:

Direct Selling Association
1730 M St., N.W.
Suite 610
Washington, D.C. 20036.

FINANCIAL REWARDS

There are two ways to make money in this field: direct sales to the individual consumer and creating your own sales force to work within the framework of the parent company. The commission range for direct consumer sales ranges anywhere from 20 to 50 percent of the retail sales price.

In conventional retail store selling, there is usually an intricate sales network involved in getting the product from the manufacturer to the consumer. The manufacturer sells to the wholesalers and distributors via sales managers and individual salespeople; wholesalers and distributors in turn employ their own sales managers and individual salespeople to sell their goods to individual retail stores and chain stores; retail stores use store managers and individual clerks to finally get the product into the hands of the consumer. Also involved in the scheme are vice presidents of sales and marketing on the manufacturing, wholesale, and retail levels.

As you can see, conventional retail store selling involves a great many professionals who share in the profit on each product. The same is true with direct home sales—with just one big difference. In conventional selling, all personnel involved are hired by the employer involved in the above-mentioned selling process. When a salesperson wants to get promoted he or she has to wait for an opening. When an opening does come up, sometimes an individual with more seniority, or one who has a more personal relationship with the top brass, gets the position. In direct selling, most companies allow any ambitious individual to develop and expand his or her own sales organization at his or her own pace. You can recruit as many individuals as you want, to sell under you. They in turn can recruit as many individuals as they want, to sell under them. You, however, are given credit for all sales stimulated by your initial recruitment efforts, no matter how remote from your original efforts. Just as a conventional sales manager or vice president of sales or marketing shares in the final purchase price of his or her company's products, you receive a percentage of the purchase price of all sales initiated by your original recruitment efforts. This method of rewarding those who produce, regardless of their background or company affiliations, is very democratic. An ambitious beginner can pave his or her own way unencumbered by company politics. There are many individuals who sell via the recruitment and direct consumer methods who earn over $100,000 annually.

ACQUIRING CUSTOMERS

There are two types of customers you should strive for: the individual consumers and those who will themselves sell and recruit through your own sales organization. Quite often your "consumer customers" will eventually decide to join your sales organization as individual sales agents and recruiters.

Almost any friend, neighbor, or social acquaintance is a potential consumer customer. Once they develop an appreciation of and loyalty to your products they will often become repeat customers, calling you on the phone when they need more products. You also have a wide field to choose from when desiring to recruit others to join your sales organization. Fellow workers on your regular job might want to earn extra money. There are many tradespeople and professional people who are on a straight salary who require additional income during these inflationary times. Advertise the opportunities you offer in the official publications that represent nurses, school teachers, meatcutters, supermarket workers, police and firemen, government employees, etc. Your librarian can probably help you put together a list of such publications. Arrange meetings in your home or apartment to inform potential salespeople of the benefits of joining your organization.

Apartment house managers can make excellent recruits. First of all, most of them can use extra income; secondly, tenants are always calling on them when paying their rent or requesting a repair. They might as well become involved selling these people cosmetics, soap, toothpaste, jewelry, or other consumer products.

As you recruit new salespeople, teach them not only how to sell, but also how to recruit new people themselves. You will profit from everyone.

FUTURE GAINS

With most sales organizations, you can travel the entire United States recruiting and training new salespeople. Remember! After you have established an organization in a locality, you will receive bonus payments on their sales. In fact, if your parent organization has outlets in Europe, you can have a lot of fun traveling over there to develop new selling groups.

It is also possible to start your own parent organization. In this manner you would either manufacture or purchase directly any item which you feel has mass sales appeal. This might include certain types of clothing, leather goods, jewelry, tools, cooking utensils, cosmetics, etc. Your methods of operation would be similar to those already discussed. The only difference is that you would be the owner and operator of the entire organization; your profits, and of course responsibilities, would be greater.

OUTSIDE CAR SALESPERSON

WHY

We live in a mobile society. In bad times as well as good, almost everyone needs an automobile—whether it be new or used. Automobile dealers depend on the people who travel to their agency as their main source of sales. These people may go to these dealerships as a result of its convenient location or the lure of newspaper and television ads. Still, there are a large number of other potential customers to be reached and secured by car dealers. This can be done through the "outside car salesperson."

The outside car salesperson is an independent sales agent, working under license to one particular dealer, who specializes in his or her spare time in selling cars to friends, associates, or anyone else he or she decides to contact.

Why would anyone want to deal with an outside agent? Many people are in need of a new or used car. Sometimes they just keep putting off looking for one. Very often, newspaper and television advertising becomes confusing and scary. Many people are intimidated by car dealers, looking upon them as a group of fast-talking, hard-driving, pushy car hustlers. But doing business with a friend is different. You can take advantage of this situation to perform an interesting, useful, profitable service for your friends and associates and yourself. Furthermore, because you will be bringing in outside business that normally would not have gone to the agency you represent, the sales manager or owner might even allow you to offer some extra discounts they normally would not give to a regular walk-in customer.

GETTING STARTED AND FINANCIAL REWARDS

A sales license can be obtained through your local Department of Motor Vehicles, at a cost of $10 per year. In this business, all of your earnings come from commissions based on a percentage of the profit from the car sold. Dealer profits range typically from 12 percent on the lower priced cars to 19 percent on the higher priced models. The lower priced cars are the subcompacts, selling for approximately $4000 to $5500 at a gross profit of 12 percent ($480 to $660); compacts sell from $5500 to $8000 at 14% profit ($770 to $1120); the mid-sized cars sell from $8000 to $9000 at 17 percent profit ($1360 to $1560); and the full-sized cars sell from

$9000 to $15,000 at 19 percent profit ($1539 to $2850). Because of the gasoline crunch, you can practically forget about the full-sized cars. However, there are still many full-sized models sitting on dealer's lots that have to be sold off. And there is a good sales approach you can use to sell them: The larger, gas-guzzling engines last longer than compacts because they don't have to work as hard to deliver the desired horsepower. What they can save the owner on repairs and frequent trade-ins can often make up for the increased use of gas.

The above figures are all approximate values, of course. Quite often you will have to offer your customers discounts to make you and your offer appear more attractive. This will cut into your sales commission somewhat. However, the increased volume of business that these discounts can generate can far offset any discounted profits. Most car dealers will allow you to discount a car anywhere from 5 percent to 10 percent off the sticker price. This is determined by the selling price of the car, with the higher-priced cars receiving the higher percentage discounts. The general rule is as follows: subcompacts—5 percent discount off the sticker price; compacts—7 percent discount; mid-sized cars—8 percent discount; full-sized cars—10 percent discount. The profit is lowered as the percentage discount goes up. The salesperson's profit is usually 20 percent of the dealer's final profit.

The following chart expresses all the preceding figures and summarizes the discount and profit picture:

SUBCOMPACTS — $4000 to $5500 (not including sales tax) at a 12% gross profit = $480 to $660
    with a 5% customer discount = $456 to $627 net profit
    with a 20% sales commission = $91.20 to $125.40 for YOU

COMPACTS — $5500 to $8000 (not including sales tax) at a 14% gross profit = $770 to $1120
    with a 7% customer discount = $716.10 to $1041.60 net profit
    with a 20% sales commission = $143.22 to $208.32 for YOU

MID-SIZED — $8000 to $9000 (not including tax) at a 17% gross profit = $1360 to $1530
    with an 8% customer discount = $1251.20 to $1407.60 profit
    with a 20% sales commission = $250.24 to $281.52 for YOU

FULL-SIZED — $9000 to $15,000 (not including tax) at 19% gross profit = $1539 to $2850
    with a 10% customer discount = $1295.10 to $2565 profit
    with a 20% sales commission = $129.51 to $256.50 for YOU

Remember, you don't always have to give large discounts to

make a sale. You will be representing a dealer and a particular make of car. Stress the fine service the dealer gives. Highlight the fine points and handling characteristics of the particular make and model of car. This can be learned quickly by reading over the manufacturer's sales literature.

All new-car dealers will have a used-car department. Your sales license will also allow you to sell used cars for the dealer. College students, families needing second cars, and people just starting out in their careers are likely candidates for used automobiles. The price and profit on a used car is variable depending on the year, make, model, and overall condition of the car. In this case, profit cannot be expressed by a percentage figure. However, the general profit range on a used car is from $300 to $1200. Again, your commission is 20 percent of the profit or from $60 to $240. When selling used cars, it is a good idea to visit your dealer's lot once a week to see and test out what is available. Write down the cars you feel represent the best values and then approach your potential customers with this information. Everyone likes to feel that someone has something "special" for them. Very often, they can test the car without your actually being present. As long as you are the initial salesperson, the commission is yours.

ACQUIRING CLIENTS

All your friends, neighbors, and working associates are potential customers of yours. Advertise your services on college bulletin boards and in newspapers. Most large organizations such as banking systems, advertising and insurance firms, and manufacturing plants publish in-house journals or newsletters allowing employees and management to communicate with each other. These often make excellent advertising vehicles and their rates are very inexpensive. Professional, trade, and union journals are also excellent places to advertise auto sales. These publications include the magazines representing nurses, teachers, government workers, meatcutters, construction workers, retail store employees, etc. Your librarian can help you locate the publishers of these magazines. Have fliers made up advertising your services and even have special "deals of the week" on certain new and used cars. These fliers can be placed on the windshields of parked cars that look like they've seen better days.

FUTURE GAINS

If you like this type of work, you can eventually become a full-time salesperson. In this capacity, you can earn anywhere from

$15,000 to $50,000 a year. You can even advance to sales manager and earn more. Eventually as you prove your competence, you may even be able to arrange with an automobile manufacturer to own your own dealership.

"SWAP MEETS" OR "FLEA MARKETS"

WHY

These events, which I will for simplicity's sake refer to as swap meets are today's version of the marketplace of years gone by. They are places where people with goods to sell rent spaces to do so, and people looking for bargains come to shop for these goods. Swap meets are places to get good deals. The original purpose of a swap meet was to provide a facility for people to "swap" or sell personal possessions they no longer needed. The concept proved so popular, that many entrepreneuring individuals went out and bought new merchandise from manufacturers, wholesalers, and other suppliers for resale at the meets. In fact, today, a large portion of the goods sold at meets are brand-new. Because selling space at swap meets can be obtained inexpensively, concessionaires can often sell their merchandise at prices lower than conventional discount stores who have to pay high rents in shopping centers and downtown areas.

GETTING STARTED

A swap meet requires a large amount of space. Therefore, many municipalities and private entrepreneurs will set up a swap meet on a county fairground when there are no county functions taking place. Sometimes the owner of a large piece of undeveloped property will utilize it for swap meet purposes until he or she decides to build on the land. Very often an outdoor drive-in movie company will use its parking area for swap meet activities during the day when movies are not shown. One thing is for certain, though: Swap meets are held regularly in almost every community in the country, if not throughout the year, then at least during the warmer seasons. Typically, they are held on weekends. However, many meets extend for three to four days including the weekend.

LOCATING SWAP MEETS

To find out where swap meets are held in your area, you can consult the yellow pages under the heading "Swap Meets," the editorial office of your local newspaper, or even the state highway patrol. (They usually have to patrol swap meet areas and know where each one is located.) Another source of information is the publication:

Swap Meet USA
P.O. Box 200
Grover City, California 93433.

This magazine gives sources of merchandise suitable for swap meet sale as well as the names, locations, selling times, and business terms for numerous swap meets held across the country.

Selling space for swap meets generally is sold on a daily, weekly, monthly, or seasonal basis. A 100-square-foot selling space plus adjoining room for your car or truck usually rents from $5 to $6 a day. Consult the management or operators for their terms and policies.

SELECTING ITEMS FOR SALE

Almost any type of merchandise, new or used, will sell at a swap meet. Before you get directly involved, however, attend a swap meet and observe the display of merchandise. Notice which concessions receive the most activity. Keep one thing in mind: The cost of living is getting ridiculous; people are looking for bargains. They go to swap meets in search of basic necessities as well as novelty items. Some of the staple items successful at swap meets are tools, casual clothing (jeans, sweaters, sports shirts, etc.), auto accessories, and household goods such as tableware, kitchen utensils, and bed linens.

The swap meet operator can advise you on the proper procedures for the collection of state sales tax. Usually, he will take care of collecting it from each concessionaire and turning it over to the state.

The rules for obtaining merchandise are the same as for other retail ventures. Consult the yellow pages under wholesalers, manufacturers, and distributors of the products you desire to sell. The *Thomas Register of American Manufacturers*, located in your library, contains lists of every type of product manufactured in the United States and the names and addresses of each manufacturer.

See if you can start out selling on a consignment basis, whereby you pick up your merchandise from a supplier's warehouse, display it at the meet, and then return the unsold goods paying only for the items sold. After you build up a working profit and obtain a better idea of what will sell, you may desire to start purchasing your goods in advance, especially if you can receive a better discount from your supplier. Not everyone will allow you consignment privileges. However, there are ways to impress potential suppliers with your honesty and integrity in developing these consignment relationships. Supply them with personal references from your banker, previous and present employers and/or business associates, attorneys, and friends.

Very often retail merchants have an oversupply of merchandise they have to liquidate and are willing to sell these items at sacrifice prices. Contact these merchants; they can be another source of sale merchandise.

Swap meet selling can be fun. You can meet a lot of interesting people and enjoy the fresh air of the outdoors.

FINANCIAL REWARDS

If you obtain merchandise at the right price, there is a lot of money to be made in this venture. Many swap meet dealers report making profits of $200 and more in just one day of selling.

ACQUIRING CLIENTS

Naturally, you depend on the foot traffic generated by the swap meet to attract buyers. Nevertheless, there are many things you can do to attract large crowds to your booth. Take out ads in the local newspaper pointing out your special bargains, the location of the swap meet, the dates you will be at the meet, and the exact location of your booth. Support these ads with some local radio spots. Your satisfied customers will often recommend that their friends, neighbors, and co-workers come to you. If you rent the same space for consecutive meets, you may have large crowds of repeat customers shopping at your booth.

FUTURE GAINS

Swap meets are big business. You can even start and operate your own meets. Quite often, the owners or operators of large parking lots, fair grounds, drive-in theaters, or empty city and county lots do not wish to get into the swap meet business themselves but desire to capitalize on their properties when they are not in use. You can arrange to lease these properties for a percentage of the gross income (10 to 20 percent) at designated times for swap meet use.

Next you would advertise the meet to potential sellers in the "business opportunity" section of your newspaper. Many people travel large distances to shop at swap meets. It is easy to accommodate at least 150 sellers on a good-sized lot. At $5 to $6 per selling space per day, this will create $750 to $900 in daily revenue. In addition, it is customary to charge the shoppers attending a meet a $1 admission charge. It is typical for at least 1000 people to attend a meet in just one day. This adds another $1000 to your daily income for a total of $1750 and $1900. If you allow $600 for advertising the meet and a 10 percent rental payment to the property owners, you are left with a daily profit of $975 to $1110. At a 20 percent rental payment to the property owners, you are left with a daily profit of $800 to $920.

After you develop the expertise to start and run swap meets, you can work with many property owners in developing swap meet operations thoughout an entire county or state.

GIFT SERVICE

WHY

One of the biggest annoyances for some people is having to select, purchase, and send gifts. Many people are obligated to send gifts to friends, relatives, and business associates. This is especially true in the corporate world where executives are often required to send tasteful and thoughtful gift items to clients, associates, superiors, and subordinates. If you can relieve them of this burdensome task by providing a gift purchasing and sending service, you can develop quite a profitable business for yourself. Your profit is derived by purchasing the gift items at wholesale and billing your client at retail.

GETTING STARTED

As in other retail sales endeavors, you must obtain a city business license. To purchase products from wholesalers, you will also need a resale number, which you can obtain from your local board of equalization. If there is a sales tax charged in your state, a state board of equalization resale permit is required. This permit is not necessary when acting as an independent sales representative for another company; just when you are the prime seller. In many cases, you do not have to pay any advance money for a resale permit. You must, however, keep accurate records of all your sales involving the sales tax and periodically turn this money over to your local state board of equalization.

You will have to use your own imagination and ingenuity in

determining what type of articles will make suitable gift items. Just browsing through a boutique or gift shop can give you numerous ideas. The next step is to develop a dependable source of supply. Since jewelry items make up a large bulk of the gift-giving business, establish yourself with some jewelry manufacturers and wholesalers. As in other selling endeavors, it is advantageous if you are not required to carry an expensive inventory of the products you desire to sell. You want to be able to purchase each item at wholesale as you receive an order for it. Wholesalers want to sell their merchandise in volume to produce a suitable gross profit for themselves. However, if you keep dropping in with repeated single orders that can amount to a sizeable sum at the end of the year, quite often a wholesaler or manufacturer will welcome your business on a unit-by-unit basis.

After you visit a number of suppliers and get an idea of what type of items you will be selling, make up a list of your popular items along with the retail prices and pass or mail out copies of it to business offices. In some instances, your supplier will be able to provide you with pictures or catalog sheets to pass out. Often it is not necessary to contact the sender of the gift directly, but rather his or her secretary whose responsibility it is to handle gift giving chores.

Offer to mail the gifts also, to completely eliminate all red tape on the part of your client. Remember, you are selling convenience. When billing your clients, some tact will be required. In all business dealings, it is naturally preferable to be paid at the time of service. However, important business executives might be irritated if asked to pay in advance. Therefore, you might have to bill these people. In most cases, you will have no trouble getting your money when they pay their monthly bills. You may want to require a down payment for some individuals. One tactful way to get around the whole matter is to offer all clients a 10 percent discount if a check accompanies their order. This might cut down on your profit somewhat, but it can eliminate billing procedures and any possible collection problems.

You can also arrange with some of the major credit card companies to utilize their services to bill their customers and then turn over the charge slips to them for reimbursement, less a percentage charge for the service. With most credit card companies, this charge is approximately 3 percent of the sale. With many credit card companies it is not even necessary to have the client's card. All the client has to do is give you his or her card number. You in turn write up the charge form inserting the number in its proper place, and send the card along with a stamped self-addressed envelope to them for their signature and immediate return to you.

When you advertise your services in newspapers and magazines, leave room on the order form for the customer's credit card number and signature. If the customer fills it out and sends it to you, you will be supplied with all the prerequisites necessary to ensure your receiving your money from the credit card company. For extremely high priced orders, check with the credit card company to verify credit. Your bank can assist you with the details of obtaining a credit card affiliation. When mailing the merchandise out, insure it for its face value, so that if necessary, you can prove the recipient actually received it since he or she will be required to sign for it.

FINANCIAL REWARDS

Most people are willing to pay from $20 to $50 for a thoughtful gift. Whatever price you obtain these items for, the difference in price represents your profit. The wholesale price of most conventional name-brand items is approximately 60 percent of the suggested selling price. Thus, a $40 retail item wholesales for approximately $24 and leaves you a profit of $16. For attractive nonbrand items with no definite predetermined selling price, it is easy to triple and even quadruple your investment. This is especially true of jewelry items such as gold chains, pendants, and bracelets. Leather goods such as briefcases and wallets can also fall into this category.

ACQUIRING CLIENTS

It would be a good idea to advertise in the business section of newspapers as well as in various industry, business, and professional journals. For a list of these journals, consult *Ulrich's International Periodicals Directory*, found in most libraries. As business increases, so can your advertising budget.

You do not have to depend exclusively on the business community for sales. Many busy people obligated to give wedding, birthday, anniversary, or religious confirmation presents will welcome your service. Therefore, it would be advantageous to advertise in the newsletters of religious, social, civic, and fraternal organizations.

FUTURE GAINS

This type of business can be expanded on a national level. You can have a catalog made up, featuring your inventory. You can then advertise this catalog in national business journals and newspapers such as the *Wall Street Journal*. It is customary to charge a token fee for such catalogs to cover production costs and ensure that only serious shoppers request it. You can obtain a toll-free (800) number from the phone company allowing your clients to conveniently place their orders from anywhere in the United States. You in turn bill the client via his or her credit cards as discussed, and then send the merchandise directly to the intended receiver.

You can also hire other salespeople to represent you on a commission basis calling on business executives and selling from your catalog or a sample case of merchandise. Their commission would depend on your profit margin. If you allowed them to keep 40 percent of the profit as commission, you could induce good people to work for you while still retaining a satisfactory profit for yourself.

MAIL ORDER BUSINESS

WHY

Many consumers like to shop for unique and interesting items through the mail. First of all, it is convenient. Because of the postal laws, if they are ever dissatisfied, they can return their merchandise to the mail order dealer for a refund. This feat is usually only accomplished with a great deal of aggravation through conventional retail outlets. Secondly, there are a lot of manufacturers and distributors of superior quality merchandise that do not have the facilities to sell through retail stores; they therefore can only serve the public through the mails.

Fortunes have been made in mail order. If you click with a good item, it can be a very easy and lucrative way to make money, right from the comfort of your home. If you do not make it, however, there are several things you can do to keep any losses to a minimum.

GETTING STARTED

Obtain a business license from your local city hall. It will cost you approximately $65. If the state in which you conduct your business has a state sales tax, you will also have to obtain a resale permit from your state board of equalization. It will be your responsibility to add and collect the state sales tax and turn it over to the state via the state board of equalization office in your community. The resale permit allows you to purchase items from your suppliers without having to pay any sales tax until the items are resold by you. Additionally, you should have business cards made up.

SELECTING ITEMS FOR SALE

What items should you handle? Obviously there are no sure-fire formulas for guaranteed sales. There are, however, a few categories of items that are generally always successful when sold through the mails. One such category is the "convenience" group, items that make certain everyday tasks such as household chores easier to perform. Included in this group are kitchen aids such as vegetable peelers, slicers, and graters. Cleaning pads and brushes that make housecleaning easier are very popular. Any item that can aid in organizing paperwork is a good bet. This would include home bulletin boards, file folders, and recipe holders.

Certain types of jewelry and electronic items are very successful via mail order, including inexpensive digital watches, pocket radios, and cassette recorders. Gift and boutique items sell well. Books should not be overlooked, especially those offering instructions on building things and other "how to" books.

The preceding is just a random sampling of items you might consider handling. For more ideas, go through the mail order section of various newspapers and magazines, observing the items which appear most frequently. Browse through the aisles of department, variety, and gift stores picking out items you think are interesting and would be successful via the mail order approach.

OBTAINING MERCHANDISE

Look in the Yellow Pages under the headings for the items you are considering handling; then look under the subheadings: wholesalers, manufacturers, and distributors of these items. These headings will be right next to the retail listing. Approach the wholesalers personally, presenting your business card and resale permit. Find out what your best prices would be and whether the item you want would be constantly and continually available. Do not buy yet! First, place your ad in the newspapers or magazines you select. Once the orders start coming in, then purchase your merchandise. In this manner, you get your money first, then pay for the merchandise and pocket your profit. If your promotion is not successful, then all you lose is the cost of the ads. In many cases, you can probably obtain lower wholesale prices if you buy large quantities of an item and pay in advance. However, in the beginning, it is better to give up a few percentage points in profit in return for security.

If you decide to handle books, go to a large bookstore and browse through the "how to" departments. Pick out the books you think would sell via mail order. Write the publishers and find out your price as an independent distributor. If they are willing to sell to you at a good price, follow the process described above: First place the ad, then purchase the merchandise according to incoming orders.

The *Thomas Register of American Manufacturers*, found in most libraries, is another instrument in finding sources of supply. This publication is actually an encyclopedia of almost everything manufactured in the country, with the names and addresses of the manufacturers. If you find items you like in this publication, write to the manufacturers and find out their terms. Again, sell first, then buy.

There are firms that specialize in supplying mail-order operators with mail-order merchandise. One such firm is:

Specialty Merchandise Corp.   —Dept. 322
6061 DeSoto Avenue
Woodland Hills, California 91635

Write and ask for their catalogs. Compare their prices with those of your other sources. If you find some good items at the right price from these organizations, it can be an excellent and convenient way of doing business, for much of the legwork involved in obtaining merchandise can be eliminated.

You can sometimes obtain free advertising by making special arrangements with fraternal, civic, social, professional, trade, and religious organizations who desire to raise money for their worthy projects. They give you free advertising space in the magazines, journals, or newsletters sent to their membership. In return, the customer orders are sent to them. They keep an agreed-upon amount of money from each order and then send you the balance and the name and address of the customer to whom the merchandise is to be sent. In this way, both you and the organization share in the profits; and you don't have to risk any advertising monies.

The way your ad is written can also play an important part in your sales success. Use as few words as possible. Have a caption in bold print calling attention to your product. For instance, if you are advertising a potato peeler, your first line might read: "SLICE POTATOES EASILY AND EVENLY." An ad for an onion peeler could start out with: "AT LAST, NO TEARS!"

FINANCIAL REWARDS

There is a general rule for pricing items sold via mail order. To allow you to cover your advertising and mailing expense and earn a decent profit, whatever you pay for an item should be doubled to arrive at a selling price.

ACQUIRING CLIENTS

The placing of your ads is a big and important step toward acquiring customers. A well-written ad placed in the proper newspaper or magazine can be the key to a large response. There is no sure-fire formula telling what publication to advertise in. To complicate things, some items are more popular in some parts of the country than in others. However, there are newspaper and magazine advertising agencies that can assist you in placing ads in almost any type of newspaper or magazine in the country since they deal directly with these publications. Then all you have to do is deal with just one source—the agency. They can suggest publications and areas of the country best suited for your product. Furthermore, you pay no extra money for this service, just the advertising rate of the publication. The service agency obtains its profit by receiving a trade discount from the publications represented. Two such advertising services are:

National Mail Order
Classified
P.O. Box 5
Sarasota, Florida 33578.

Jay Reiss Advertising
Agency
Suite 2100
16930 Blackhawk Street
Granada Hills, California
91344.

FUTURE GAINS

It is possible to arrange for "dropship" services with some suppliers. In this process, your customer mails you the money for the item, you keep your profit and mail the rest to your supplier along with the name and address of your customer. Your supplier then mails the product directly to your customer naming you as the supplier. Through this system, you do not have to become involved in the actual handling, storing, and mailing of your products.

Once you do enough business to become properly capitalized, there are numerous ways to expand your business. You can import large quantities of merchandise manufactured here or abroad at volume discount prices and place prominent ads in national magazines to secure a large volume of orders. You can eventually carry a wide enough selection of merchandise in one or several categories to have attractive catalogs produced featuring it. The catalogs can be advertised in national publications for free or a small charge to cover production. The people who receive the catalogs can then order as many items as they want as frequently as they want.

If desired, you can act as the major supplier to smaller mail order operators who will pay for their own ads featuring merchandise they can order from you, upon receiving responses from their ads. In this manner, although some of the profit is shared, you eliminate having to pay for ads. In essence, you are acting as a "wholesale" mail order operator to smaller "retail" operators selling direct to the consumer.

An excellent book on mail order is:

How to Get Rich in Mail Order
by Melvin Powers
Published by Wilshire Book Co.
12015 Sherman Rd.
North Hollywood, Calif. 91605

ADVERTISING REPRESENTATIVE FOR NEWSPAPERS AND MAGAZINES

WHY

Advertisements are of prime importance to most periodicals. The selling of commercial advertising space is the major source of income and profit for most publications. In fact, in many instances, a magazine is created and published just as a means of securing advertising revenue. The subscription revenues usually pay just a portion of a paper's large overhead. There are many innovative ways to take advantage of a magazine's or newspaper's need for advertising revenue.

Some large national publications maintain their own sales staff. Others maintain their own sales staff but also utilize the services of independent professional sales organizations. Many medium-sized publications such as trade and professional journals use independent sales organizations exclusively. Smaller publications such as neighborhood dailies and weeklies will usually maintain a small permanent sales staff supplemented by some additional part-time sales people.

GETTING STARTED

There are several paths of entry into this field. To gain some preliminary experience, you can contact a neighborhood daily to work on a freelance part-time basis. In this position you would call on retail merchants, institutions such as banks and insurance companies, service businesses such as dry cleaners, and any other local business or professional concerns who could benefit by announcing their goods or services to the readers of the local publication. You may build up a large following of loyal clients and decide to remain in this capacity.

Or, you may decide to work as a part-time or full-time employee for a national trade, professional, or consumer journal. An example of a trade journal would be a magazine representing and catering to the needs of the baking industry, prime advertising candidates for which would be the many manufacturers of baking equipment, utensils, and ingredients such as flour and flavoring agents that go into preparing baked goods. Journals for nurses and doctors are an example of professional publications. Manufacturers of medical equipment benefit by advertising in these magazines. A consumer journal is one directed to everyday consumers who purchase toothpaste, soap, clothing, food products, and other everyday items. The manufacturers of these items are the prime advertisers in these types of publications.

Another area of involvement is to work for a "sales agency" which handles the advertising sales for publications who choose not to maintain their own sales staffs. No matter which area you become involved in, the work is always the same—*Selling!*

In most cases, past experience is not a major prerequisite for obtaining assignments in magazine ad selling. The most important criterion in this field is enthusiasm. You must like serving people, you must enjoy the challenge of selling, and most important, you must not become discouraged when you get a lot of refusals. Everyone gets them. Those who remain confident and maintain a positive attitude usually ride out the storm and profit handsomely.

When starting out with a magazine, read some of the back issues. In fact, read some of your competitors' back issues. In this manner, you will become familiar with the field your magazine writes about. You may approach clients in person or via the telephone. There are two main points to remember when calling on a client: First of all, make sure you are talking to the right person—the person who can authorize the ad. Come right out and ask who that person is. It will usually be the president of the company, the vice president of sales or marketing, or the advertising or product manager. Secondly, do not be afraid to admit that you are new with your publication and are not familiar with your client's products. Just communicate the fact that you would like to know more about your client and would like to increase his or her sales via an ad in your magazine.

FINANCIAL REWARDS

In most cases, you will receive a percentage of the sales you obtain. This percentage is generally from 10 to 20 percent. An ad in a publication can run anywhere from $300 a page to $5000 a page, depending on the market it serves, the circulation of the magazine, and whether the ad is in black and white or color. As you can see, your commission on a one-page ad can run from $30 to $1000. On partial pages, the rates and earnings are adjusted accordingly. Quite often on just one sales call, you can obtain an order for the next three to six issues of that publication. This can all add up to tremendous profits. In fact, it is not unusual for good advertising space salespeople to earn over $50,000 a year or more.

ACQUIRING CLIENTS

There are two types of clients you will want to acquire. First is your own direct client—the magazine or agency you will sell for. You may have experience working in a certain field or trade. For example, if you are a school teacher, you may be a natural at selling ad space in a teaching journal to textbook publishers and manufacturers of teaching aids.

You may see a magazine on a newsstand that you would like to represent. On the inside cover of all magazines is a section giving the name, address, officers, editors, and other important people involved with the publication. Included in this section is the name of the advertising sales manager or the name and location of the independent sales agency representing the magazine. Call the appropriate party and inform him or her of your desire to increase their advertising revenues.

To get an idea of all the different types of magazines published and the addresses of their editorial offices, go to your library and browse through the following two books: *Ulrich's International Periodicals Directory* and *Standard Rate and Data*.

After you secure an association with a publication, the first thing is to find out who the potential clients are. The owner of the magazine or independent sales agency you associate with can provide you with much of this information. Reading competing magazines and seeing who their advertisers are will supplement your knowledge. In the case of trade and professional journals, there are often directories listing numerous manufacturers and distributors serving that field. For example, for medical journals, there are directories naming the suppliers of different types of medical equipment. These are your potential advertisers.

FUTURE GAINS

After you gain sufficient experience in this field, you can start your own independent sales agency representing one or several magazines in a variety of noncompeting fields. Your success is limited only by your desire to grow. The more magazines you represent and the more commissioned salespeople you recruit to sell under you, the greater your income. In this capacity, it is customary to pay your salespeople from 10 to 20 percent of the sales they generate, and to charge your magazine clients from 40 to 50 percent of the gross revenues your organization generates for them. You also, however, have to pay your own office rent, telephone, and bookkeeping expenses. This will generally amount to 20 percent of your sales volume. After deducting these expenses, your net percentage profit will range from 10 to 20 percent of your revenues. A good salesperson should be able to generate at least $200,000 a year in advertising volume in either one or several magazines assigned to him or her. If you have a staff of five salespeople working for you, total sales can easily amount to $1,000,000 a year or $100,000 to $200,000 for you.

TELEPHONE SALES

WHY

With the high cost of gasoline and overnight lodging, telephone selling is becoming an important part of the sales process. As the name implies, it involves the selling of merchandise via the telephone. It allows an organization or person to sell to potential buyers located anywhere in the United States, all from one location. A large number of customers can be contacted in a relatively short period of time. This cuts down on sales overhead as it eliminates the need for airplane, automobile, gasoline, and motel expenses necessary to keep salespeople on the road for personal calls.

GETTING STARTED AND ACQUIRING CLIENTS

There are basically two types of organizations that utilize the services of telephone salespeople; the first is the company that actually makes or distributes the products being sold. They hire people to utilize the telephone in selling their products exclusively. The second type is an independent sales organization representing the products of a number of manufacturers or distributors, strictly on a fee-for-service commission basis. They can be thought of as "manufacturers' telephone representatives." Many of these firms will specialize in just one industry, representing noncompeting lines of several manufacturers. In this manner it is easier for them to gain a more comprehensive knowledge of the products they sell—essential in any good sales presentation.

Because a visual presentation of a product cannot be made over the phone, the items that generally sell best are those that are already familiar to the customer. Office supplies sell well on the telephone. When you mention a certain type and quality of paper, people on the other end of the line usually know what you mean. The same is true for file folders, staple machines, typewriter ribbon, etc. Fluorescent lights can be sold over the phone to retail stores, factories, warehouses, showrooms, and other facilities that use fluorescent lighting and periodically have to change worn-out bulbs.

To be an effective telephone salesperson, you should possess a thorough knowledge of the product. This knowledge can be acquired through the manufacturers' catalogs and product brochures. The secret of a good sale is to get the customer talking as much as possible to encourage him or her to become involved with you, the product, and an eventual sale. Ask the customer what his or her needs are, and then show how you can fill them with your products. Your employer will suggest effective approaches for the products you sell. Enthusiasm is probably the main prerequisite for a successful sale.

To find people to work for, look in the classified employment section of your newspaper under "Telephone Sales."

FINANCIAL REWARDS

When working for the actual manufacturer of a product, you might receive a base salary plus a percentage of your sales. If you participate on a part-time basis, most likely you will be paid strictly on a commission basis. The typical sales commission ranges from 5 to 30 percent, depending on such factors as the selling price of the item and the amount of profit represented in this selling price.

When working for an independent telephone sales organization, your income will most likely be based on a percentage of your sales—again represented by a 5 to 30 percent range. Depending on how successful you are, your salary can range from $10,000 to over $50,000 a year.

FUTURE GAINS

After gaining experience in this field, you can start your own independent sales organization. To keep your risks to a minimum in the beginning, you may want to operate as the only salesperson and use a standard telephone system, paying the usual long distance rates. Almost any type of manufacturing firm is a potential client of yours as long as the products they produce can be sold in large quantities to commercial users. In this business you do not sell on a unit basis to individual consumers. There would not be enough financial return per average sale to warrant your time and expenses. You generally sell to retail stores for consumer resale by them, to other manufacturing companies who might require a particular part or parts in their manufacturing processes, or maybe to an institution such as a hospital. You might for instance, supply hospitals with thermometers, disposable examining gowns, or other items used routinely in large quantities.

The *Thomas Register of American Manufacturers*, found in your library, can provide you with an excellent list of potential clients. This publication contains the names and addresses of every type of manufacturing firm in the country, categorized by product type. When calling on manufacturers, point out that you can help their business, as they only pay you on a fee-for-service basis, after you actually consummate a sale for them. You can offer your service as a replacement of or adjunct to their regular sales staff. Your client's and your own intuition can help you determine who are the most likely buyers to call.

As your business expands, you will want to hire additional employees and utilize telephone WATS lines to reduce your telephone expenses. When you own your own service, you generally charge your clients 10 to 60 percent sales commission which is then split evenly with your employees. Thus, whatever an employee earns is also duplicated and earned by the owner of the service. Therefore, if you have five full-time employees, each averaging $25,000 a year a piece, and you are one of the employees, your gross income will be approximately $170,000 a year (four employees = $120,000 for you, plus your own $25,000, plus the $25,000 your company—you—earns from this $25,000).

Your biggest expense will obviously be your telephone bill. This can be reduced considerably through the use of independent telephone services that offer you discounted long-distance rates.

If you expand your operation to include five full-time salespeople, each working 40 hours a week as mentioned, it would be advantageous to purchase the second plan, which would average out to approximately 10¢ a minute. This would amount to $64,800 a year. Based on the previously mentioned $170,000 commission earnings of your five salespeople, this would leave you with $105,200 gross profit before rent expenses.

INDUSTRY RECRUITING

WHY

City, county, and state governments depend on the influx of new industry to generate thousands and sometimes even millions of extra dollars in tax revenues. In addition, these industries employ the local citizens, decreasing welfare subsidies and creating even more revenues through personal income taxes. It is not always easy for localities to attract new industry. This is especially true in cold-weather communities where heating costs are expensive. As yet, there is no official occupational title "Industry Recruiter." However, creation and innovation are the mainstay of our economic system. One of the fundamental principles of business is: Find a need, then fill it. If you are an inventive salesperson with an understanding of corporate business, the recruiting of industry to certain localities could prove to be very lucrative.

GETTING STARTED AND ACQUIRING CLIENTS

First, you have to find localities that are in need of new industry. This should not be hard to do, since most are. Then you have to approach the chamber of commerce of that community and propose they use your services to help recruit new industry into that area. This will take a great deal of salespersonship on your part, since this is a new field. The secret, as in all sales endeavors, is to show the chamber of commerce your enthusiasm for their area. Inform them how much you feel their area could be beneficial to numerous industries and how you would like to personally contact these industries and induce them to move to or set up a new division or branch office in the area. Most chambers of commerce advertise their area in business publications such as the *Wall Street Journal, Business Week, Fortune Magazine,* and numerous other journals. Nevertheless, it often takes the "personal touch" of having an aggressive and knowledgeable person contacting and selling various industries on the idea of locating in a particular area.

When deciding on which communities to call on first, it would be a good idea to start with those who are already advertising their areas in the business journals. They have already expressed their need. Your local librarian can provide you with a selection of recognized business publications to help you start your search. In addition, send a letter describing your services to all chambers of commerce. To find the names and addresses of all the major chambers of commerce in the country, consult *Worldwide Chamber of Commerce Directory,* published by Johnson Publishing Company. Follow up with a telephone call to the head of each chamber.

To induce a chamber of commerce to utilize your services, you might start out with an offer they can be comfortable with. Request they give you a six-month trial period to recruit some industry into their area. This should be acceptable to them. After all, they might already have been trying for six years to get someone to move into their area.

After an agreement is confirmed, the next step is to approach appropriate industries to either move to or at least develop pending branch operations in that area. The first thing is to find industries who are already planning complete or branch operation moves to new areas. The best way to do this is to constantly read such major business publications as the *Wall Street Journal* and others already mentioned in this chapter. In fact, place small ads in these publications informing industrial concerns of your expertise in locating areas profitable to their operation. After you locate some likely firms, place a call directly to the president. And don't worry, it is sometimes easier to talk to the president of a company than to the janitor. Obviously you will first have to talk to the executive's secretary. So, put your best foot forward and impress her or him with the importance of the call. Another option is to go to your library and look through *Standard and Poor's Register of Corporations*. This book lists all the major corporations in the United States and describes their business functions. You may find a corporation whose main business function could greatly benefit from a move to one of your client communities. Attend industrial trade shows and contact and communicate with company heads at their booths or cocktail parties. In fact, throw a couple of good parties yourself and see that these important people are invited. To find the dates and locations of these shows, contact the official trade associations representing these industries. They are listed in the *Encyclopedia of Associations*, which can be found in most libraries.

When selling a community to a corporation head, always stress the profit benefits of being located in that area. If the community is in the snow belt, point out that lower land and labor costs there could far offset heating oil expenses. Because the price of fine homes is often considerably lower in snowy areas, it will be easier for that company to recruit top-notch management. And after all, all snow belt areas still have spring, summer, and fall, in addition to winter. A community might be located in the vicinity of an ideal shipping area such as a seaport or railroad line important to a company. Or it might be in close proximity to important consumer markets. There are benefits to every community. Develop and discuss these benefits with the chamber of commerce you will be representing.

FINANCIAL REWARDS

There is no set formula for determining financial return for this type of work. However, remember, you may be the one responsible for bringing in hundreds of thousands of dollars of increased tax revenues to that area. You are therefore definitely entitled to a small percentage of that revenue for the duration of that company's stay in the community. For example, if the taxes on an industry recruited by you are $100,000 a year, you should receive approximately 10 percent of that or $10,000 annually, even though you will have nothing more to do with the situation after the move is completed. Does this seem overly rewarding? It is not. After all, it will take a lot of time and effort on your part to finally effect an industrial move. If you arrange enough industrial locations for enough client communities you could easily create an annual salary of $100,000 or more for yourself.

FUTURE GAINS

After you effect one or two company relocations, your reputation will travel quickly in the chamber of commerce community. It should then be easier to attract clients. After you build up a sufficient client list, you can even hire other salespeople to work for you and share in the profits.

10

VENTURES THAT REQUIRE ADMINISTRATIVE SKILL

RETAIL ART SHOW

WHY

Every community has its budding artists. Many would like to practice their specialty professionally and make a name for themselves. Others would just like the satisfaction of having others appreciate their talents so much, they are willing to pay them the supreme complement—pay money for their work. Many of these artists turn out quality work worthy of sale. In fact, many unknown artists can turn out work equal to that of some celebrated artists whose works command large sums of money. They just need a chance to become recognized.

The problem is finding a place to display their creations commercially and economically. One method is through a "consignment shop," discussed in the next chapter. However, you can provide a service by arranging for the use of a large public gathering place for an art show and then subletting individual selling spaces of approximately 200 square feet each to individual artists.

GETTING STARTED

A high school, college, or YMCA or YWCA gymnasium can provide you with the necessary space at a very reasonable cost, usually from $200 to $300 for approximately 12,000 square feet. At 200 square feet per exhibit, this area would accommodate 60 exhibitors. A large field or parking lot not used on Sunday can also be an excellent facility. A major convention center in a large

172

city or town can be the most effective place to hold such an exhibit as they are usually centrally located, easy to get to, and known by everyone in the community. These facilities charge the most money: approximately $700 for 12,000 square feet. Nevertheless, this breaks down to just 5.8¢ per square foot or $11.67 for each 200-square-foot exhibiting space. When you consider that this type of facility can contribute greatly to the success of your project, it might be the best way to go. Artists will be more inclined to subscribe to your services and the general public will be more prone to patronize the event if held at a convention center. Contact the facility you want to use at least four months before the proposed date of your event. This will ensure the acquiring of the space and leave you sufficient time to solicit renters and advertise the event to the public.

FINANCIAL REWARDS

You can add an entrepreneurial charge of $48.28 to the $11.67 cost of each of the 60 200-square-foot display spaces. This brings the rental fee to $59.95 per rental client. It also provides you with a preliminary gross profit of $2896.80 for the event ($48.28 × 60 spaces). You should allow approximately $600 for advertising publicity. (A lot of extra publicity can be attained "free" as will be seen under Acquiring Clients.) You can recoup your $600 advertising expense (and even more) by charging a $1.00 admission at the door.

ACQUIRING CLIENTS

Once you establish your location and date, you have two important goals: acquiring rental clients and promoting the attendance of the event to the general public. Your rental clients can be solicited from the many arts and crafts classes at various night school, community college, and university programs in your community. Have inexpensive fliers announcing your event made up and pass them out to artists patronizing smaller events. In addition, advertise your event in local artistic publications circulated throughout your community.

You must have two basic rules for your renters: They must pay their rental fee at lease 30 days before the event and they must agree to a maximum price per art object. An ideal maximum is $59.95. It allows you to promote the event as a "bargain opportunity" to people seeking fine works of art.

To make the event successful for your renters, encouraging them to patronize future events produced by you, it behooves you to do everything in your power to induce as many people as possible to attend the event. And as mentioned, if you are charging a $1.00 admission fee, the more people that attend, the more money there will be for you. In turn, the admission charge also induces more people to attend your show because people often tend to appreciate an event more if they have to pay to get in.

Contact as many interior decorators as possible, advising them of your event; they might want to buy up a lot of your renters' creations for future resale to their own clients. When you produce an event that benefits both the public and aspiring artists, this is news. Contact all local radio and TV stations and newspapers and magazines informing their newspeople of your event. Their mention helps accomplish the solicitation of both artist renters and consumer attendees. What's more, it is free advertising. In addition, contact all civic and religious organizations for some free publicity in their member newsletters. Many store, restaurant, and theater owners will allow you to place posters announcing your event in their facilities free of charge. Supplement all this free publicity with well-placed ads in newspapers and magazines, and well-selected radio spots.

FUTURE GAINS

Your artist clients will constantly be creating more works of art. If your events are successful, they will patronize you on a continuing basis. And once your shows gain the reputation of having high quality artwork at reasonable prices, they will attract a large following. In fact, have each attendee write down his or her name and address at the door. This can be used to compile a large mailing list announcing future shows. You can eventually utilize even larger facilities to increase the size and financial return of your events.

As your knowledge of art increases, you may decide to open up your own art gallery. In this endeavor, you would acquire the paintings of fine artists either by direct purchase or through consignment, and then resell them.

CONSIGNMENT SHOP

WHY

All over the country amateur craftspeople and artists are creating original and high-quality handicraft items. Paintings, needlepoint, jewelry, ceramics, sculptures of clay, marble, metal or wood, furniture, leather goods, and wood articles are only a few of the varied items handcrafted by people in their homes and workshops. Practically every night school program is filled with people from all walks of life learning about and producing every type of handicraft imaginable.

Many people who create handicrafts would like to see their products for sale in the marketplace. In addition to providing them with extra income, it gives them a feeling of creative worth when they see a public demand for their efforts. Moreover, there are many consumers constantly searching for new and imaginative gift items and decorative objects for their homes, apartments, and offices. This can provide you with an opportunity to act in a liaison capacity between craftspeople and consumers via your own "consignment shop." In this capacity, craftspeople would place their goods in your store for eventual sale by you. When a sale is transacted, you keep a percentage of the sale price for your services and efforts, and return the balance to the craftsperson.

GETTING STARTED

There are two prerequisites for starting this type of business: a retail store location and a continuing source of merchandise. It should be relatively easy to find craftspeople to supply your store. You can contact the arts and crafts programs in every high school and college in your area. From this source alone there should be an abundance of people only too willing to place their creations in your store; your main concern will be to select from among their creations the high quality items that will tempt discriminating shoppers. Advertising in handicraft magazines can also aid in obtaining the works of fine independent craftspeople.

Your store does not have to be in the high-rent district of your community. There are many shoppers who will travel to remote areas in search of interesting and unique items. You will not require expensive fixtures; however, the interior should be clean and neat. The walls of the store should be properly painted, the shelving and other fixtures used to display the merchandise should be acceptable in appearance, and the store should be well lighted to properly show off each item.

FINANCIAL REWARDS

The attractive aspect of this type of business is that you pay for your merchandise only after it is sold, thus eliminating the expensive inventory problems characteristic of typical retail operations. When a craftsperson places his or her work with you, agree on a retail price and offer a receipt for the item. After a sale is transacted, it is quite reasonable for you to keep 40 percent of the sale price for your services.

ACQUIRING CLIENTS

To attract shoppers to your store, place ads on the radio and in local newspapers that might be worded as follows: "Are you looking for that special gift or a unique item for your home or office? Stop in at [name of your store] and browse through hundreds of beautiful and interesting items very reasonably priced." After a while, word will spread throughout the community of your very special store.

FUTURE GAINS

Eventually, you can expand your operation to comprise multiple locations in numerous communities. In addition, this retail experience can provide you with the knowledge to open up conventional retail stores featuring exotic and fashionable merchandise imported from all over the world.

SPECIAL PURCHASE BROKER

WHY

Every day throughout the country, department stores, discount stores, supermarkets, and other types of retail outlets feature special merchandise on sale at very low prices as a means of attracting shoppers. Most of this merchandise is not available from their regular suppliers; the store buys it from manufacturers who for one reason or another are willing to sell a quantity of their goods at extremely low prices. These low prices then allow the retailer to resell this merchandise at correspondingly low retail prices to attract customers. There are several reasons a manufacturer might offer a quantity of goods at "sacrifice" prices: The manufacturer might be overstocked due to improper inventory control or sales forecasting, financial problems might require an immediate liquidation of a quantity of merchandise, or a quantity of goods might be slightly damaged or flawed making it unsuitable for conventional sale but attractive for a "special sale" of merchandise commonly referred to as "seconds."

There are thousands of manufacturing and distributing companies throughout the country. It is not always easy for retailers to keep abreast of every special offering of every manufacturer in the country. Likewise, many manufacturers concentrate their main efforts on production and do not have the marketing facilities to contact every retail store when they have a special offering for sale. This situation can provide fine profit opportunities for individuals who are willing to keep abreast of what is happening in the marketplace and to contact retail stores concerning these special opportunities.

GETTING STARTED AND ACQUIRING CLIENTS

There are two fundamental prerequisites for getting started in this business: Make yourself known to as many manufacturers of consumer merchandise as possible and keep abreast of their special closeouts. Concurrently, make as many retailers as possible aware of your services and keep them abreast of your special offerings.

Go to the *Thomas Register of American Manufacturers*, found in most libraries, for a list of every product manufacturer in the country. Have stationery printed with your business letterhead and send letters to as many manufacturers as possible informing them of your services to them—that is, finding customers for the merchandise they want to dispose of. Likewise, send letters to retail stores announcing that you have access to many types of sale items at very low prices. There are directories listing the names and locations of most major retail stores and chain headquarters throughout the country. One very good ones is *Fairchild's Financial Manual of Retail Stores*, published by Fairchild Publications.

After you send out your letters, do not sit back and wait for people to ring your telephone or knock on your door. Be creative and inventive. Contact a number of manufacturers of popular consumer merchandise (housewares, apparel, house tools, etc.) and find out specific items they are willing to release at special prices; then personally contact or call a number of retail stores advising them of the specific items you can obtain for them and the corresponding prices. When people can focus on several specific items instead of generalities, they are more likely to agree to a purchase. Conversely, call on retailers and ask them what type of "special sale" items they are looking for and then call up as many corresponding manufacturers as possible to see if you can locate such merchandise at an attractive price. After you build up a reputation for your services, then both manufacturers and retailers might call on you to accommodate their needs.

FINANCIAL REWARDS

In this business, you are acting as a broker or liaison between manufacturers and retailers. You do not have to become responsible for the actual purchase, shipping, or resale of any merchandise. Your primary function is to bring both parties together. The fees you can charge are variable. If you find a terrific buy for a retailer, you might just charge the retailer a percentage of the purchase price of the goods as your commission fee. If the manufacturer, although selling at a sacrifice price, can still make a suitable profit on his or her merchandise, you might just charge the manufacturer a percentage of the sale price as your commission fee. In many cases, you will be able to charge both the manufacturer and the retailer a percentage of the sales price as your professional fee. The percentage commission you charge is also variable. If the sales amount is large, for example $100,000, your fee might be 5 percent of this figure, or $5000. If the sales amount is small, for example $20,000, you might want to charge a commission fee of 10 percent or $2000 for your efforts. Everything is negotiable. In the beginning, charge as high but also as reasonably as you can. Eventually, experience will tell you just how much you can charge and to whom.

FUTURE GAINS

There are hundreds of consumer manufacturing companies in this country and hundreds of thousands of retail stores. The potential in this business is almost limitless. You can specialize in just one class of merchandise (house tools, footwear, etc.) or service all categories of consumer merchandise. As your business increases, you can expand your operation by hiring additional salespeople to personally call on or telephone clients. The commission fees can then be shared with these people. The amount you share will depend on your overhead, such as telephone expenses. It is realistically possible to earn well over $100,000 a year in this endeavor.

APARTMENT HOUSE MANAGER

WHY

This can be an excellent opportunity for a young couple to get one foot up on the cost of living—eliminating the high cost of apartment rental. It is ideal for a husband and wife team if one or both are college students or are operating a second business from the home. In this manner they can always be on call for their management responsibilities while attending to their second income.

GETTING STARTED

The main prerequisites for managing an apartment house is to be conscientious, personable, desirous of serving people, and a problem-solver. A typical apartment house requires someone on duty at all times six days a week during the daytime. This is why it is ideal for a married couple or even two roommates. Although not difficult, there are a lot of responsibilities in this type of work. Vacant apartments have to be shown to prospective tenants, rents have to be collected, janitors, gardeners, and all repair people have to be supervised. Repair problems in each apartment have to be recorded and reported to the owners or management company responsible for the complete maintenance of the property.

FINANCIAL REWARDS

The typical compensation for an apartment house manager is approximately $20 per unit. Therefore, if you manage a 30-unit building, your monthly compensation would be $600. If each apartment rents for $400 each, you would then receive your apartment free and receive an additional $200 per month from the owners. If you are married or have a roommate as your partner, each of you can have an outside financial interest as long as someone is on duty during the daytime. Of course, arrangements can vary with each situation.

ACQUIRING CLIENTS

The best way to obtain a management assignment is to make contact with the owners of apartment buildings. This can be done very easily by attending local meetings of apartment house owners groups, contacting real estate agents who specialize in apartment house sales, and calling on building management companies who take responsibility for the total management of investment properties.

FUTURE GAINS

After managing an apartment house for a while, you may become interested in the total management of real estate properties, whether they be apartment houses or office buildings. People from all walks of life purchase apartment houses and office buildings as sound business investments. Sometimes just one individual owner or a group of partners are involved in the ownership. In most cases, the owners are very busily involved in their primary vocations and do not have the time or expertise to attend to the responsibilities involved in the total management of their investment. This has given rise to the need for professional management companies to attend to every detail involved in the proper and profitable management of an apartment house or office building.

As the operator of your own management company, you would hire the individual apartment house manager, secure the services of a janitorial and gardening service, and, when repairs have to be made, arrange for plumbers, carpenters, electricians, roofers, and so on. In addition, you would be responsible for all rentals, rent collections, the payment of all service people, and the keeping of all financial records for the owners.

This can be a very lucrative endeavor. Although you arrange for the work, all the expenses for service people and materials are paid for by the owners. The general fee for the professional management of an apartment house or office building is 11 percent of the gross rentals. Therefore, if you are responsible for a 30-unit apartment or office complex where the average rent is $400 a month, this amounts to an annual rental of $144,000. At 11 percent your fee would be $15,840 a year.

If you become responsible for the total management of ten apartment or office complexes of similar size and revenue, your gross income would be well over $150,000 a year. Naturally, you will have to maintain a small office and hire several other people to assist you with your responsibilities.

Eventually, you could obtain a real estate broker's license and specialize in the purchase and sale of apartment and office buildings. As long as you are managing the building, if the owner decides to sell it, you might as well get the assignment. And when you venture to sell a client's building, you can offer prospective buyers a worry-free turn-key operation. After all, when you sell a building, your customers don't have to worry about maintaining the building—you are already doing it. The commission for the sale of an apartment or office building is approximately 6 percent of the total sale price. This is one way fortunes are made in the real estate profession.

11

PROMOTIONAL SERVICES

PRODUCT DEMONSTRATION AND MODELING

WHY

All products are sold through salespeople. Nevertheless, many companies assist the efforts of their salespeople through product promotion. This promotion might be in the form of live demonstrations in retail stores in which that item is conventionally sold, demonstrations at trade and consumer conventions, and advertising in television, magazines, newspapers, and catalogs. These promotional methods require the services of men and women to demonstrate or model the products. If you meet the requirements for this type of work, it can provide you with excellent part-time income opportunities and the chance to meet interesting people. In addition to making this field a vocation, there often are opportunities to learn about new product fields and develop career relationships with a company you might demonstrate or model for.

GETTING STARTED

The main prerequisites for this type of work are to be well-groomed, to possess an outgoing personality, and to like working with people. Each specialty has its own specific requirements and financial rewards.

RETAIL PRODUCT DEMONSTRATION

This job primarily entails the demonstration of consumer products in retail outlets such as supermarkets, department stores, and discount stores. It might involve showing how effectively a vacuum cleaner, food processing machine, or silver cleaner works. In a supermarket, you might demonstrate how easily an instant soup mix can be prepared and how delicious it tastes. The age range for this type of work is from 18 to 65.

CONVENTION DEMONSTRATION

Quite often the public or an industry is exposed to a product via a convention in a large hotel or convention facility. For instance, manufacturers of printing presses might display their equipment to the management and owners of commercial printing firms via a trade show sponsored by that industry. Manufacturers of medical equipment might demonstrate their new instruments to physicians at a medical convention. On the consumer level, shows might be sponsored by manufacturers of ski equipment, camping equipment, or recreational vehicles and attended by the public with a corresponding interest in one of these fields.

The manufacturers who exhibit their products at conventions want to show these items in their best light. Not only do they design and set up attractive display booths, but they also desire attractive and personable people to draw attention to their booths and to discuss or demonstrate their products. Because of this, there are more restrictions in this area. Primarily, very attractive women between the ages of 21 and 35 are sought for this type of work.

MODELING

One of the most popular ways to expose the public to products is through advertising. This advertising might be in the form of a television commercial, newspaper or magazine ad, or a product catalog produced and distributed by a company. In advertisements, almost all products are either worn by, pointed to, discussed by, or highlighted by a model. The age range for models is anywhere from an infant to a person in his or her eighties, depending on the product advertised and the image the manufacturer wants to convey to the public.

FINANCIAL REWARDS

Demonstrators in retail stores generally earn from $4 to $6 an hour for their services. Convention demonstrators generally earn from $8 to $16 an hour for their services. Models for television commercials, newspaper and magazine ads, and catalog illustrations earn anywhere from $10 to $300 per hour depending on their popularity and whether an ad is for local or national distribution.

Note: 10 to 15 percent must be deducted from the above figures as payment to the agency that obtains your assignments.

ACQUIRING CLIENTS

All demonstration and modeling assignments are usually obtained through agencies specializing in this field. Look in the yellow pages of your phone book under "Convention Services," "Modeling Agencies," "Demonstration Services," and "Market Research Services." Have some 8″ × 10″ black and white glossy photos taken of yourself in several poses and put together a fact sheet specifying your age, weight, height, and physical measurements. Visit as many agencies as possible, and leave copies of your photos. As your reputation for fine service develops, you can look forward to repeat requests for your talents.

FUTURE GAINS

As previously mentioned, your exposure to numerous industries might result in a full-time career opportunity in a particular industry. Additionally, you might decide to start your own agency serving the needs of industry (discussed in the next chapter).

PRODUCT DEMONSTRATION AND MODELING AGENCY

WHY

As discussed in the previous chapter, there is a tremendous need for product demonstrators, convention-booth hostesses, and models to service the promotional and advertising needs of the business world. It would be virtually impossible for models and demonstrators personally to contact all the possible companies they could work for. Correspondingly, it would also be impossible for every manufacturer to become personally aware of all the demonstrators and models that could serve their marketing requirements. This has given rise to the need for special agencies to solicit and screen demonstrators and models for their industrial clients.

GETTING STARTED

It is quite possible to develop a multiservice agency providing product demonstrators for both retail and convention purposes and models for the advertising media. Obtaining a large listing of demonstrators and models is not going to be done overnight; but it can be accomplished eventually. All you will need to get started is a small office, which you can set up in your home, to coordinate your activities from. There are a lot of attractive and intelligent people on college campuses who can contribute to your personnel needs. Place classified ads in local newspapers under the headings: "Modeling," "Special Announcements or Services," "Public Relations Opportunities," or "Sales." Contact the operators of beauty salons informing them of your needs. Many of them might have some customers who could fit your requirements and would welcome the opportunity to do so. Also, take out listings in the yellow pages of your phone book under "Convention Services," "Demonstration Services," and "Modeling Agencies." Many people automatically look in these sections to find work.

For convention demonstrators and modeling aspirants, have each applicant supply you with several black and white glossy photographs of themselves in different poses, and a fact sheet listing their age, weight, height, measurements, and past professional assignments, if any. It will be important to make up your own brochure featuring the people who represent you. This brochure can then be sent to potential client companies to impress them with your staff and provide them with a means of selecting those who appeal the most to them. The requirements for retail product demonstrators are not as stringent, and usually your personal recommendation will suffice for placing an employee with a client. Once you have a suitable number of applicants, you can start soliciting business clients.

FINANCIAL REWARDS

As discussed in the previous chapter, there are three different categories of workers in this field and they fall into three general income categories. You will bill your client for the services of your employees and then pay them their fees, less 10 to 15 percent which you keep for yourself for your services. To review, the fees and your commissions are as follows: retail store demonstrators— $4 to $8 per hour, at 10 to 15 percent agency fee, amounting to $.40 to $1.20 per hour for you; convention demonstrators—$8 to $16 per hour, at 10 to 15 percent agency fee, amounting to $.80 to

$2.40 per hour for you; modeling—$10 to $300 per hour, at 10 to 15 percent agency fee, amounting to $1 to $45 per hour for you.

Keep in mind that you can assign many employees to numerous assignments at the same time, thus enjoying an accumulative hourly income for yourself.

ACQUIRING CLIENTS

Because each client might have different requirements at different times, we will distinguish and describe the solicitation of clients in each of the three sectors, retail demonstration, convention demonstration, and modeling.

RETAIL DEMONSTRATING

Many manufacturers of consumer products can benefit from retail demonstration of their goods. However, find out and approach the companies that are already doing this. Very often a company will give a newcomer to the field a chance to prove his or her worth. Contact the headquarters of all department stores, discount stores, and supermarket chains in your area to find out which companies are conducting product demonstrations in their stores. In addition, browse through the *Thomas Register of American Manufacturers*, located in your library, and contact the management of the manufacturers of all consumer products that you feel could benefit from in-store demonstrations.

CONVENTION DEMONSTRATING

Call on all the hotels, convention halls, and convention bureaus in your area to find out about upcoming conventions and trade shows. Find out the names and addresses of the organizations sponsoring the conventions and shows. They in turn can furnish you with the names, addresses, and telephone numbers of participating exhibitors. Call or write these firms informing them of your services. List yourself in the yellow pages of the telephone directory under "Convention Services." In addition, convention bureaus in major cities usually prepare a brochure that is sent to all prospective organizations to encourage them to hold their conventions or trade shows in their locality. Be sure to place an announcement of your services in your community's convention brochure.

MODELING

Contact advertising agencies, commercial photographers, catalog production companies, and the advertising departments of manufacturing companies in your area. Send them a brochure featuring the pictures and statistics of the models who represent you. Browse through consumer catalogs and observe the ads in newspapers and magazines and the television commercials in your community. See which firms use models to highlight their products. Contact these firms and their advertising agencies advising them of the contributions you can make to their future ad campaigns.

FUTURE GAINS

If you develop a well-run agency with numerous accounts, it is quite possible to earn well over $100,000 a year in this venture. If you desire, you can also establish multiple operations in numerous cities with each office staffed by a competent manager who would also share in the profits he or she creates.

12

THE ENTERTAINMENT FIELD

PERSONAL MANAGER

WHY

Entertainers specialize mainly in developing and performing their talent. They require personal managers to put together and coordinate the many facets of their careers. The personal manager possessing ingenuity can put together an artist's career, launch it, and advise and direct it to success. He or she can take a talented truck driver or department store clerk and turn him or her into a star. The personal manager will usually obtain the booking agent (or artist's manager, discussed in the next section), a business manager for handling financial affairs, a lawyer for contract writing, people to assist in setting up for a performance, and other personnel necessary to the functioning of a person or group on the rise. In essence, the personal manager is responsible for the total professional needs of the artist. He or she arranges publicity and gets recording companies, night club owners, and concert promoters to see and evaluate their client. However, the personal manager never directly procures work for the artist. That task is left exclusively to the booking agent.

GETTING STARTED

As with the artist's manager, an intuitive feeling for the entertainment industry is probably the prime prerequisite for success in this field. The entertainers already at the top are not likely to solicit your services. So, as with so many other endeavors, you must be able to recognize the beginners who possess talent and learn how to market them. They need you and you need them. Frequent the same establishments as the artist's managers do— nightclubs, discotheques, cocktail lounges, amateur contests, etc.

FINANCIAL REWARDS

The personal manager usually receives 10 percent of the entertainer's professional income for his or her services. You can see how a fortune can be made by a personal manager who has the knack of organizing and promoting people.

While it is typical for booking agents to have a large roster of clients as any employment agency would, the personal manager has a limited number of clients. Quite often, due to his or her extensive responsibilities, a personal manager will deal with just one client. Nevertheless, there is still a considerable amount of money to be earned, as you will receive 10 percent of the artist's total professional income: live engagements, television appearances, records, product endorsements, etc.

ACQUIRING CLIENTS

The methods of acquiring clients for yourself have been discussed under "Getting Started." This section is dedicated to acquiring "work" for your clients. This is best accomplished by retaining the services of a good booking agent. As mentioned, the areas frequented by booking agents are the best places to locate and establish relationships with them. Obviously, it is not always possible to get the top agents to observe your artist or group when they are performing. Therefore, invest a few hundred dollars to make some "demo" tapes of your client's talents. Then you can call on established agents and have them listen to a few minutes of your tape. (This is not to infer that the beginning agent with desire and drive cannot also do a satisfactory job for you.) After a good agent is contracted, work with him or her in creating publicity for your client. It eventually results in working engagements and money for everyone. You can then go on and acquire a good business manager, attorney, and other important personnel for your client.

FUTURE GAINS

As soon as you develop a successful artist or group, your reputation and financial situation in the entertainment field will be pretty well established. With concert and television appearances, record albums, and product endorsements, an entertainer's income can reach well over $1,000,000 a year, and concurrently, your income well over $100,000 annually. And don't worry about your client's fading in popularity; if it happens—and it sometimes does—your reputation and expertise can always attract another good artist or group.

ARTIST'S MANAGER OR BOOKING AGENT

WHY

Each year a number of unknown musical groups and individual musical artists take their place in the world's spotlight of fame and fortune. Although it may sometimes seem like it, the rise to stardom is not achieved overnight. It takes insight, supervision, and direction from the "artist's manager" to recognize the potential talent in a beginning group and then direct their progress through the solicitation of a long series of engagements. The artist's manager is primarily an employment agent specializing in entertainment employment. He or she might represent one or several groups or individuals. Entertainers perform; the artist's manager sees that they get work. From the first job in a smoky nightclub to the million dollar concert tours, television appearances, and record albums, the artist's manager sees to it that his or her clients make it to the top, and once there, stay there. Because of their importance to the careers of entertainers, many artist's managers, also known as "agents" or "booking agents," have made fortunes in this type of work.

GETTING STARTED

Artist's managers or agents come from all backgrounds. Some have college degrees, others learn their craft by starting out in the mailroom of a recording company. Many cover nightclubs, discotheques, college campuses, cocktail lounges, and other arenas where struggling entertainers might be performing. The prime prerequisite for this type of work is to be "street smart." You must possess a "feel" for what will sell and know how to communicate with both the entertainers and the people that hire them. One place to start in this business is to announce your services as an artist's manager in the trade magazines that cater to the recording industry. *Cashbox* is one of the prime journals in this field. The names of others can be obtained by consulting *Standard Rate and Data* and *Ulrich's International Periodicals Directory,* both available in most libraries.

In the past, New York City, Nashville and Memphis, Tennessee, and Los Angeles, California, have been the unofficial headquarters for the entertainment industry. However, things are now spreading out. Talent is universal with no locality having a monopoly on it. You can find recording studios in every major city in the country. All communities have nightclubs, discotheques, and cocktail lounges which employ local talent to draw patrons. Many cities and towns have music centers and other facilities suitable for concerts.

Contact all the recording studios in your area. Quite often a young group without any management will use these facilities to record one of their numbers. Talk with the owners of these studios as to their opinion of a group that has possibilities. Obviously, frequent all the nightspots where groups might be temporarily working. Everyone needs better management! And don't forget the colleges; place an announcement of your services in all local college newspapers. The word will soon get around.

After you locate one or several artists or groups with whom you have a mutual feeling of trust, you can begin to do business. It is extremely important, however, to have a beginning group sign an "exclusive contract" with you, ensuring that you are being retained as their agent. This can prevent a lot of problems when they start their climb to the top.

FINANCIAL REWARDS

The standard fee for an agent's services is 10 percent of the artists' fee. It is customary for an artist or group to receive at least $100 for an evening's work. After the artist or group develops a reputation, the fee can climb to at least $200 and more a night. This represents anywhere from $10 to $20 or more an evening for you as the agent. If your client is scheduled for three nights a week on a continuing basis in a club, this represents a continuing commission of from $30 to $60 or more a week. As an agent, you can handle several individual artists or groups at the same time, thus acquiring commissions that can accumulate into large sums of money. As some of your artists or groups become popular and start to approach fame, their entertainment fees will rise and, accordingly, so will your agent's commission. It is quite common for a top artist or group to command $1000 to $5000 for a performance: $100 to $500 for the agent. And once an artist or group does become popular, it then becomes easier to command higher fees for them. In addition, when you arrange for the production of record albums, the earnings and your commissions can become phenomenal. It is not uncommon for a top artist or group to earn $1,000,000 and more a year in record albums and concert dates— $100,000 for you.

ACQUIRING CLIENTS

After you sign one or several artists or groups, the hard part then arises—finding them work along an upwardly mobile path. If an artist or group is not presently working, the main thing is to get them their first job regardless of the pay. While they are performing at this job, arrange for as many potential employers representing larger facilities in the area to come and see them as possible. In this manner, if your client pleases these people, you can save a lot of time and legwork in securing future and more lucrative engagements. And don't forget the local disc jockeys— they can be instrumental in making a major recording company aware of your clients. The recording companies are constantly appealing to disc jockeys to play their records. If you can persuade a disc jockey to make a pitch for your clients the next time his record company contact calls, you and your clients may be well-rewarded.

When you are properly capitalized, arrange for your artist or group to make a demonstration (demo) tape recording at a local recording studio. The typical fee charged by a well-equipped studio is $60 an hour, and includes an engineer who can operate the controls and "mix" the recording tracks to produce a professional sounding product. For approximately $400, you can arrange for a studio to make a number of duplicate cassette tapes. Distribute these tapes to recording companies, disc jockeys, concert promoters, and proprietors of nightclubs and other establishments that utilize the services of entertainers to attract patrons.

Arrange for your clients to perform at local charity benefits. At least several times a year, a local television station will host a telethon to raise money for worthy charitable causes. Volunteer your clients' services for such causes; the exposure can be tremendous. If you are consistent in doing everything possible to gain momentum for your clients, they can eventually gain stature in the profession.

Musical artists are not the only performers that can use a hand in getting engagements. You can expand your search for clients to the ranks of dancers, mimes, and comedians, all eager for that lucky break. Let them concentrate on their performance; you concentrate on launching their careers.

FUTURE GAINS

The most obvious gain in this field is to represent one or several prominent artists or groups. Once a client of yours attains some national recognition, it will be easier to attract and sell your other clients to the public. With one or several of your clients consistently in the limelight, it is not unrealistic to command an income of over $500,000 annually in fees for yourself from their television appearances, concert tours, record albums, etc. Eventually you could even start your own recording company. In this capacity, you would utilize the services of a recording studio to produce records and tapes for your clients and even other artists or groups for consumer distribution. The general procedure is as follows: a master tape is made at the studio; a record manufacturing company is subcontracted to manufacture records and tapes from the "master"; the recording is promoted via newspaper ads, disc jockeys, and personal appearances of the recording artist or group; the records and tapes are sold to wholesale distributors and rack jobbers for resale to the public. *This is how fortunes are made!*

CONCERT PROMOTER

WHY

Everyone likes good entertainment. In addition to the entertainment provided in nightclubs, discotheques, and similar facilities, there is the "concert" type of entertainment where hundreds and even thousands of people congregate to hear one or several entertainers or groups. There is nothing as exhilarating as a live band elevating the mood of a large crowd. Furthermore, it is quite common for music fans to pay $10 and more for an admission ticket. This bringing together of entertainers and listeners is performed by the "concert promoter."

GETTING STARTED

One of the prime prerequisites of this field is to know what the listening audience will pay to see and hear. Obviously, a contemporary big-name group will always draw a large crowd. However, in the beginning you may not have the experience or reputation to negotiate with and arrange a concert with the "big-timers." Top artists can be very temperamental, selfish, and hard to do business with. There is much paperwork and many legal matters to be dealt with, with just one big-name rock concert. Quite often, if a contract is not worded just right, a performer or group does not even have to show up for the performance, leaving the audience and promoter stranded. In due time, however, you can develop the expertise and know-how required in performing such tasks. In the meantime, start out small, start with entertainers that *need you!* People do not always have to have big-name performers to be entertained. There are many highly talented unknown groups waiting for their break, gladly willing to perform at a concert for a reasonable fee. These groups can be contacted through their booking agents or personal managers. You can rent an auditorium or hall with a 500-person capacity for approximately $500 or less. Tickets can sell for a conservative and affordable $10 each—not much more expensive than an everyday movie.

PROMOTING THE CONCERT

Your concert can be advertised inexpensively in school and local newspapers and via posters on college campuses. Many retail store owners will graciously let you place a poster announcing your event in their windows. Free publicity can be obtained through the news departments of television and radio stations and in the "Where to Go" sections of newspapers and magazines. And don't forget the talk shows. Today, almost every radio and television station has at least one or two talk shows airing daily. They have to get interesting guests and information every day. News of your concert and the people who will be performing is important and newsworthy information. If your performing group lives close to the local radio and television stations in the vicinity of the scheduled concert, arrange for the members to be interviewed on as many talk shows as possible. Everyone likes to hear entertainers being interviewed. They also are induced to later attend their performances. And if it is not feasible for a performing group to personally appear on a talk show before a concert, it is often possible for them to be interviewed by a radio talk show host or disc jockey via telephone.

FINANCIAL REWARDS

It is quite possible to acquire the services of a good beginning group for $500. After all, they can not only use the money, but also the exposure. If you sell 500 tickets at $10 each, this gives you a gross amount of $5000. If you deduct $500 for rental of the auditorium, $500 for advertising expenses, and pay the group $500, this leaves you with a profit of $3500. You may want to utilize two alternating groups for just one concert. This would cut your profit down by another $500, leaving you with $3000; however, it would further ensure the success of your venture.

Remember too! You don't always have to work in one locality. All communities have a school auditorium, outdoor theater, or movie theater which can be rented for a concert performance. After you develop your expertise and reputation as a concert promoter, you could quite possibly book two concerts a month, utilizing the many communities at your disposal. At $3000 profit for just a small concert, this could amount easily to over $70,000 a year in income for you.

ACQUIRING CLIENTS

As mentioned, you can get in touch with a group via their personal manager or booking agent. If you hear a record of a group whom you would like to arrange a concert with, the recording company can usually put you in touch with the proper people for negotiation.

FUTURE GAINS

As your finances increase from the success of your smaller concerts, you can retain the services of a good entertainment attorney to negotiate the intricate contracts required in working with nationally and internationally known artists. For these groups, you will need a large amphitheater that can hold thousands of people. Don't worry! They're around. As with smaller groups, contact the personal manager or booking agent for these famous groups. As big as they are, they want to stay that way. They will most likely talk to you. After all, in addition to making extra money for one night's work, live concert performances can help them sell more record albums. With a famous group, you will probably have to promise them a percentage of the receipts. That's okay, too. A good group can command a $20-per-person admission fee. If 3000 people pay $20 a piece to see a famous group, this amounts to $60,000. If you give half of this to the performing group, this leaves you with $30,000. A good amphitheater can be rented for approximately $5000 an evening and another $5000 should be allotted for advertising publicity. This leaves you with $20,000 profit for one concert. It is not uncommon for a good concert promoter to earn over $500,000 a year arranging numerous concerts for numerous groups.

THEATRICAL PRODUCER

WHY

Every once in a while people like to break away from movies, television, and video cassettes and enjoy "live" entertainment—performed right in front of them. Many people who have never seen or been interested in live theater will become interested in it once properly introduced to it at reasonable admission fees. If you are a drama enthusiast and either have or can obtain some experience in the theater arts—acting, staging, and costuming—you can participate in putting on stage productions for your community.

GETTING STARTED

You will have no trouble obtaining performers. Every community has it's acting classes. They may be part of a program conducted by a college, high school, civic, social, or private group. Contact the students of these programs advising them of your goals. They will be only too happy to participate. The next thing is to decide upon a play. Your best bet at the beginning is to keep your selection to plays with few characters and simple sets. The library is full of books with plays from all interest categories, including the complete dialogue and stage movements. Or, there may be someone in your community who has written an original play worthy of production. Then a good director will be required. You may be qualified to do this yourself. However, you may prefer to devote your time to coordinating all the facets of a theatrical production and concentrate primarily on advertising and promoting the play to the public. In this case, it would be advisable to find an individual seriously interested in directing.

After the play, the performers, and the director are selected, the next thing is to find a facility in which to stage your production. In most communities there are many sources for this: a high school or college auditorium; a movie theater (which might be rented for several evenings, especially if movie attendance has been off). Large hotels sometimes have auditorium facilities for business conventions. Many communities have abandoned theaters which might be suitable for production. The facilities are there, it just takes a little searching.

FINANCIAL REWARDS

An auditorium with a 500-person capacity can be rented for approximately $500 for a 24-hour period. An admission fee of $6 per person is quite reasonable. In fact, it is little more than the price of movie. If you fill the theater to capacity, this means $3000 in revenue for an evening. And if your play becomes popular, an afternoon matinee can mean another $3000 in revenue—$6000 for the day.

Obviously there will be promotion and production expenses. Inexpensive promotion methods will be discussed under "Acquiring Clients." With good acting and directing, it is not necessary to have expensive sets. Your actors have to be paid. You can arrange to pay them a percentage of the gross receipts. Beginning actors will generally require little financial remuneration. They perform primarily for the enjoyment and the chance to be discovered. If your play requires only four or five actors, acting expenses can be kept to a minimum and your profits at a maximum.

ACQUIRING CLIENTS

For a play to be a success, it must have patrons. Therefore, we will refer to the attracting of an audience as "Acquiring Clients."

When promoting a production, in addition to advertising in local newspapers and magazines, put up posters in the vicinity of the theater. Stores and restaurants in the area will usually allow you to place well-designed posters on their premises, free of charge. In addition, contact civic, social, religious, and fraternal organizations. They are always looking for ways to raise money. Offer to give them a group rate for viewing your performance. They can charge their members the full admission price and put the difference in their treasury to support their worthwhile activities.

Remember the free publicity available from local newspapers, magazines, and radio and television stations. They are always looking to do feature stories on what is going on around town. In addition, arrange to have your performance reviewed by newspaper and television reviewers.

Restaurant and café owners are always looking for new and innovative ways to increase business. Your production might be adaptable for presentation in a roomy and suitably arranged dinner restaurant or café. Just as they have dinner shows in Las Vegas and other entertainment capitals of the world, this same principle can be implemented in smaller but comparable situations. Usually an entertainment admission price is charged, with one dinner followed by a show and then a subsequent dinner-show.

A situation which cannot only be profitable but can also allow you the satisfaction of performing a humanitarian service, is to offer the management of senior citizen and convalescent homes the opportunity to obtain your services in bringing your production to their facilities for presentation to their guests. Many of these facilities are very profitable business operations. Their owners can afford to pay your company a reasonable fee to perform. In addition, it is good public relations on their part when striving to keep present guests and attract new ones. Contact Veterans Administration hospitals; they are usually budgeted to present entertainment programs for their patients.

FUTURE GAINS

If your show is a hit, it can be taken to other communities. The admission price can be raised slightly to cover increased costs and add to your profit. Contact the managers of summer theaters to either obtain their facilities for a share of the profits or have them secure your entire show for a fee.

TELEVISION RECORD PACKAGING

WHY

The record business is a multibillion-dollar-a-year industry offering rags-to-riches possibilities not only for the songwriters, recording artists, producers, and managers, but also for people in ancillary fields such as "record packaging." The term "packaging" does not mean putting the record in the actual package or container, but is an industry term referring to the putting together of an album consisting of a series of already released songs, quite often by different artists or recording companies. These albums usually have a central theme such as romantic, country and western, rock and roll, songs from popular movies or plays, or "oldies-but-goodies." The primary purchasers of these albums are people over 30 who do not care for all of the currently popular music, but often prefer the music from 10, 20, or more years ago—songs they can relate to, melodies that bring them back to a beautiful part of their lives. These songs are often not available in record stores, or if they are carried by a store, they are usually hidden amid a vast inventory of other records and hard to find.

There are many people over 30 and there are thousands of songs from the past these people relate to, enjoy, and are willing to purchase if approached properly. This has given rise to a dynamic and lucrative arm of the recording industry—"television record packaging." Songs from a particular era with a central theme can be put into one album and sold via television mail order advertising. It is a touch-and-go business, but if you put the right combination together and excite the interest of the viewing public, you can have a 100,000 or more seller at your fingertips.

GETTING STARTED

The prime prerequisite for this type of endeavor is a "feel" for the right combination of tunes that will interest a specialized but large segment of the public. Putting a good record album together is like baking a good cake—it's the combination of ingredients that makes it a winner. There is no college training program that can prepare you to do this. If you feel you have your hand on the pulse of the public, you can engage in this business on a part-time basis aside from your regular job or profession. If you are between jobs and do not have a regular vocation, this business can be learned from the ground up. You can start in the recording business as a mail clerk, warehouse person, typist, bookkeeping clerk, or some other position that allows you entry into the field and the chance to observe and get a "feel" for what is going on. You can learn a lot of "rules of the road" in this manner. A lot of wealthy record tycoons started this way.

The most important step is thinking up a group of songs that, when sold as a "package," will have great marketability. You can put from 10 to 12 songs on one record. A typical television package will consist of one or two records. Remember! The entire package must have a central theme. You might package 10 to 20 of Elvis Presley's past hits, but you wouldn't combine Elvis Presley with Louis Armstrong. Examples of themes are "24 Wonderful Hits of the 50's," "20 Wonderful Cowboy Hits," "The World's Most Beautiful Love Songs," etc. Write your ideas down on paper, then ask yourself "Do I have a hit here?" Only you can decide.

After you put your ideas on paper, you then have to find out what record company owns each song you want to produce and which publisher has the copyright on the song. Your local record shop can assist you in determining the recording company for each song. Then you contact their business affairs manager and inform him or her of the song or songs you would like to use. Propose to pay a certain amount of money per song. They will either say yes or no. A typical fee for a song is anywhere from 2¢ to 10¢ per album sold, depending on it's popularity. If the recording company says yes to you, you then must go to the publisher (copyright holder) of that song for permission to use it. They cannot refuse you permission to use the song if you pay them the statutory royalty rate of 2¹/₂¢ per song per album sold.

Once you make a deal with each recording company and publisher representing all the songs you want to use, you are in business. You then pick up the master recordings from the record companies and take them to the company who will undertake the actual manufacture of the records. They will make pressing plates from the masters and then press the actual records for you. There are companies that specialize in this type of work exclusively. Because of the popularity of cassette tapes, you should also go to companies that specialize in tape reproduction. The recording companies that supply you with the masters can help recommend good manufacturers to you for both records and tape.

As will be illustrated under "Financial Rewards," you must sell approximately 10,000 albums to break even. This is the quantity that should be originally ordered and produced. If you have a hit and the orders keep coming in, it is easy to have more records and tapes run off the assembly line.

The cost of television advertising will vary from station to station depending on how many viewers are reached. Before you spend money on the more expensive stations in the larger cities in the country, you can test-advertise your product in smaller cities that represent a good cross section of the American public and also have lower television advertising rates: for example, Columbus, Ohio, and Memphis, Tennessee. If the results are poor, take your losses and forget the whole thing. If the response is good, you can then expand into an aggressive television campaign in large cities all over the United States and shoot for 100,000 to 500,000 in sales. As orders come in, you can use the revenues to finance additional advertising.

FINANCIAL REWARDS

First of all, you need $30,000 to finance a 10,000 record and tape production and a test-advertising campaign. Do not let this amount of money scare you if you don't have it. There are ways to

200

have other people finance the deal with you sharing in the profits. This will be discussed under "Acquiring Clients."

The following is an example of a typical successful record package: The typical selling price for a 24-song, 2-record album is $8.95.

> Expenses: (Typical)
> Recording Company—5¢ per song
> Publisher—3¢ per song
> TOTAL permissions cost for a 24-song album—$1.92 per album
>
> Manufacturing price for each record album—50¢
> Jacket for each album—20¢
> American Federation of Musicians trust fund—5¢ per album
> Art work amortizes to 2¢ per album
> Mailing expense—70¢ per album
> Advertising expense amortizes to $3.00 per album
> TOTAL COST—$6.39 per record album

Net profit computes to $2.56 per record album. If you have a hit of 100,000 sales this computes to approximately $250,000 profit. Obviously, more sales means more money and less sales means less money.

ACQUIRING CLIENTS

Because the clients are the customers who purchase your albums, and we have already discussed how to attract them (via television advertising), we will dedicate this section to the ways of attracting financial backers to eliminate any risk on your part. Of course, the profits will then have to be shared, but on a successful package, there will be plenty of money left over for you.

Approach accountants with your package. Many have clients who are in such a high tax bracket that if they were to lose $30,000, tax-wise it might amount to only $6000 out of their pocket. And if the album were successful they could take their large profits and invest them in real estate or other popular tax shelters. There are also many wealthy people in the record business who might share your entrepreneur's enthusiasm for the proposed album and be willing to finance the project.

Once a backer is found, it is customary to share the profits 50-50 with them. Thus, on our proposed 100,000 unit sales representing $250,000 profit, your share would be $125,000.

In addition, there are marketing companies specializing in television mail order sales whether it be record albums or can openers. Approach these television marketing companies with your proposed package. If they like your idea, they will retain you to contact the recording companies, publishers, and manufacturers to put the deal together. They will then take complete responsibility for the television marketing. In this type of situation, it is typical for you, the original entrepreneur, to receive 20 percent of the profits—$50,000 of our $250,000 profit illustration—but you have much less work.

FUTURE GAINS

Once you put a successful package together, whether on your own or through financial backers, you can use your profits to produce more albums. You can even hire other talented people to think up marketable packages. As new songs are written, there will constantly be an increasing backlog of past songs that an increasing older population will desire to hear again. It's the old story—find a need, then fill it.

FILM SHOWING BUSINESS

WHY

Almost every week in every community in the country, social, business, fraternal, religious, civic, and youth organizations hold meetings. One problem most of them have is getting a large turnout of members to attend. A lot of people are just not turned on by the reading of the minutes of the last meeting or listening to arguments on who should head different committees or projects. One way to attract a large turnout of members is to feature some type of entertainment as a major event of the meeting. Frequently, guest speakers are used. This presents some problems, however. Very often a speaker is hard to get; he or she may be expensive, boring, or both. There is an ideal solution to this, one from which you can profit. In lieu of guest speakers, informative and entertaining movies can be shown. They can be obtained free of charge and shown on a large colorful screen with a 16mm projector.

GETTING STARTED

There are movies available on almost every subject imaginable. Many athletic organizations, industrial associations, and manufacturing companies produce public relations films regarding their functions, to promote their image and activities. These organizations are only too happy to allow various groups the privilege of seeing them. Most public libraries, in addition to books, provide films covering a wide range of interesting topics on business, careers, sports, youth activities, do-it-youself projects, wildlife, etc, which can be obtained free of charge. There is one catch, however: most organizations providing free films for viewing do not want the viewers to be charged an admission fee for seeing them. Therefore, you must be careful not to charge for the films per se; but you can charge for the service you are rendering: the use of your projector, your selecting and procuring the film, your screening the film to make sure it contains nothing offensive and is appropriate for the group and your traveling to the meeting to show the film.

SOURCES OF FILMS

As mentioned, the public library can be the easiest and most practical source for films. Contact major manufacturing companies to see if they have any public relations films for public viewing. The names and addresses of these firms can be found in the *Thomas Register of American Manufacturers* in your local library. While at the library, browse through the *Encyclopedia of Associations* to find the names and addresses of various trade and industrial associations. Many of these organizations will have films available for you. When writing these firms, address your letters to the attention of their public relations department.

Almost everyone likes sports! People from all walks of life and every age group have a profound interest in athletic events. Here is where you can really win! Many major athletic associations provide free films covering the highlights of the many famous contests in their sport. The following are the names and addresses of the major athletic associations representing several popular sports:

American Baseball League
280 Park Avenue
New York, New York 10017

National Baseball League
20 Montgomery Street
San Francisco, California 94104

National Hockey League
920 Sun Life Building
Montreal P.Q. Canada H3B 2W2

National Basketball Association
2 Pennsylvania Plaza
Suite 2010
New York, New York 10001

National Football League
410 Park Avenue
New York, New York 10022.

FINANCIAL REWARDS

A reasonable fee to charge for a half-hour film is $50 and for a one-hour film, $80. In place of a one-hour film, you can always show two half-hour films in sequence for the same $80. The cost of a good 16mm sound projector is $800 new or $600 used. In the beginning of your venture, you can rent a projector for approximately $10 for a 24-hour period. Look in the yellow pages under "Movie Projectors." Eventually, you can purchase your own projector with your earned profits.

ACQUIRING CLIENTS

Practically every club and religious, civic, fraternal, youth, and athletic organization in your community is a potential client of yours. As a starter, look in the yellow pages under "Clubs," "Organizations," "Fraternal Groups," "Churches," "Synagogues," etc. Contact every listing under these headings. Call on every YMCA, YWCA, Jewish Community Center (JCC), and similar organizations. The editorial office of many newspapers can provide you with a list of various organizations in the community. In fact, just reading the social section of local newspapers can furnish you with plenty of sources to solicit.

When contacting these organizations and groups, be clear. Do not tell them that you have a lot of films in which they might be interested. Instead, pick out certain films you feel their membership would be interested in and mention these specific films to them. Sometimes when you give people too much of a choice, they become confused and do not buy or subscribe to anything. When you allow them to focus on just one or two items, they are more apt to respond. These clubs and organizations meet periodically, providing you with the opportunity for repeat business. After you finish a filming, talk to the people in charge about other films for future meetings. You can offer to locate films for them on request.

Another client source is the business community. Every business organization is in existence for one sole purpose—to sell something. That means they have salespeople. The talents of these salespeople can mean the difference between failure and financial success. The skills and motivation of their salespeople can always be improved upon. Many industrial associations and libraries have films on successful selling techniques either for a particular industry or for general use. Contact industrial associations (listed in the *Encyclopedia of Associations* in your library) about the availability of sales and motivational films. Then notify

companies in the corresponding industry about your availability
to show sales and motivational films to their salespeople.

FUTURE GAINS

This type of business can blossom to the point where you might
even purchase several projectors, hiring other people to perform
the actual projection work for you and concentrating your efforts
primarily on the procuring of films and the solicitation of clients.
For this type of arrangement, a fair financial compensation would
be to split the fees 50-50. For a $50 charge for a half-hour film, this
leaves you and your operator with $25 each. Likewise, a one-hour
performance at $80 allows $40 each for you and your operator. As
you can see, if you schedule ten or more showings per week in
your area or surrounding communities, fees can really add up.

13

INSTRUCTIONAL
SERVICES

INSTRUCTIONAL SERVICES

WHY

People are constantly looking to expand their knowledge and
know-how. Sometimes they want to learn a new skill to embark
upon a new income endeavor. Other times an individual may want
to learn a new hobby or gain new information for self-satisfaction.
Whatever the situation, we live in a dynamic world with millions
of people from all walks of life looking to improve themselves.
This provides numerous opportunities for an educationally
minded, qualified individual to provide instruction. You may
teach some programs yourself or hire other qualified instructors
to teach their specialty.

You might ask: "Why would a potential student of mine not
enter a night school program for instruction?" There are several
reasons. Quite often a school program is not compatible time-wise
with the work and family responsibilities of the intended student.
High school and college night school instructors are not always
creative in organizing and communicating a good program to students. How many times have you been put to sleep by a knowledgeable but dull instructor who is not organized in his or her
presentation? If you can meet the deep-seated needs of your students, there is a chance for you to become very successful in this
enterprise. For instance, if your program teaches a gourmet
cooking class, teach the students how to make money in this skill
via a personal catering service. If you teach arts and crafts projects, show people how to market their products. If you teach a
typing or bookkeeping program, show the attendees how they

can profit from starting their own secretarial or bookkeeping service. In other words, if you think and teach in "concepts," your program will stand out and become far more successful than existing programs.

Furthermore, many existing high school and college night school programs are expensive. It is not unusual to pay $85 for a six- to ten-session course. You can charge these same fees, or even less, and offer a lot more.

GETTING STARTED

Think about your experience. Have you become proficient or nearly proficient in any activities other people would enjoy learning from you? If you have a general background or interest in a special activity, you can easily supplement your present knowledge with additional reading on the subject or by indulging in short training programs conducted by college and university extension divisions. You can then use your own ingenuity to expand and improve upon the training to offer superior courses of your own. Remember one important thing: You do not necessarily have to be an expert in a subject or activity to provide competent instruction in it. The most important thing is your organizational and teaching ability. If you can analyze a subject, breaking it down into its basic components, and then present the information in a logical and easy-to-understand manner, you can often provide instruction better than the so-called "experts" in that field can. In fact, you can soon develop a reputation of being an "expert" yourself.

As mentioned, you can hire qualified people to assist you. You may have them teach entire courses that they are proficient in. Eventually, you may just become involved in the organizing of courses, soliciting students and proper instructors. In essence, your role would be that of a "Principal," "Headmaster," or "Executive Head" of an efficient teaching program. Almost any skill or subject that can attract a class of 30 people is suitable for presentation.

Finding facilities for your instructional services should not be hard. Every class does not have to be taught in the same location. Rooms in YMCAs, YWCAs, churches, and commercial halls can be rented very reasonably. Quite often, the rental fees are almost negligible in contrast to your tuition income. Some fields which have proven to be very popular with the general public are:

PHOTOGRAPHY

Find a good photographic instructor and have him or her also show your students how to market their photos to magazines, advertising agencies, greeting card companies, or the general public. See also the chapter on "Child Photography" in this book.

ADVERTISING COPYWRITING

There are many qualified writing instructors around who would like to supplement their income by working for you. Just contact the writing department of a good college, high school, or university. Furthermore, many people want to learn how to write and how to sell their pieces. You don't necessarily have to teach people how to write the "great novel." The instructors can alert students to the numerous opportunities to write advertising copy for advertising agencies or private companies. You may want to conduct a program in advertising copywriting and then instruct your students on how to secure writing assignments and maybe eventually own their own advertising agency. See also the section on "Writing Opportunities" in this book.

ARTS AND CRAFTS

Training in skills such as painting, sculpting, pottery making, needlepoint, jewelry making, metal work, etc., is in great demand. After a course is completed, you can stage a commercial sale of your students' creations to give them a feeling of accomplishment in their efforts. This will also build up further interest in your arts and crafts program. Show your students how they can make substantial amounts of money in such specialties as jewelry design (see the chapter on "Jewelry Manufacturing" in this book).

FASHION DESIGN

New designs keep the apparel industry moving at a dynamic pace. There are four fashion seasons in every year (fall, winter, spring, and summer). Each season and year has its new styles to keep shoppers shopping. This calls for a steady influx of new creations from talented designers. Many a successful designer has launched his or her career through a well-constructed instructional program in fashion design. You can teach this program and show your students how to market their creations. (See also the chapter on "Agenting" in this book.)

ASSERTIVENESS TRAINING

Many people in this world are talented but do not know how to be assertive in their professional, business, and social dealings. Teaching people to be more assertive (forceful, aggressive, confident, self-assured) in their actions has become an important field. Secure the services of a competent psychologist, psychiatrist, social worker, or even successful businessperson to teach this program. Have your instructor show the participants how to use their assertiveness training to advance in their business career or improve their social life.

GOURMET COOKING

Food preparation is looked upon as an art. The preparation of food which is tasty, healthy, economical, and easy is attracting wide support. The high cost of dining out, in addition to an increased interest in personal health has strengthened this interest. Cooking can be taught in the home of someone with suitable kitchen facilities, or such facilities can be rented from an organization housing proper cooking equipment, such as a civic, social, or fraternal group. You can even teach your students to profit from their new expertise through the creation of their own catering service. See also the "Personal Catering" chapter in this book.

TENNIS

Today, everyone is conscious of physical fitness and games which require and produce it. Tennis is now the rage; there are virtually unlimited opportunities for the proper teaching of this sport. Naturally, you will require the use of a tennis court. Due to the popularity of the sport, free time on courts is becoming harder to obtain. It is sometimes possible however, to purchase blocks of time on some tennis courts and then incorporate this expense into your fee. In addition, some private homeowners have tennis courts on their property. Sometimes they are willing to rent their courts out to qualified instructors in return for tennis lessons or a monetary fee.

SELF-DEFENSE

Due to the increase in crime, more people are becoming interested in the art of self-defense. If you have been in the military, you may be proficient in this already. If not, it should not be hard to find someone who is, who would be willing to act as one of your instructors. For this type of instruction, it is advisable to take out a liability insurance policy. Contact your local insurance agent for information or look in the telephone yellow pages under "Insurance, Liability."

EXERCISE CLASSES

Today, there is an increased awareness of good health and what the average individual can do to promote and ensure his or her physical well-being. This provides tremendous opportunities to conduct exercise classes. It is advisable to inform the potential participants of what type of activities will be taking place and have them sign a waiver relieving you of any responsibility if their physical condition is not compatible with your program. Usually a visit to their doctor will inform them if they are in suitable condition to participate in a vigorous exercise program. Your program can be supplemented with a list of doctor-approved diets to assist in any necessary weight loss. Special lectures designed to motivate people to eat properly can also be provided. Fortunes have been made by people involved in this type of physical fitness program.

TUTORING HIGH SCHOOL STUDENTS

There are many high school students having difficulty with subjects important to their graduation and acceptance into college. Quite often, their difficulty is not due to a lack of native intelligence or academic ability, but rather to confusion and poor communication between teacher and student. Today's teaching system does not always allow a small teacher-to-student ratio. Quite often, a potentially good student drowns academically in a sea of students taught by an impersonal instructor.

If you or any of your instructors has a thorough background in languages, higher math, science, history or other subjects taught in high schools, and possess the ability to analyze a subject, breaking it down into its components or themes, and then present the information in an organized and interesting manner, you can be of great help to many distressed high school students. You can organize groups of students having trouble with the same subject.

When advertising your tutoring services, go to all the high schools in an area informing the principals and teachers. In many cases they will welcome your services, and recommend you to students with temporary learning difficulties. Many schools are underfinanced and understaffed and therefore are not equipped to handle all learning problems.

Concerned parents will welcome your skills. The money spent to aid their children will be well worth it to them. Temporary learning difficulties can seem gigantic problems to young people. Your assistance may be the answer to their overcoming such problems and ensuring academic and emotional growth. Advertise your services in all high school newspapers.

SUMMARY

Almost any topic can be developed into an interesting classroom program appealing to people from all social and economic levels. Go through a college "extension division" catalog and observe the courses being taught. See if you can teach the same courses in a more interesting and productive manner. You may find out that you can actually charge less money per course, pay your instructors more money than the college, and still end up with more profit for yourself. As a further guide to developing instructional programs, many of the endeavors described in this book can be learned and developed into areas of a large private teaching program.

FINANCIAL REWARDS

As a general guideline, you should structure your fees so that you receive at least $50 an hour for your services. A typical course will involve ten three-hour sessions for a total of 30 instructional hours. At $50 per hour, you will want to receive $1500 in fees from your students. If your average class contains a typical 30 students, a fee of $50 (quite reasonable) would be charged each student ($1500 ÷ 30 = $50). If a course requires less than 30 instructional hours or there are fewer or more than 30 students in a class, you can adjust the admission fees accordingly to maintain your $50-an-hour professional fee.

When you utilize the services of other instructors to teach your programs (and most likely you will), you can divide the student admission fees 50-50 with your instructors. This amounts to $25 each per student for both you and the instructor. If desired, you can maintain your services at $60 an hour and use the extra $10 per hour for advertising promotion and rental charges for your teaching facilities. In this case, it would be permissible and only fair to still pay your instructors at the rate of $25 per hour. After all, the extra $10 per hour is going to promote your program which will mean extra assignments for them.

ACQUIRING CLIENTS

There are a variety of ways to announce and promote your instructional services. We have already discussed the methods of promoting a high-school tutoring service. Professional advertising in local newspapers and magazines is a good starting point. Additionally, most newspapers, magazines, radio, and television stations have "Community Billboard" segments informing their subscribers of various events taking place in the community. Community bulletin boards in supermarkets and Laudromats can also attract patrons.

Quite often, local restaurants, coffee shops, and retail stores will allow you to place attractive posters announcing your programs in their facilities.

Be sure to place ads in the newsletters of various civic, youth, social, religious, trade, and fraternal organizations. In fact, it might be advisable to offer members of certain organizations special group rates, with the savings being turned over to their treasury to be spent on worthwhile projects.

FUTURE GAINS

Eventually, you can have your own course catalog made up and mailed to all the residents of a particular community. If you offer enough courses, and receive $25 per hour per course, you can develop quite an income for yourself. As an example, if 30 courses are taught at 30 hours per course, that comes to 900 instructional hours. At $25 profit per hour for you, this amounts to $22,500. You can keep adding courses to your catalog and expand your program to other communities. As you can readily see, even teaching can be a business. It can also be a good one, with you, your instructors, and your students all profiting.

14

TRAVEL
SERVICES

CAMPER AND
RECREATIONAL
VEHICLE GUIDE

WHY

The pioneering spirit of the early days of our country was exemplified by the wagon train moving west. The romance of the early wagon train is now captured by the recreational vehicle. These vehicles now allow people to explore new places in the United States and bordering countries with the constant provision of lodging, bathing, and food preparation facilities. Although gasoline is expensive, the number of people that can travel in a camper, coupled with the fact that the expense of lodging is eliminated, make recreational vehicle travel an economical way of vacationing.

Just as the wagon trains had "wagon masters" to lead people through strange territories, there is now a need for competent people to lead recreational vehicles and camper caravans to new and unfamiliar places. This is especially important for travel to foreign countries such as Mexico and Canada. The younger camping families might not at first appreciate the caravan and leader concept. However, mature or retired couples who want the adventure of the open road but desire the security of supervision and guidance, quite often wish to be part of a caravan with a leader.

GETTING STARTED

To qualify for this type of endeavor, one should own a camper or other form of recreational vehicle and have some experience in camping. It will not be necessary to have actually visited all of the places you will guide people to. You should, however, read up on the locations and places to be traveled to and visited, and be prepared to handle situations and problems as they might arise. Organizational and supervisory abilities are paramount, in addition to liking and getting along well with people. Some mechanical knowledge is an asset to aid caravan members who might experience minor problems with their vehicles. Also essential is basic knowledge of first aid, and of the locations of hospitals in the regions you choose to visit.

To aid you in becoming familiar with places to travel to and visit, here is a partial list of books that can provide you with general background information:

Fodor's Travel Books
By Eugene Fodor
published by David McKay Co.

The Motor Camper's Guide to Mexico
By Richard Carroll
published by Chronicle Books

The Rand McNally Road Atlas
published by Rand McNally
Rand McNally's Campground & Trailor Park Guide
published by Rand McNally

Roughing It 2
By Dian Thomas
published by Warner Books

Woodall's Campground Directories
published by Woodall Publishing Co.
and distributed by Grosset & Dunlap

*Trailer Life's 1981 R.V. Campground and Services Directory
for the United States, Canada, and Mexico*
(1156 pages of useful information)
published by Trailer Life Publishing Co., Inc.
23945 Craftsman Road
Calabasas, California 91302.

The above books, and many more, are available in most general bookstores. In addition, the government publishes a booklet providing complete information on camping sites in the national park system. For a copy write to:

Superintendent of Documents
U.S. Government Printing Office
Washington, D.C. 20402

Ask for *Camping in the National Park System,* Stock No. 024-005-00668-1. The cost of this booklet is approximately $1.75.

To find out the locations of hospitals near your selected campgrounds and along your routes, contact that area's Chamber of Commerce and the State Highway Patrol.

When planning a trip, it is important to make everything as convenient as possible for your caravan members. Make up a list of desirable clothing and equipment to bring. Make sure your own vehicle is equipped with a complete first aid kit. It would also be a good idea to take a basic first aid and CPR course with your local chapter of the Red Cross or fire department.

Make reservations far in advance with each campground you plan to visit. The previously mentioned books will tell you who to contact. Once at a campsite, plan side trips to nearby scenic areas, towns, and historical landmarks to enhance the pleasure of your clients. The Automobile Club of America can offer you further assistance in this area. To ensure everyone's staying together, suggest that everyone have a citizens' band (CB) radio. This also makes the trip more fun and adventurous. Most camper families already have them. As a last precaution, arrange rendezvous points in case some members of the group get lost. This venture can not only be profitable, but can also be exciting for both you and your guests.

FINANCIAL REWARDS

A typical caravan should include from 10 to 20 vehicles. A charge of $25 a day per vehicle is reasonable, allowing you a gross profit of from $250 to $500 a day. It is customary to pay a guide approximately $100 a day and keep the rest for yourself.

ACQUIRING CLIENTS

Take the bull by the horns. People who own RVs are sometimes confused and lack the initiative to start an adventure. Plan predetermined trip and then advertise the availability of it. Recreational vehicle magazines are an excellent place to start. Your local library can provide you with a list of these publications. Visit recreational vehicle supply stores and place bulletins in their shopping areas advertising your trips. The management will usually welcome the opportunity to inform their customers of your services for it generally means more supply sales for them. Also, contact the dealers of new, used, and rental vehicles. Knowledge of the existence of your service can inspire more people to purchase or rent recreational vehicles.

Contact and advertise in the newsletters of social, civic, religious, and fraternal organizations. Offer to present short speeches concerning your activities to these groups. And most important, advertise in senior citizens' magazines and visit their meetings. These people have been planning and saving all their lives for such ventures. Write to the owners of recreational vehicles; the State Department of Motor Vehicles can usually provide you with such a list.

FUTURE GAINS

As one individual, you can only guide one trip at a time. However, you may receive more applicants that you can personally handle. In this case, you can solicit the services of other experienced campers who would welcome the adventure and extra income of acting as one of your guides or "wagon masters." As mentioned, a fair financial arrangement would be to pay your "wagon masters" $100 a day.

TOURING SERVICE

WHY

People of all age groups, incomes, and social levels like to take short trips for recreational diversion on weekends or in other leisure time. Many people, however, develop a certain amount of apathy when it comes right down to formulating and carrying out plans. Additionally, the high price of gasoline and of automobiles and their upkeep stops many people from taking recreational trips. Depending on the car, it takes anywhere from 7.5¢ to 15¢ worth of gas per mile plus an extra 5¢ for wear and tear to operate a motor vehicle. A bus can transport a person a lot cheaper and in greater comfort. You could fill a tremendous need by renting commercial buses for the day and arranging numerous tours for all types of people and interest groups.

216

GETTING STARTED

Your prime prerequisite for this type of business is the ability to obtain the use of a commercial bus. This is easy. Just check the yellow pages of your telephone directory under the heading "Buses, Commercial Charter." You will most likely find many charter bus services only too happy to accommodate you. Rates vary. However, in general, you can obtain a modern air-conditioned bus with a 40-person capacity, equipped with restroom and driver, to travel 150 miles round trip for approximately $400, averaging out to about 3¢ a mile per person. Included in this fee is accident insurance.

Where do you travel to? You might take a group of families to an amusement park, zoo, or historic center. A group of senior citizens might desire to see a stage show locally or in a nearby community. If you obtain a list of all the interesting places to visit in your area within a day's travel round trip, your imagination will allow you to match a variety of groups to different travel opportunities. Obtaining ideas for places to travel is relatively easy. Write your state or the adjoining state chamber of commerce to obtain lists and brochures of interesting places to visit. Contact your local office of the American Automobile Association. The organization publishes booklets on every interesting place to visit throughout the country. And don't forget your local bookstore. You will most likely find several books depicting interesting places to visit in your vicinity. You will be surprised at all the travel opportunities in your area. Most people do not take the time to do this on their own. And if you do, it can become quite profitable and enjoyable to arrange travel opportunities for people.

FINANCIAL REWARDS

As mentioned, a bus with a 40-person capacity, complete with driver, costs approximately $400 for a 150 mile round-trip excursion. Shorter trips will be less. Longer trips will obviously require more money, but they cannot be completed in one day. In the beginning, it would be advisable to limit your trips to one-day excursions. As you increase your expertise in this field, you can then experiment with longer trips. Using a 150 mile round-trip excursion (300 miles) as an index, this comes to $10 per person. Admission, dinner, and other fees at the focal point of a journey must also be calculated. However, these are fees that people must pay even if they travel by themselves. In some cases, you might be able to arrange for a discount rate for your group. To allow a reasonable profit for yourself, add an extra $150 to all expenses. This computes to $3.75 per person. This is quite a bargain for each traveler and allows a sizeable amount of profit for yourself.

ACQUIRING CLIENTS

Your potential list is extensive. Contact every social, civic, religious, fraternal, and senior citizens' group in your community. Make up inexpensive fliers for each proposed tour. Ask these civic groups for their mailing lists and do a bulk mailing to members. And don't forget about neighborhoods. After a hard week's work, many parents in a community would welcome the opportunity to load themselves and their children on a comfortable bus for a no-hassle drive to an interesting location. As mentioned, single people are always looking for new opportunities to meet each other. Arrange for special "singles" trips to nearby resorts, restaurants, or scenic areas for a day of enjoyment and socializing. Pin up your flyer on local bulletin boards.

Many divorced people do not know how to entertain their children on their days of custody. What a perfect opportunity for you to serve their needs with an interesting trip that can relieve a parent of the pressures of planning absorbing activities. You can take care of this task allowing them to concentrate on their relationships with their children.

Sometimes, an opportunity is in your own backyard. A group of sports enthusiasts might desire a trouble-free ride to an athletic stadium. A club may want to go for a picnic in the country. As your business starts to develop, you will come up with more ideas and clients.

FUTURE GAINS

After you develop a fine trip for a group of people, you will most likely get them back numerous times as repeat customers. In the beginning, you should accompany as many excursions as possible to learn first-hand the little things that can be done to make a trip enjoyable. Eventually, you can arrange multiple trips on the same day to numerous places. For this, you will need a knowledgeable supervisor/sightseeing guide to accompany each trip. It would be mutually profitable to split your $150 fee with your trip supervisors. At $75 each, you should have no trouble obtaining people to fill your needs. Each trip you arrange will mean approximately another $75 for you. Eventually, you can devote your time to the soliciting and coordinating of activities, leaving the actual travel responsibilities to your supervisors.

218

TRAVEL AGENT

WHY

Each year, millions of people travel to millions of places in numerous ways. The trips may be for pleasure, for business, or both. The vehicles used may be plane, train, bus, car, boat, or ship. The trip may involve a distance of several hundred miles or an elaborate excursion around the world. In any case, travelers usually need guidance and assistance in planning the most routine business trip or the most lavish vacation voyage. This service is provided by the travel agency business, and the individual arranging the itineraries for travelers is known as a "travel agent." As a professional agent, you may work for an agency out of your home on a part-time or full-time basis. In addition, there are other lucrative and exciting job opportunities in the travel business, such as being a tour guide, which will be discussed later in this chapter.

Today, tourism is the largest combined industry in world trade, and in the United States it ranks among the top three industries in our nation. It is the second highest retail expenditure among Americans. With increased leisure time and more disposable income, the continued and staggering growth of this industry is assured—as is the increase of the travel job market. In 1980, in spite of spiraling inflation, an economic slowdown, soaring fuel costs, airline deregulation, airline strikes, and financial losses among some of the major airlines, travel agent sales increased 23 percent and agency commissions increased 30 percent over 1979. What does all of this mean? The travel agency business is as stable as a rock and is here to stay.

GETTING STARTED

The main piece of equipment you will need to conduct agency business at home is a computer which interfaces with the agency's computer. Your agency can recommend a model. These machines can be purchased for $3,000 or leased for $88 a month. To succeed in this profession you must like people and be concerned about their welfare, possess an enthusiasm for your work, and be able to pay attention to detail. Theoretically, there is no formal training required for this type of work. You can walk into any travel agency and if they like and accept you, you can develop expertise as an outside agent via a short period of on-the-job training. On the practical side, however, there are relatively short and inexpensive training programs that can allow you to get a headstart in this profession and enter the field on a higher and more profitable plane as an independent outside agent. This field is complex; that is why there are so many opportunities in it. I recommend you receive some formal training. It will enable you to obtain a better entry-level position and, as the saying goes, "Hit the ground running."

Many universities and community colleges have day and night school programs offering courses that can prepare you for the travel business. There are also many fine vocational schools throughout the country that specialize in training people in all phases of the travel business. These schools are usually staffed by experts experienced in all phases of the industry. Many offer continuing advice, placement, and guidance following graduation. Such schools can be found in the yellow pages under "Schools, Vocational" or "Vocational Schools." To assure yourself of their credibility, make sure they are approved by your State Department of Education. Your local librarian or high school guidance office may be able to assist you in looking this up. Further assistance in this field can be obtained by contacting the *Travel Advisors Training Academy, 3926 Wilshire Blvd., Suite 300, Los Angeles, California 90010.* A typical program offers four months of training consisting of nine hours of instruction a week. Fees generally run from $600 to $700 for the entire program.

A good program will cover the technical aspects of ticket preparation, selecting and planning a travel itinerary suitable for your client, and then arranging for interesting things to do along your client's journey. After you complete your training and obtain an independent assignment from the agency, representatives from different airlines, steamship lines, hotels, and tour operators will be only too happy to further inform you of their organizations' activities and procedures.

As in so many other fields, your position and compensation in this business is largely what you put into it. You can actively go after the patronage of individual vacationers, groups, and business travelers. It does not cost a traveler any more money to deal with one agent than to deal individually with each airline, steamship, train, bus, or auto rental company and all the hotels involved in a trip. More and more people are becoming educated to the benefits of using a knowledgeable and concerned agent. By the same token, most transportation and lodging facilities prefer to deal with professional agents. It cuts down on the time they have to spend with each individual traveler. Because time is money, and because a good agent can direct a lot of business to reputable transportation and lodging companies, these facilities will pay commissions to agents in return for their professional services.

FINANCIAL REWARDS

Commissions paid to agencies by transportation companies, hotels, and tour companies change constantly. However, they generally run from 10 to 20 percent of the provider's price to the consumer and, as mentioned, are paid to the agency by the provider. An airline will generally pay 10 percent commission to an agency. A steamship company or hotel may pay from 15 to 20 percent commission depending on the time of the year, and a tour operator may pay a 20 percent commission. A fine but new hotel may pay a 20 percent or even greater commission to an agency that will help it acquire new business. The same is true with a new tour operator. However, your professional decisions to advise people on various modes of travel and lodging should not be motivated by personal financial remuneration. Always provide arrangements that are in the best interests of your clients. Their repeat patronage and recommendations will ensure accumulated dividends for you.

As mentioned, commissions are paid to the agency with whom you are associated. They are then shared with you depending on the arrangements you work out with your employer. Generally speaking, however, they are usually split 50-50 between employer and agent. In other words, you will receive approximately 5 to 10 percent of all your bookings. If you book a round-trip airline flight amounting to $400 and three nights lodging in a good hotel at $80 a day for a business client, this amounts to an account total of $640. Even at only 5 percent net commission for you, this amounts to $32. If you gain the respect of the business community and book enough of these trips a day, the financial results can be fantastic. Furthermore, many of your satisfied business clients can also become your vacation trip clients when it comes time to travel with their families. A typical vacation package overseas might amount to $3000 per person. For a couple, this amounts to $6000. Because commissions generally run higher for these types of bookings, you can look forward to a 10 percent or $600 commission on planning a luxurious vacation trip for a couple. As an added incentive, you can receive from 25 to 75 percent off from the transportation and lodging companies involved in the trips you take personally.

ACQUIRING CLIENTS

To build up a large and lucrative clientele, there are two groups of people you should go after. The first is the dedicated business or vacation traveler who consciously plans on some form of travel each year. The second group is the many people who never consider traveling or keep putting off that "big trip" until another time. The first group of people desire professionals that can quickly book the trips they choose or help them plan trips they will be happy with. The second group is probably the largest; and many of its members can be sold if approached properly.

When soliciting the patronage of the first group, place ads in the business and travel sections of your local newspapers. Follow this up with professional announcements in local business and professional journals. Medical, accounting, law, and teaching journals are a few of the publications representing people with stable incomes who travel frequently. Stress to these people that you are not just an order-taker, that you are personally dedicated to the comfort of these people whether they travel for business or pleasure. You might even call personally at the company headquarters of business organizations in your community. This alone shows your dedication to serve. It is not always necessary to talk directly to the head of the company. Quite often, an executive will assign travel responsibilities to his or her secretary. An executive secretary has enough on his or her hands without the added responsibilities of making complicated travel arrangements. Contact these secretaries, present them with your card or brochure, and inform them of how you can take all of their employer's travel requirements off their shoulders. If handled properly, you can become a welcome associate. With the high cost of doing business, many business organizations like to economize wherever possible. Because of recent airline deregulation and increased competition, wide differences in airline prices are occurring. What's more, they change from day to day and from airline to airline. It is difficult for a business traveler to constantly check each airline every time he or she must arrange a trip. However, as a professional who deals exclusively in travel, it will become second nature to you to constantly keep abreast of changing rates enabling you to arrange the most economical trips for your clients. Communicating this point to the business world can also help you solicit a large clientele.

And now for the second group of people—the large group of nontravelers. Remember! Everyone can be sold if approached properly, especially when you are selling pleasure and maybe even excitement. Use all your resources to develop interesting speeches describing exciting trips. Offer to give these speeches to all senior citizens' organizations, and civic, social, religious, and fraternal groups. The operators of the various airlines, steamship lines, bus companies, package tours, and vacation resorts can often provide you with literature and pictures to make your speech interesting and saleable. You will be surprised at how many stay-at-homes and stick-in-the-muds you can induce to become involved in the rewards of travel.

There are also many special tours that you can arrange and induce specialized groups to take part in. For instance, the tomato growers of America might be interested in a trip to Europe to learn about the techniques of the tomato growers there. The tomato growers in Europe might be highly honored to have their American contemporaries as guests in their country. This gives many tomato growers who never considered traveling, an excuse to take that "big trip." After all, it's for business. And if they have a little fun, well, that's okay too. What's more, a lot of the trip is probably tax deductible—another inducement. When planning such a trip, it would be your job to arrange travel, lodging, entertainment, and local tours to the farms of European tomato growers. This is all a big responsibility; but when you consider at least 30 tomato growers each spending a minimum of $2000 with you, this amounts to $60,000 worth of business and a net commission of $6000 for you. Do this for a number of specialized groups, and you are floating down that old money river.

Tomato growers were just used as an example. There are literally hundreds upon hundreds of specialized organizations in this country, listed in the *Encyclopedia of Associations* found in most libraries. Contact their national headquarters. Ask about their goals and problems. Many specialized groups have counterparts in Europe and Asia. Meeting with their associates abroad can provide new insight and dimensions in achieving their goals, not to mention a lot of additional enjoyment.

If you can take an interest in the needs of any individual or group of people and take pleasure in providing arrangements to make their lives more exciting, you will soon develop a large clientele. As an added measure, you can also keep track of the names and addresses of all the people you serve and eventually develop a newsletter informing past clients of new and interesting travel adventures awaiting them.

FUTURE GAINS

An aggressive travel agent working in the employ of an agency can earn from $40,000 to $50,000 a year. And as the owner and operator of your own agency, the sky is the limit. You can keep the entire commission of all the trips you personally arrange and share in the commissions of the agents who work for you. If you develop a large staff of motivated agents and constantly strive to keep them abreast of new ways they can serve their clients, you can develop a lucrative business earning you over $100,000 annually.

TOUR CONDUCTOR

When starting out in the travel business, you do not necessarily have to work for an agency. There are over 600 tour operators in this country. They arrange complete travel packages for groups of people to every place on the globe. These packages are sold through travel agencies. To ensure the enjoyment of the participants of a tour, a tour conductor is employed by the tour operator to accompany each group of travelers and oversee the tour. It is not uncommon for a tour conductor to earn from $175 to $200 a day taking a group of people through a part of a country, an entire country, a group of countries, or maybe an entire continent. Many tour operators provide trips to all parts of the world. After completing one assignment, it is possible to request a tour to another part of the world. In this manner, after several years of this activity, you can not only accumulate a fine sum of money, but your experience as a serious world traveler can provide you with the expertise to become a highly knowledgeable travel counselor resulting in a large clientele and bank account.

If desired, you can specialize in just one country, learn every facet of it: every restaurant, hotel, resort, scenic area; every package tour, airline, train, bus, and boat going through it. You can then act as *a wholesale travel agent operating your own "wholesale travel business."* In this capacity you would prepare and wholesale itineraries to retail travel agencies who deal with individual consumers. It is not possible for an individual full-service agency to become totally knowledgeable about every country in the world. Nevertheless, the operators want to provide expert advice and service to their clients, and you could help. For example, if you specialize in France, travel agencies in the United States can turn to you to provide every conceivable type of travel arrangement for their individual clients or client groups who wish to travel there. You would obtain travel and accommodations at special wholesale prices and then resell these accommodations to individual agencies for eventual resale to their retail clients. Obviously, you would have to work on a small mark-up to allow suitable profits for your client agencies. However, if you serve enough agencies, these small profits can accumulate to huge sums of money.

As in so many businesses, the possibilities in the travel field are as great as the imagination and desire to serve others. What's more, this business can be a lot of fun.

15

UNIQUE AND INTERESTING SERVICES

ASTROLOGY READING

WHY

Fact or fiction, reality or fantasy, the science of astrology and the preparing of personal astrological charts is becoming extremely popular. Even people who profess not to believe in it, often have a deep-down curiosity on what the stars predict for them.

Astrology is the most ancient of sciences, present from the beginning of man's recorded history, and is based on the premise that the position of the sun, moon, stars, and planets, in relation to each other, affects the favorability of certain days and the fortunes of individuals. There is now considerable evidence proving that humans are influenced by the cosmic environment.

Astrologers believe that the electromagnetic and gravitational patterns of the solar system at the time of one's birth definitely mark one's personality and character. At the exact moment of one's birth, from that specific location, the sun, moon, and all the planets of the solar system were in specific positions in relations to each other. A horoscope is a map or diagram of the heavens for that event, showing the relative positions of the sun, moon, stars, and planets. To make up an individual's horoscope, or chart, the astrologer must know the exact date, time of day, and place of his or her birth. Each of the twelve signs of the zodiac is believed to be associated with definite aspects of character, temperament, physiology, and aptitude. By establishing the relative positions of the heavenly bodies at the exact time of a person's birth (constructing a chart), astrologers claim to be able to predict his or her future or give advice on courses of action or decisions. There are fine profit opportunities for people seriously interested in this science.

GETTING STARTED

The construction of an astrological chart (horoscope) definitely requires some expertise and knowledge of the principles of astrology. There are a number of books that can teach you this, and in addition, there are many classes given by experienced astrologers. Many such programs are now conducted in the night school divisions of colleges and universities. Two books that can be very informative in orienting you to this field are: *A Time For Astrology*, by Jess Stearn, and *Write Your Own Horoscope* by Joseph Goodavage, both books published by The New American Library. In addition, there are numerous books in many public libraries covering all aspects of astrology. Several organizations represent the interests and advancement of the astrology profession:

American Federation of Astrologers
P.O. Box 22040
Tempe, Arizona 85282

Astrologer's Guild of America
P.O. Box 75
New York, New York 10011

National Astrological Society
127 Madison Ave.
New York, New York 10016.

The National Astrological Society also conducts a School of Astrology.

FINANCIAL REWARDS

It is common for an astrologer to charge from $10 to $300 for a reading depending on the clientele serviced and the detail put into a reading. Once you become fairly accomplished in this science, you can do a person's chart in approximately a half to one hour.

ACQUIRING CLIENTS

To promote your business, advertise in the yellow pages of the telephone book under "Astrology Readers." Since this business can also be conducted through the mail, it would be advisable to advertise under "Personal Services" in the classified section of various newspapers and magazines. All the client has to do is tell you the date, time and location of his or her birth and you can prepare the chart and mail it. It would be a good idea, however, to have the client send his or her money with the order. If you charge just $10 per chart, you can build up a lucrative business via the mails.

Do not be afraid to advertise in sophisticated business journals. You will be surprised to find out how many executives cannot resist finding out if the stars support their business decisions. A lot of business will eventually be derived from word of mouth advertising by satisfied clients.

Since astrology is such a popular topic, offer to give lectures on it to business, social, civic, and fraternal groups. There will always be several members of the audience who will desire to see you later for a private consultation. Call on all the radio and television talk show hosts in your area. They are always looking for interesting and informative guests to appear on their shows. Such an appearance always promotes some eventual patronage from the listening and viewing audience.

FUTURE GAINS

Your astrology service can be developed on a very high professional plane, whereby you would have your own office for private consultations by appointment. On this level, you would charge at least $100 for your services. There are many professional astrologers who feel, and communicate to their clients, that if you know what obstacles confront you, you can then plan to handle them properly.

HANDWRITING ANALYSIS (Graphology)

WHY

A person's handwriting gives an insight into his or her personality and character. The formation of loops, swirls, slants, thrusts, and pressures indicates emotions, moods, abilities, intelligence, aspirations, attitudes, drives, and character. In addition to being an interesting topic for conversation, handwriting analysis has commercial applications.

When hiring an employee, whether it be a stock clerk, salesperson, or top executive, the personnel officials of any organization are interested in many facets of the candidate. Is he or she ambitious? Honest? Creative? A self-starter? Can he or she work well under pressure? Does he or she get along with others? Quite often previous employers do not wish to mention the negative aspects of a former employee for fear of a possible lawsuit. Frequently, they may not even be aware of the negative attributes. Polygraph (lie detector) tests are illegal in several states. However, by having a prospective employee fill out an application form in longhand, many employers are finding a new way to aid themselves in selecting honest employees with the proper attitude. Graphology can also be used to help place personnel in the proper departments.

This type of service can also be useful to private individuals, for instance, those desiring a deeper insight into people with whom they are considering being associated, such as a potential business partner or even a mate. Sometimes all it takes is a scribbled note for a handwriting analyst to be able to offer a general character outline of someone.

The person who learns to analyze handwriting can create fine profit opportunities for him or herself serving the needs of industry and private individuals.

GETTING STARTED

Graphology can be learned in a relatively short period of time via night school programs in many colleges. A typical course consisting of twelve meetings of three hours each can provide an intelligent individual with the rudiments of operating a commercial handwriting analysis service. A handwriting analysis service can be operated through the mail, expanding your customer source area to the entire United States.

FINANCIAL REWARDS

There are many variables that determine the fees for this service: the financial position of the client, the depth of the study required, and the significance of the results. A company deciding on the hiring of a key executive can easily be charged $300 for an in-depth study of an applicant. This type of analysis would take at least an hour to perform. On the other hand, a supermarket desiring to know about the honesty of a cashier or stock clerk would be charged approximately $30 for a brief 20-minute analysis of the person's general character. A psychologist or psychiatrist should be charged at least $100 for an overall study of the general characteristics of a new patient, but an individual with a mild curiosity to find out more about him or herself would probably only be willing to pay a $10 to $15 fee for a brief personality description derived from a short note. This type of income can also be earned by setting up a small booth in the lobby of a restaurant, or receiving permission from the management to visit the tables of the guests.

ACQUIRING CLIENTS

Your market for customers is any business employing at least one person. Just going through the yellow pages of your phone book can provide you with an enormous list of potential customers to contact. Advertising in business journals is another fantastic clientele source. To find a list of business journals, consult *Ulrich's International Periodicals Directory* or *Standard Rate and Data*, in your library. An inexpensive ad can be placed in the classified sections under "Business Services." Television talk show hosts are always looking for interesting guests to interview. Volunteer to appear on as many shows as possible, talking about your specialty, and even analyzing the handwriting of the host or hostess and some of the other staff members or guests of the show.

FUTURE GAINS

Eventually, you can develop a nationwide commercial service through the mails, serving the needs of industry and private individuals.

SINGLES DANCES

WHY

There are millions of single people in this country. And regardless of one's economic station, age, looks, or personality, finding compatible people of the opposite sex can be an extremely difficult task. Loneliness is like a silent disease. Many are not aware of it or don't like to admit to it; nevertheless, it is there. Blind dates can be uncomfortable, singles bars and discotheques superficial, and computer matching downright degrading and wholly inaccurate. In fact, even singles dances can be a turn-off if it connotes a lonely hearts event. However, when a singles dance is sponsored as an elegant social event, it can take on an aura of acceptability in the higher-class circles of any community.

GETTING STARTED

You need two things to sponsor a dance: a dance hall and a band. The dance hall should be in a good part of town and the band should be professional and capable of playing everything from swing, rock and roll, and disco, to romantic. Having a good location and a good band focuses attention on the entertainment side of the event and takes away from any implication of its being a rendezvous for the forlorn. Most high class hotels and country clubs have banquet rooms which they are glad to rent out for dance and other social events. In fact, these facilities can be rented quite reasonably if the management is allowed to retain the liquor and soft drink concessions. This makes for quite an acceptable arrangement, as your guests will expect refreshment facilities. The hotel or country club will also be able to suggest several good bands for the event. If you live in a small town, select a location that is equidistant from several small communities so you can attract participants from each area.

To attract a good crowd, your event should have a theme. In the fall, you might call it Center City's (name of your community) Harvest Moon Ball, or maybe the May Cotillion, or June Promenade or the April Shower Ball. The possibilities are numerous. Everyone feels comfortable going to an event sponsored by a reputable charity—the March of Dimes February Ball can provide an exciting event for singles to attend. Naturally, you must obtain permission from the charity you select and give them a portion of your proceeds; 10 percent is quite sufficient. Your local librarian can refer you to reference texts listing popular charitable causes that will be glad to cooperate with you.

After the location, date, band and theme are selected, the next step is to design a tasteful announcement of your event which can be used as a flier for distribution or as an advertisement in selected publications. A sample announcement is shown on page 232. Notice that the announcement is simple and to-the-point. It mentions the event is for singles but does not keep stressing it. This makes everyone comfortable.

Note: You may want to offer a reduced admission price for those who mail in advance reservations and payment. Advance sales would give you peace of mind and assurance that you will have

THE MAY COTILLION
For Sophisticated Singles

Friday Night, May 22nd 8 to 12 midnight
at the
WEST SIDE HILTON
(Address)
Dance, meet, and have fun to (name of band)
Swing, jazz, rock and roll, disco, and ballroom dancing
Ages 25 to 50
Admission $10.00
Sponsored by: Your name and phone number
(for those needing further information)

enough money to pay for the facilities and band. However, don't worry; a well-planned, well-publicized event will attract a large group of people on the arranged-for evening.

FINANCIAL REWARDS

As noted in the sample announcement, $10 is a reasonable and acceptable admission charge. Your expenses will be approximately $500 for rental of the facility, $500 for the band, and $500 for advertising. You should have four attractive hosts and/or hostesses to collect the money at the door and greet the people. Payment of $25 each ($100 total) is quite sufficient for this task as it is a fun assignment and puts these individuals in a prime position to meet everyone. A well-planned event should draw at least 500 people. This gives you a gross of $5000, less $1600 in expenses, for a net profit of $3400. If you sponsor this event in cooperation with a charity, deduct 10 percent of the gross ($500) from this figure.

ACQUIRING CLIENTS

Most local professional journals and newsletters offer very low advertising rates. Place the illustrated sample ad in local nursing and medical journals to attract single doctors, dentists, nurses, technicians, medical secretaries, etc. Ads in legal journals will likewise attract legal secretaries and attorneys. The company newsletters of manufacturing plants, insurance companies, bank chains, etc., will attract secretaries, engineers, accountants, and other professional employees of these organizations. If there is a major airport in your community, contact each airline and advertise in their employee newsletter to attract flight attendants, pilots, sales personnel, and other professional personnel. In fact, have an $8^{1}/_{2}" \times 11"$ flier made of your announcement and attach it to the employee bulletin boards of these organizations, or mail at least one flier to the offices of each facility.

As people enter the admission area in the evening of the dance, have them sign a guest book giving their name, address, and phone number (optional). This can provide you with a mailing list to be used as an additional marketing source for future events.

FUTURE GAINS

Socializing is a continuous activity in our society. If your first dance goes well, it will induce even more people to attend future events. Good news travels fast. In fact, you can even schedule one a month. Of course, give every dance a new theme and try to vary the location in order to present each event as a "new experience."

As you gain experience in sponsoring these social events, you can expand the affairs to other communities (also on a once-a-month basis). Naturally, you can't be in more than one place at a time. Nevertheless, you can plan the format and marketing for each location and hire a supervising host or hostess to assist you with each affair. A good temporary employment agency in a distant community can provide you with the right person to act as your senior supervisor for the dance.

As mentioned, your net profit can come to approximately $3400 for each affair. If you paid your senior assistant $400 (quite reasonable) for each event, this brings your net to $3000 per occasion, less any monies due a charity when their name is used to help sponsor an affair. If you sponsor a dance a month in just five communities, this comes to $180,000 a year in earnings for you.

Additionally, you can utilize your acquired mailing lists and marketing expertise to sponsor vacation trips, cruises, and other events for singles. This is accomplished by purchasing space on cruise ships, airplanes, hotels, resorts, etc., at wholesale prices and selling these spaces on a retail level via a "package" price for the event. This can be conveniently accomplished by working with a licensed tour operator or travel agent.

If you are innovative and creative in providing quality events for single people, the opportunities for profit and satisfaction can be almost endless.

PARTY ENTERTAINMENT SERVICE

WHY

People of all ages enjoy parties. But in order to be effective, a party must be organized. One cannot just throw a group of people together and expect them to have fun automatically. There must be a catalyst to get things rolling. This catalyst is often in the form of organized and well-coordinated games or other entertainment which can spark spontaneous fun among the guests. It is easy enough for a well-meaning host or hostess or organization to give a party. Yet, it takes a special talent to plan and supervise the activities to provide a state of merriment among the guests. This goes for people of all age groups. You can offer this service in the form of an independent business endeavor for yourself. People go through a lot of expense in providing food and other refreshments for a party. They might as well spend a little extra to ensure the success of the party. People cannot have fun on food alone.

GETTING STARTED

A party service can be offered to parents planning birthday parties for their children, a group of married couples wanting to have a party to add some merriment to their everyday routine, a church or fraternal group wanting to provide an afternoon or evening of fun for its members, a club or charity wishing to provide entertainment for a membership or fund-raising drive, an office or business organization wanting to have a picnic for its members or clients, a senior citizens home wishing to offer their residents an afternoon of fun, or a group of single people wishing to have a party and provide for some fun ways for people to meet each other. All of these people (and more) offer you the opportunity to serve them creatively and commercially. When planning a party game routine, the activities must be coordinated to the age group and theme of the party or picnic. The games and activities must be presented to the party-goers in such a manner so as to induce them to want to participate. Nothing is more of a turn-off than to have games forced on one. Put yourself in the role of an invited guest. Very subtly ask the other guests if they would like to take part in a fun idea you have. More likely than not, they will be lined up to do so. For large parties and picnics, the games and activities should be set up in advance.

Libraries and bookstores are filled with books on games and activities for people of all ages. One book that is extremely informative and enlightening is the *Complete Book of Games*, by Clement Wood and Glorida Goddard, published by Doubleday. This book contains information on over 1500 party activities for children and adults, including details on party games, athletic games, and card games for both indoor and outdoor events.

For some of the outdoor parties you can include such activities as relay races, horseshoe and beanbag throwing, throwing baseballs at objects on a stand, or throwing an object such as a Frisbee for distance. To make things more exciting, you can give out prizes to the various winners in each event. These prizes can just be inexpensive trophies purchased with a small portion of your fee. For activities at an event where money is being raised for a church, charity, or other cause, you can have professional or amateur palm readers, fortune tellers, and astrologists come to perform their mystic magic for the participants on a fee-for-service basis. The fees can then be split between these artists and the sponsoring organizations. In events such as bean bag and baseball throwing, each participant can be charged a small fee for the chance of winning a prize, with the proceeds going to the sponsoring organization. The cost of the prizes can be deducted from the proceeds going to the organization. (This is the same principle on which carnivals operate.)

Practically all of these games can be set up inexpensively by you. For instance, for the bean bag toss, you can purchase some simple beanbags, set up small boxes of varying sizes at varying distances, and have each one represent a certain number of points, with the smaller ones carrying more points than the larger ones. For the baseball toss, you can set up some bowling pins or other indestructible objects on elevated platforms and have participants try to knock them down for prizes. With some white powder you can draw a series of circles around each other in a target fashion with the center bull's-eye representing the highest point and each subsequent larger circle representing a proportionately decreasing point value until the outside circle is reached. The participant can then stand at a predetermined distance and throw a series of baseballs at the target. As the balls land on the various circles, the total number of points are added up, with the highest total providing the participant with a prize. Everything is fun, everything is simple!

You can also organize indoor parties to serve the needs of local businesses: office parties, holiday parties, employee incentive parties, sales parties, etc. Choose a theme—a place, an event, a holiday—and plan your food, decorations and entertainment around it. Since businesses often have large entertainment budgets, this can be a very lucrative opportunity for you. As stated previously, libraries and bookstores are filled with books offering you scores of ideas for parties. As you get proficient and experienced in this type of work, you can innovate and utilize many of your own party ideas.

FINANCIAL REWARDS

The charge for your services is variable and will depend on many factors: the size of the party, the length of the party, the type of group to be entertained, etc. For a large picnic where a lot of supervision is necessary in handling the many events, judging winners, and giving out prizes, a number of assistants will be necessary, thus requiring a larger fee. In general, a $50 to $100 charge for a small children's birthday party would be very reasonable and a $150 to $300 fee would be acceptable for a large church or company picnic.

Commercial parties can be extremely lucrative. Many businesses and industries have large entertainment budgets for public relations. It is customary for a company to spend from $5,000 to $20,000 for just one party. If you can select many of your props and services for relatively low prices, it is possible to keep your expenses at 50% of your fees thus earning from $2,500 to $10,000 for just one party.

ACQUIRING CLIENTS

Think up a catchy title for your service: "Party Time," "Playtime," "Fun Services," etc. Personally call on and send out fliers to business, church, charity, civic, and fraternal organizations. Lists of these can be found in your local telephone book yellow pages and quite often at the editorial office of your local newspaper. When calling on fund raising committees of charity organizations, inform them that one of the best ways to raise money for their cause is to throw a party that people will look forward to attending, with the admission and other proceeds going to the charity. Call on food caterers. They can recommend your services to their own clients. After all, after people eat, they look forward to other forms of entertainment. When soliciting children's birthday parties, try to find out about upcoming birthdays and then send out announcements of your service to the parents. Birthdates can sometimes be found through local census bureaus, birth records at the local city hall or county courthouse, school records, and sometimes through commercial mailing services.

Call on the presidents and public relations officers of major businesses and industries in your area. Find out who their potential clients are, do they have any plans to increase employee morale, improve relations with the consumer public, etc. Then contribute your creative ideas on how you can help them achieve their goals. Call on banks to develop customer parties for new branch openings.

Tell the local newspaper office what you are doing. Your service can provide material for a feature story. The same is true for local television. This whole venture can be both profitable and exciting.

FUTURE GAINS

You can organize several parties taking place on the same day by utilizing assistants to supervise each function. College students would enjoy earning extra income in this manner. A fair financial arrangement would be to split the net income from each party 50-50 with each party supervisor. Do not confuse a "party supervisor" with an individual that might help out in some of the events of a party or picnic. The helpers should receive only a minimal fee for their efforts. It is the party supervisor that shoulders the main responsibility for the success of a party.

In a large community it is very feasible to cater 20 parties a week. After paying your party supervisors their fees, if your average net after expenses is $75 per party, this amounts to $1500 a week or $78,000 a year for you.

If you can develop a loyal clientele amongst business and industry clients, you can earn well over $100,000 annually.

CHILD ATTENDING
FOR SHOPPERS

WHY

All parents love their children, but not necessarily while shopping. When parents go on their routine shopping tours in the department stores and shopping centers of this country, they usually have to bring their small children along. Looking after the constant attention needs of their offspring can be very demanding

237

and tiresome, and can diminish some of the pleasures and cut down on the efficiency of shopping.

Baby sitting is conventionally thought of in terms of teenagers looking after little children while the parents are out to a movie or party. This role can be expanded to looking after children in department stores and shopping centers, freeing the parents to concentrate on and enjoy their shopping responsibilities. People with small children shop every day, opening up interesting profit opportunities for you.

GETTING STARTED

In this endeavor, you would look after a number of children in one area while the parents are shopping. The beauty of this is that you can charge a nominal hourly fee for each child, but enjoy an accumulative hourly income looking after a number of children at the same time. The main prerequisite for this type of work is that you enjoy working with small children. And it can be fun, especially when they are not your own.

You will need an area in which to look after the children. This can be accomplished by renting a small space in a busy shopping center or department store. Contact the management of these facilities and express your intentions to them. In many cases, they will be very happy to provide you with some low cost space in which to operate your business. After all, if parents have a place to leave their children while shopping, it will encourage them to do their purchasing in that particular shopping center or department store. This adds to the business of everyone in that center or store. The fact that there is a child facility in a shopping center makes it easier for the management to rent and get the highest prices for their retail spaces.

When parents leave their children with you, you cannot just let them sit there; you have to provide them with activities that will absorb their attention. This does not mean watching television! There are many games and activities for every age group that involve the participation and attention of several or more children. Many of these activities can also be quite educational. Your local library and bookstore have scores of books on activities to keep small children busy.

In addition, consult your insurance agent regarding liability insurance in case a child becomes injured.

FINANCIAL REWARDS

A fee of $3 per hour per child is quite reasonable for you to charge. After all, people now pay almost that to park their cars. If you maintain an average of ten children an hour in your facility, this amounts to $30 an hour for your services. You should have at least one supervisor for every ten children. Therefore, if your average hourly class is over ten children, you will need additional help. There are many housewives, retired people, and high school and college students who would enjoy this type of work and the extra income it would provide them. Wages of $3.50 to $5.00 an hour are quite sufficient compensation for the services of these individuals.

ACQUIRING CLIENTS
To attract the patronage of shoppers with children, place large posters in every store in a shopping center. This alone can provide you with an almost instantaneous response. The management of these stores will most likely provide you with a prominent area to display your signs. After all, if their shoppers can safely deposit their children somewhere, it means more shopping time and dollars spent in that store. In addition, advertise your services in all community newspapers and shopping bulletins. After a while, you might obtain the business of a lot of parents who will desire a safe place to leave their children while they are doing things other than shopping, such as going to the doctor, playing golf or tennis, or just plain staying home and resting.

FUTURE GAINS
This type of business can be expanded into a major enterprise with multiple locations. Contact the management of all busy shopping centers or department stores in a city. A service like yours is most welcome in today's hectic and busy society. You can eventually have a location in many different shopping areas in a community, with each location supervised by one of your trusted employees. You can pay each supervisor an hourly salary plus a percentage of your gross receipts per location.

SEX SURROGATE

WHY
Sex is one of the most popular topics around. There are jokes about it, conversations about it, books written about it, movies made about it, and a host of other forms of speculation about it. Finally all the words fade into the background and the individual is left alone with his or her problems. Sexual dysfunction is one of the most common and frustrating problems facing mankind.

Although there are still no foolproof methods for treating sexual dysfunction, sex therapy, with the use of a sex surrogate, has had a reasonable amount of success with the problem.

A sex therapist is preferably a licensed psychologist or psychiatrist who may treat all of the emotional problems of an individual or just specialize in sexual problems. The sex therapist does not become involved physically with the patient. He or she talks with and counsels the patient in an effort to resolve problems. Nevertheless, having the patient experience a constructive sexual experience with a trained and understanding partner can prove very useful in providing corrective measures. This is where the sex surrogate comes in. *Surrogate* means a person supplied in place of another, in this case the patient's chosen sex partner.

There are many married, single, and divorced people who want to resolve their sexual problems in a safe atmosphere with understanding and caring people before encountering what might be called the "outside world." Very often, a sexual encounter with an uncaring and insensitive person can compound one's problems.

The surrogate is the therapeutic arm of the therapist. After the therapist sees the patient, he or she will then communicate with the surrogate about the nature of the patient's problems. The patient will then see the surrogate to practice sexual techniques and discover new dimensions about themselves. These techniques are not necessarily different sexual positions, but rather methods of teaching the patient to appreciate the sexuality of his or her own body and that of a partner. This is usually done just by the simple caressing of every part of the body in addition to other loveplay. When this is perfected, it is a big accomplishment. One of the biggest reasons a person loses interest in or "turns off" to a partner is that the partner does not necessarily fit the total or perfect image that is imagined of him or her.

When an individual can finally recognize and appreciate the sexuality of every inch of his or her body and that of a partner, the sexual arousal or "turn-on" becomes self-perpetuating. The act of penetration and other intimate acts then become an exciting extension of the caressing and loveplay. When the surrogate helps the patient achieve an appreciation for the sexual potential of the bodies of both participants, that patient can then achieve the same fulfillment from other partners he or she has feelings for.

GETTING STARTED

Approximately 10 percent of sex therapists in this country utilize the services of sex surrogates in the treatment of their patients. In southern California alone, there are over 300 therapists who utilize the help of surrogate partners for their patients. Of the surrogates in practice today, 80 percent are women and 20 percent are men. The age range is from 25 to 55. What these people have in common is a sensitivity to the needs of others and a sincere desire to help them.

Although there are no standard training requirements for becoming a surrogate, you should undergo some form of responsible training before going into practice. There might be a program in your area for this type of work. Your local associations for psychologists or psychiatrists might be able to provide you with information concerning a training program in your community. Also, consult the magazine *Sexuality Today* for information on training programs. Write *Sexuality Today*, 2315 Broadway, New York, N.Y., 10024. There are two professionally recognized training programs in southern California. One is sponsored by Ms. Barbara M. Roberts, a licensed therapist who works with surrogates in her practice. Her address is P.O. Box 155, Tarzana, California 91356. The other program is conducted by the International Professional Surrogates Association. For information on this program write: IPSA, P.O. Box 74156, Los Angeles, California 90004. Both programs provide approximately 80 hours of formal training in this profession.

Once in practice, you will be working under the supervision of a practicing therapist, in the treatment of his or her patients. This may be done in the therapist's office, but it is also acceptable to work with patients in your own home or any other location where you prefer to practice.

FINANCIAL REWARDS

The general fee range for surrogate work is from $35 to $75 per session. A typical session lasts from one to two hours. The number of sessions needed is determined jointly by the therapist, patient, and surrogate.

ACQUIRING CLIENTS

As mentioned, a surrogate works in conjunction with psychologists or psychiatrists in the treatment of their patients. The best way to establish yourself is to communicate with the professional practitioners in your community to let them know of your training and availability.

Most communities have professional associations for both psychologists and psychiatrists. All of the professionals in these organizations might not work with surrogates or believe in them. Attend some of their meetings to inform them of the benefits of surrogate therapy. Whenever possible, give examples of "case histories" where surrogate therapy has proved beneficial. In addition, place announcements in their professional journals informing them of your services. It would also be professionally acceptable to have a simple brochure printed up and mailed to the therapy professionals informing them of your expertise. You might turn some nonbelievers into believers. After all, the more patients they help, the more their practices can grow.

FUTURE GAINS

There have been numerous instances where a surrogate has become so interested in the treatment of emotional problems, that he or she has returned to college to earn credentials as a licensed psychologist. Obviously, because of your surrogate experience, you may decide to specialize in problems of sexual dysfunction. The amount of further training required will depend on whether or not you have had any previous undergraduate college training, and if so, how many psychology courses were included in your program.